ABA Career Series

The
Legal
Career
Guide

FROM LAW STUDENT TO LAWYER

Fifth Edition

Gary A. Munneke | Ellen Wayne

AMERICAN BAR ASSOCIATION

Law Practice Management Section | Law Student Division

Commitment to Quality: The Law Practice Management Section is committed to quality in our publications. Our authors are experienced practitioners in their fields. Prior to publication, the contents of all our books are rigorously reviewed by experts to ensure the highest quality product and presentation. Because we are committed to serving our readers' needs, we welcome your feedback on how we can improve future editions of this book

Cover design by Andrew Alcala, ABA Publishing.

This book is adapted from the 1992 ABA Career Series publication, *The Legal Career Guide: From Law Student to Lawyer*, which was influenced by two earlier books, *From Law Student to Lawyer*, by Frances Utley and Gary A. Munneke, published in 1984 by the American Bar Association, and a briefer 1973 version by Frances Utley, entitled *Where Do I Go From Here?*

Printed in the United States of America

12 11 10 09 08   5 4 3 2 1

Library of Congress Cataloging-in-Publication Data

The Legal Career Guide, Fifth Edition. Gary A. Munneke and Ellen Wayne. Library of Congress Cataloging-in-Publication Data is on file.

ISBN: 978-1-60442-260-3

Discounts are available for books ordered in bulk. Special consideration is given to state bars, CLE programs, and other bar-related organizations. Inquire at Book Publishing, ABA Publishing, American Bar Association, 321 North Clark Street, Chicago, Illinois 60654-7598.

www.ababooks.org

Contents

CHAPTER 20
Organizational Practice 237

CHAPTER 21
Judicial Clerkships 243

CHAPTER 22
Pro Bono and Public Service 255

CHAPTER 23
Law-Related and Nonlegal Professional Services

CHAPTER 24
Substantive Practice Areas

CHAPTER 25
The Future of Law Practice

CHAPTER 26
Where Do I Go from Here?

Appendices

Index

About the CD

Charts

About the Authors

Gary A. Munneke is a professor of law at Pace University School of Law in White Plains, New York, where he teaches courses in Professional Responsibility, Torts, and Law Practice Management. He is active as a leader of the American Bar Association, having been elected to the ABA Board of Governors for a term from 2006–2009, after serving as a member of the ABA House of Delegates, as chair of the Law Practice Management Section, as chair of the Section's Publishing Board, and as a member of the ABA Standing Committee on Publishing Oversight. He has also served as president of the National Association for Law Placement and participated in a number of other committees for the ABA and other professional associations. Professor Munneke is the author of numerous books and articles about current issues on the legal profession, the practice of law, and legal career issues, including:

- *Barron's How to Succeed in Law School*
- *Barron's Guide to Law Schools*
- *Nonlegal Careers for Lawyers*
- *Careers in Law*
- *Opportunities in Law Careers*
- *Seize the Future: Forecasting and Influencing the Future of the Legal Profession*
- *Materials and Cases on Law Practice Management*

- ◆ *Law Practice Management in a Nutshell*
- ◆ *The Essential Form Book: Comprehensive Management Tools for Lawyers.*

Professor Munneke is a frequent speaker at seminars and conferences on topics related to his teaching and writing. A 1973 graduate of the University of Texas School of Law, Professor Munneke is a member of the Texas and Pennsylvania bars, the New York State Bar Association, and the Association of the Bar of the City of New York. He is the New York Co-Chair of the Fellows of the American Bar Foundation and a Fellow of the College of Law Practice Management.

Ellen Wayne is the Dean of Career Services at Columbia University School of Law, New York, New York. She has served in this position since 1994. In this position, she advises and counsels students and graduates; sets and implements policy; serves as the office's liaison to employers, professional organizations, and media; develops and produces Career Path orientation and skills training programs; produces podcasts of instructional and resource-related programs; and supervises and manages major recruitment programs since 1994.

Dean Wayne has authored many publications, including Job Strategies, a bi-monthly back-page section for the *New York Law Journal* (NYU), which was reprinted in Law.com, NLJ.com and the *Legal Times.* She has authored two books for the American Bar Association Law Practice Management Section: *Nonlegal Careers for Lawyers* (Munneke, Henslee, and Wayne, Chicago, IL 2006) and *Careers in Labor Law* (Chicago, IL 1985). She has also written articles for the *New York Law Journal Summer Associate Supplement:* "Evaluations Are Not Just for Employers: Evaluation from Both Sides" (2002); "Get Prepared for a Real Challenge" (2001); and "No Offer Received: Spot the Hints, Use the Experience" (2001); as well as "Successful Associates" for *NYU Associate Supplement* (2001), and "Technology and the Job Search" (1999) for *Law School Supplement NYU.*

Among many professional presentations, Dean Wayne was a speaker at the Convocation on the Legal Profession, Committee on

Professionalism and the Court of Appeals of the State of New York. The Plenary Session was for law school deans and state court judges and was entitled: "Future Trends in Legal Employment" (2000). The convocation remarks were published and made available on the Court of Appeals Web site.

Dean Wayne has also spoken for many organizations concerning the recruitment and career paths of law students and attorneys. She is a frequent presenter at the National Association for Law Placement, speaking about international students and global employment issues, marketing a law firm to law students, and Faculty Clerkship Committees, among other topics. She has spoken at the International Bar Association meeting in Amsterdam, Netherlands, concerning "Recruiting for Attorneys in the United States" for the ABA Business Law Section on Managing Recruiting and Understanding New Associates, and the Northeast Association for Pre-Law Advisors on International Recruitment of Lawyers.

She currently serves as the chair of the Career Paths Task Force for the ABA, Law Practice Management Section, where she was also vice chair of the Education Board. She was an officer of the National Association for Law Placement, where she also served as chair of the Education Board, the Publications Board, and the Nominations Committee, among others. She has also been inducted into membership in the College of Law Practice Management.

Acknowledgments

Professor Munneke wishes to thank a number of individuals. The first edition of *The Legal Career Guide* was written by Frances Utley in the mid-1970s and, over the years, many individuals have worked to produce the next four editions of the book and other titles in the ABA Career Series. Among the editors whose insights have guided the authors are Professor Joan Bullock, Theodore Orenstein, and Monica Bay.

Numerous American Bar Association staff members have supported the work of the authors and editors. These professionals have included Patricia Brennan, Neal Cox, Tim Johnson, Yasmin Waring, Beverly Loder, Sherry Gouwens, Kathy Wiley, Jane Johnston, and Paula Tsurutani. In addition, various officers and leaders of the Law Student Division, as well as Professor Munneke's students at Pace Law School, have reviewed and commented on the early drafts of this book, particularly Kristina Ivtindziosky and Jennifer Yuen. Professor Munneke also wishes to thank his Pace Law School Faculty Assistant, Denise Acevedo, Assistant Dean for Career Services, Rachel Littman, and Amy Gewirtz, Career Services Associate Director, for their work in preparing this manuscript and resources. Without these individual contributions, it would have been impossible to keep the information in this book current and relevant.

Lastly, Professor Munneke thanks his wife, Sharon C. Walla, a practicing lawyer, who provides real-life examples to illuminate his writing, support for his never-ending projects, and light along the pathway of life.

Dean Wayne acknowledges the advice and assistance of many colleagues from career services offices nationwide, as well as the support of a number of individuals from Columbia Law School: former Dean Lance Liebman, Professor Lou Lowenstein, Brian Donnelly, and the staff of the career services office, particularly Stephen Buchman, Anna Colliton, and Administrative Assistant Harriett Jordan. She also recognizes colleagues J. Kirkland Grant, Carol Phillips, Anton Mack, Elaine Bourne, Clyde (Skip) Rankin, John (Jack) Kerr, Roger Melzer, Hon. Kristin Booth Glen, M. Dee Pifer, Norma Cirincione, Carol Kanarek, and Marty Africa.

Dean Wayne would also like to thank co-author Professor Gary Munneke for being her mentor, teacher, friend, and colleague through the years. His creative energy always pushes her to do her best and often to go beyond her comfort zone both profession-ally and personally—always, as he tells her, in his best interest. Together, they have participated in many professional events, pro-grams, committees, and family activities. She has always appreci-ated his support and advice.

Finally, Dean Wayne expresses thanks to four individuals who have been of great influence in her life and are no longer with us: Peter Kutulakis, Salvatore Luiso, Francis Heuston, and her father, Benjamin A. Wayne.

Both authors express special thanks to Professor Bill Henslee, their co-author of the sequel to this book, *Nonlegal Careers for Law-yers,* and an anchor for the Career Series since its inception, and they convey their appreciation to Major, Lindsey & Africa, Robert Half and Associates, and the National Association for Law Place-ment for permitting their materials to be included in the appendi-ces of this volume.

Preface

The American Bar Association's Career Series is designed to give students and beginning lawyers practical information on choosing and following career paths in the practice of law. Books in the series offer realistic, first-hand accounts of practicing law in specific substantive areas and guidance on setting and reaching career goals.

The Career Series was created during the ABA's 1982 Annual Meeting as a joint project of the Section of Economics of Law Practice (now the Section of Law Practice Management), the Law Student Division, and the Standing Committee on Professional Utilization and Career Development. The Career Series has produced timely, practical, career-oriented books for law students for over two decades. The goal of the Career Series is to help lawyers secure satisfying jobs in their chosen areas of practice. To this end, the Career Series Steering Committee presents this publication to complement the Career Series.

Planning for a Legal Career

After Law School: What Next?

Questions, Questions

Every year, law students return to the halls of America's 200 or so law schools (the number continues to creep up). The first-years begin their studies full of enthusiasm, aspiration, and idealism. The second-years have hunkered down to the pragmatic concerns of signing up for fall interviews through the career services office. Those whose marketability took enough of a hit with first-year grades are scrambling for alternatives or getting involved in activities that will restore a patina to their tarnished résumés. The third-years, if they have not yet gotten the job offer of their dreams, are beginning to feel the pangs of panic that somehow they will never, ever get a job. Although many students will find employment along the way, some of these students will experience a crescendo of fear that escalates through graduation, the bar exam, and the months waiting for results.

Here is the good news: Almost all of you will find work. Some will do it sooner than others; some will get more money than others; some will find jobs with more prestige than others; some will be happier with where they land than others. But you *will* find a job. For over thirty years, the National Association for Law Placement (NALP) has surveyed the nation's law schools and reported that over 90 percent of those seeking employment find it within approximately six months of graduation. Many others whose employment is not captured by NALP also get jobs. The fact that you will ultimately find a job does little to assuage the nagging fear that you will be the one left out in the cold, $100,000 in debt, and panhandling outside Grand Central Terminal just to stay alive.

The truth is that lawyers are an adaptable lot who will find ways to succeed. If some graduates end up penniless and forgotten, it will not be the lawyers. This may be little comfort when the one person who matters most to you—you—does not have a job. The reality that all your pavement pounding will eventually pay off does not eradicate the knot in your stomach that tightens up every time you call an employer for an interview.

These are the pressures of the process and they go away only after you graduate, pass the bar, settle in behind your new desk, and cash your first paycheck. Trust us on this one. Even the golden ones, running around with twenty job offers from fall interviews, will experience significant levels of stress going through the process.

Actually, the real danger is not that you will fail to find a job, but that you will find the wrong one. On this account, there is some reason to be concerned. A high percentage of law graduates changes jobs within the first two years of graduation, and lawyers who go to work with one firm and stay with that firm throughout their careers are practically non-existent.

Part of the problem is that until you actually try something, it is difficult to know if you will like it. No amount of hypothecating and planning can replace the experience of working in a job day after day. A central premise of this book is that you can improve your chances of making a sound career choice. But let's face it— there are no guarantees.

Take Liza. Liza had a strong academic record in law school, was well-liked by classmates, and was an articulate communicator.

She wanted to make sure that she made the right career choice, so she read all the books she could locate, talked to everyone she could corner, took all the personality inventories and other tests she could find, and put in the requisite introspection to come up with a perfect career plan.

Everything Liza studied told her that she should find an in-house counsel position with a major corporation and handle transactional matters. She was particularly drawn to the energy field, so she sent out her résumé and signed up for campus interviews with oil, gas, and related companies. Her efforts were rewarded with what appeared—on paper—to be the "perfect job."

To make a long story short, Liza hated the job and quit after six months. While she was unemployed, a friend of hers working in the district attorney's office told her that the DA needed to hire some temporary lawyers because of a backlog of cases. Liza decided to do it because she needed the cash, but she knew that the one thing all her planning had told her was to stay away from litigation. To the surprise of everyone, especially Liza, she loved it. She applied for a permanent job in the office, was hired, and went on to a successful career as a criminal prosecutor.

An even bigger challenge for law students is that there are so many things you can do with a law degree. The *American Bar Foundation Lawyer Statistical Report* says that just over 60 percent of the one million-plus lawyers in the United States engage in the private practice of law, either in law firms (as owners or employees) or as sole practitioners

The ABF figures are drawn from the *Martindale-Hubbell Law Directory* records, which account for just over half of all law school graduates. Thus, it is easy to surmise that the majority of law school graduates do something other than practice law.

Why should you care? First, you should recognize that it is very likely that, at some time during your career, you will do something besides deliver legal services to clients working in a law firm. To get into the right mindset for beginning the career planning process, you need to acknowledge the realities of the marketplace for lawyers, as opposed to the marketplace for law firms. If you focus only on the private practice of law, you will inevitably draw your horizons too narrowly.

Unfortunately, the law school culture does little to encourage you to think broadly about careers in law. From the first day of law school until graduation, you will encounter a bias—sometimes subtly implied, sometimes stated outright—that you are somehow not a success unless you go into private practice. In fact, in some circles, you may get the feeling that unless you go into litigation, you are somehow less than legally whole—real lawyers try cases, don't they?

You will get this from your professors, from your classmates, from your family, from the career services office, and from the law firms themselves: The investment of three to four years of your life and lots of money have been expended to prepare you for this one great calling—to practice law. Like a thoroughbred trained for the Kentucky Derby, you owe it to yourself to pursue private practice first. If that doesn't work out, *then* you can try something else.

In the end, you may be one of the 25,000 graduates who enter the private practice of law annually, or you may be one of the 15,000 who choose to do something else. For many of these graduates, private practice is a good career choice. For others, it is not. This is not a diatribe against private practice. It is merely a statement that legally trained individuals can and do work in a variety of settings, and that private practice is just one of many opportunities.

The pace of change has accelerated in the legal profession, just as it has in other fields of endeavor. New experimental models for delivering legal services are appearing. Many nonlegal organizations, such as accounting firms, banks, real estate companies, financial planners, and technology enterprises are providing services that were offered exclusively by lawyers in past decades. Alternative dispute-resolution mechanisms, such as mediation, arbitration, private judges, and dispute-resolution rooms on the Internet, compete with traditional litigation as viable approaches to problem solving. Multidisciplinary firms in many parts of the world offer integrated professional services and "one-stop shopping" for business solutions.

Not only are law firms not the only game in town, they do not hold all the cards. It has become increasingly difficult to prosecute nonlegal service providers for the unauthorized practice of law.

There is no bright line separating the practice of law from business advising with legal implications. Perhaps the right to represent others in court remains as a remnant of the professional monopoly but, in many jurisdictions, the willingness of people to represent themselves *pro se* produces inroads into litigation practice.

What is sometimes overlooked is that it is not lawyers who are losing the business—it is the law firms. If you look at banks, real estate companies, online service providers, and accounting firms, who do you think you will find working in the legal side of the business? If you guessed lawyers, you are right. Every year, more law school graduates choose these so-called nonlegal careers and, increasingly, lawyers leave the private practice of law to utilize their legal skills in one of these alternative arenas.

In an era of change, legacy does not necessarily dictate consumer choices. Clients will not go to a law firm because their parents did. They will make choices based upon their perceptions of who provides the best service at the best price. Look at travel agents. Before the Internet came along, they were complacent in their role of helping travelers arrange transportation, lodging, and amenities. With the advent of Web sites like Expedia and Travelocity, hotel, car-rental and airline Web sites, and other online tools, travel agents have lost a major chunk of their business.

Are we, as lawyers, comfortable in saying, "It could happen to the travel agents, but it could never happen to us. We're *so* special and our services are *so* unique that we are simply not prone to the same economic forces that ravaged the travel industry, right?" If you believe that one, you may be in for a rude awakening.

In times of transformational change, an omnipresent economic Darwinism governs the marketplace. Less efficient service providers will be supplanted by more efficient ones. Natural selection will dictate that organizations with favorable adaptations will survive, while those with inefficient adaptations will die out. In such an era, traits of adaptability, strategic visioning, innovation, and creativity will be worth more than market dominance from an age that no longer exists.

An old Chinese proverb says, "May you live in interesting times." Well, these times are interesting. There are no certainties about the future. On the positive side, in this complex, interconnected, global, and changing society, people are confronted with legal problems in everything they do. As long as there are legal problems, society will need people with legal training.

Choosing a Career vs. Finding a Job

People go to law school for a number of reasons other than money and status. Many students choose law to influence public policy or the outcome of events. Many seek the intellectual challenge of legal studies or the problem-solving aspect of lawyering. Because the legal profession is diverse, and because law schools seek diversity when they recruit students, there are countless reasons why people pursue legal careers. Although it is probably futile to generalize about the psychological attributes of law students and lawyers as a group, all of us have chosen law. We contemplate a career in law. We take the LSAT. We endure three or four years of law school. We survive a grueling bar examination. And we embark upon a career with great hopes for the future. Most of us find jobs as lawyers, and many of those who do not were pursuing alternative careers from the beginning.

By all accounts, we lawyers have it all. Perhaps no other field offers a comparable combination of monetary rewards, prestige, and potential satisfaction as does the law. Certainly, no other career offers as wide an array of options. Why, then, are we not happy? Despite the advantages of being a lawyer, a number of studies conducted over three decades, beginning in the late 1970s, confirm that there is a high level of dissatisfaction within the legal profession.

The key question for law students contemplating the future should not be "How do I find a job?" but "How can I find satisfaction in a legal career?" Many lawyers do find happiness in their careers. They use the law as a vehicle to develop and sustain the lifestyle they have chosen. Most lawyers would not give up their jobs to do something else. Thus, the central questions for anyone entering the legal profession should be "How do I discover the road to happiness?" and "How can I avoid the path that leads to dissatisfaction?" You want to know more than simply how to get a job; you want to know how to find satisfaction in this career you have chosen.

Look at the terms "job" and "career." A job is the sale of your skills, time, and energy to someone who compensates you for your work, and work is not always fun. Even if you are self-employed, you sell your skills to clients, and work is not always fun. A job implies that it is something you do out of necessity, for reasons like keeping food on the table and a roof overhead.

A career, however, is an identity—a series of jobs connected by a common theme. You can leave a job behind when the five o'clock whistle blows. With a career, you maintain the identity whether you are on the job or not.

When someone asks a corporate lawyer who works for an auto company what she does, her answer is not "I work for Chrysler." She says, "I'm a lawyer." Artistic types have probably mastered this better than anyone. If you ask the waiter in a restaurant down in Greenwich Village what he does, he will tell you, "I'm an actor." If you ask the clerk in the antique bookstore in Soho what she does, she will answer, "I'm a writer."

Law school does an excellent job of imparting an identity as a lawyer. No matter what you do after you graduate, you will *always* be a lawyer. You can never go back to being a nonlawyer, the pejorative term we use to describe all those who are not members of our little club.

Taking this thought a step further, there are many careers within the legal profession. In fact, there are countless alternative identities for lawyers. Lawyers are not just the generic brand, but a variety of diverse brands. Part of the process of finding happiness is discovering the unique identity within the legal profession that is particularly yours.

Richard Bolles suggests in his book *The Three Boxes of Life,* that our lives are made up of three boxes: working, playing, and learning. We all spend substantial amounts of time in each of these boxes over the course of our lives.

You should strive to meld work and play. Find jobs where work *is* play. Get paid to have fun. If Tiger Woods can do it, so can you. Too often, we are either unable or unwilling to free ourselves to enjoy what we do. We are so driven to put bread on the table that we do not allow ourselves to smell the roses, either in our personal lives or at work.

A fourth box, which Bolles neglects to mention, might be relationships. As lawyers, we spend a great deal of time working and learning. Many lawyers, however, are not good developing relationships. Yet, finding balance between our professional and personal lives is central to long-term satisfaction.

Life is too short to spend it being miserable. Even on your worst days, however, you should feel satisfied with the career choices you made. If you do not like what you are doing, then do something else. This does not mean that you should expect to be blissfully happy all the time, or that you will not encounter frustrations along the way. Rather, it means that you should experience more days when you are happy than days when you are sad.

This book will aid you in making career decisions, but career planning is not something that can be accomplished in a single session. It is an ongoing process that requires you to evaluate opportunities as they arise, reflect on changes in your personal situation affecting your aspirations, and assess new trends within the profession that impact on your practice. That very availability of options dictates the importance of each law student developing at least a broad outline of the goals he or she hopes to achieve, both professionally and personally.

Your initial career plan should start from the place you are this minute and project what you perceive to be reasonable goals for yourself for the next five to ten years. Keep in mind, however, that a typical professional's life spans fifty years or more. Because changes are inevitable, concentration on the shorter distances is a more practical approach. In a larger sense, because change is likely to be a constant in your professional life, you need to continue to focus strategically on your career throughout your life.

Profiles of Three Typical Law Students

Although it is difficult today to call any law student typical, let's look at three fairly representative but very different law students: Heather Meadows, Sally Fielding, and Bob Downing.

Heather Meadows

Heather Meadows seemed to have it all. She went to a prestigious undergraduate school, followed by graduate school at the University of Chicago, where she put together an impressive record. From there, she went straight to Columbia Law School. At Columbia, she performed with distinction, including participation on law review, and was hired as a summer associate at a prestigious Manhattan firm. At the end of the summer, Heather got a job offer from the firm, but decided to talk to other firms before making a final decision.

Here is where things got complicated. Heather was born and raised in Iowa, and her family just could not see why she did not want to return to Cedar Rapids. Her boyfriend, a fellow student at Columbia, planned to return to Los Angeles, where he had summered and received an offer from a top firm there. Without so much as asking her, the boyfriend accepted the job, and told Heather that if she *really* loved him, she would come to LA. With her record, the boyfriend argued, she could get a job with any firm she wanted. The problem was that Heather didn't want to go to LA. She had visited LA, and she hated the traffic, the lifestyle, the perfect weather, and the Biz (show business). New York was real—messy, but real. So what would it be: The family? The boyfriend? Or the Big Apple?

Then, there was the money issue. A top-tier undergrad, grad, and law school education was not cheap. Her family wasn't rich, so Heather was looking at repaying about $150,000 in student loans. She was definitely not going to make enough to live on and make loan payments in Cedar Rapids.

It was too late to get a decent clerkship with a judge. That would have been nice, giving her a couple of years to think. Maybe she could do a fellowship or LLM, but that would just postpone the inevitable decision. Why did everything have to be so complicated?

In the end, Heather accepted the offer from her summer firm. The work was challenging and the people were exciting. Despite its reputation as a place where lawyers worked long hours under high stress, she felt that it was the best training she could find. And the salary would certainly clear out her student loans. She and the boyfriend decided to try out a long-distance relationship, but he was quick to point out that if they weren't living in the same town, it would not be fair to expect exclusivity. "Sure," Heather responded, while she thought, "Blah, blah, blah!"

Sally Fielding

Sally Fielding just graduated from a small and well-regarded, but little known, private law school in Florida. She was active in a number of different student organizations, including the law school's Advocacy Program. Sally was twenty-seven, and spent three years working as an aide to a congressman before coming to law school. She was single, and flexible as to where she was willing to live.

During her first year of law school, she attended a career orientation for first-year students conducted by her law school career services director. She spent some time in the career services office after final exams that semester, meeting with the director to put together a résumé and cover letter, and to get ideas about law firms that might interview first-year students.

She sent out about a hundred letters to local law firms, none of which panned out. Several of the firms, however, interviewed her, and she was able to collect valuable information that she would use later. Through a friend, she heard about a judge who needed a clerk for the summer. It turned out that the judge wanted her to work for free, so she turned down the job, and took courses through one of the summer-abroad law programs advertised on the career services bulletin board. This not only allowed her to get away from the law school itself, but also permitted her to take some credits that would let her lighten her load during the next year.

Sally did not dally overseas, but returned in time to get a waitressing job where the hours were long, but the tips were good. She also spent some more time in the career services office, researched employers, met with a counselor to clarify some of her objectives, revised her résumé, and did a practice interview in anticipation of the real thing. That fall was crazy. Even with the lighter course load, school was just as demanding as the first year. Her commitments to student organizations, especially the required hours in the law review office, left her with no time for a personal life. She ended her relationship with a long-term significant other, who announced that Sally just didn't know how to make a commitment. Sally responded that her commitment at this time of her life was to law school. Having made that decision, many other choices in Sally's life became simpler.

To top it off, Sally's car died. It had been with her longer than the significant other. To finance a new automobile, Sally had to find another part-time job. She went to work for an eight-lawyer general practice firm where she could also work full-time the next summer. This was fortunate because, although she went to a number of on-campus interviews that semester, she didn't receive any offers.

The spring went better than the fall, as her work kept her occupied. During the summer, the only time she set foot in the law school was when she had to go for law review, having been elected to the editorial board during the spring.

Toward the end of the summer, Sally updated her résumé again, listing experience gained from her job at the firm. Instead of conducting a mass mailing like some of her friends, she sent it to selected firms she had contacted over the past two years, or firms that had been recommended to her by individual lawyers. The notes she had kept came in handy. She took a week before school started to do some interviewing resulting from her letters.

Despite what seemed to be some definite signs of interest by some of these employers, everyone seemed to hedge about making her an offer. Sally talked to the career counselor again, who suggested that those firms with formal summer clerkship programs were waiting until they made offers to their summer clerks, while the smaller firms that did not have such programs were probably uncertain about their hiring needs.

The counselor asked if Sally might expect a permanent offer from her present employer. Surprisingly, Sally did not know, but she made a note to find out. The counselor urged Sally to go through fall on-campus interviews again, which she did. Her efforts got her on the wait list for three firms but, alas, no offer.

She took a semester leave from her clerking job to work for her congressman in a re-election campaign. At the victory party, the congressman told her that if she wanted a job on the Hill after graduation, there was always room for her. When she went back to work at the law firm, she had a long meeting with the managing partner, who told her that the firm really liked her work, and would like to hire her, but would not know until after the second quarter of the fiscal year (June 30) whether it would be possible to do so.

During her last semester, while she was trying to tie up all the loose ends from law school and apply for the bar exam, Sally continued to follow up on those employers who had expressed some interest in her. She also answered several ads on the career services bulletin board and in the local law journal. No luck.

At graduation, Sally's dad asked why she did not have a job. Her mom wondered why she was not married. Sally wondered if she needed all this grief. She thought she should not complain because she did have one job offer, even if it was for the same position that she had before she went to law school.

In the ensuing weeks, she did not have time to think about much of anything except bar review lectures. She was surprised to receive a letter from one of the firms with whom she had interviewed the previous August, indicating that their needs had changed and they were making her an offer. Then, on June 30, right on schedule, she received a call from the senior partner at her old law firm offering her a job. Things were definitely looking up.

Sally's classmates thought she was lucky, but the fact was that she had been working toward getting a job throughout her law school career, not just at the last minute. She took advantage of her school's career services program and turned minor setbacks (like the car dying) into opportunities (a part-time job that led to full-time employment).

Bob Downing

Bob Downing was thirty-five years old when he graduated from Pace Law School and, unlike Heather Meadows or Sally Fielding, he had family obligations. Ever since he was a boy growing up in an urban neighborhood in Brooklyn, he had always wanted to go to law school. But with a wife and family on the way after college, law school was just not in the cards.

An engineer, Bob got a job in his field with a local government agency, and moved up the civil service ladder to become a departmental head. He worked with the town's counsel on an almost daily basis, negotiated contracts, and was frequently involved in the legal affairs of the town.

Despite his success, Bob increasingly felt the need for a new challenge. His old interest in law was rekindled through his law-related activities at work. On the home front, his family seemed to be absorbed in their own worlds. The kids, now teenagers, had their friends and activities at school. His wife had started her own career and was busy with that.

Most significant, Bob took the LSAT and, to his surprise, did quite well. This was fortunate since he had never performed at the top of his class when he was in college. He met with his boss at work and told him about his plans for law school. Bob's boss agreed not to dump any new assignments on him, but made it quite clear that when push came to shove Bob's responsibilities at work took precedence over law school. Bob agreed, because he could not afford to quit.

Nothing happened as planned. Bob worked five days and went to school four nights a week. Studying took up all of the available time on weekends. Then, as if some pernicious god wanted to test his mettle, the house needed major repairs, which took precious hours away from studying. Just when Bob got the house repaired, he learned that his office was being reorganized and moving to another location. Bob was beginning to wonder if he had made the right choice.

The first year of law school was pretty much a disaster. The highlight of the year was the miracle that Bob did not flunk out. Even when things settled down at work, Bob found that he was so far behind in school that he had to struggle to catch up. Fortunately, his business experience coping with high-pressure crises helped him survive the first year.

The second year was much like the first in terms of workload, but not punctuated with the near-disasters of the year before. Bob's grades and mental health improved considerably. His restructured job included reviewing contracts and working with outside counsel on engineering licenses and permits.

During his third year, Bob became more active in student organizations at school. He enjoyed the law-related aspects of his job, and was pleasantly surprised at the end of year when the managing partner at one of the firms with whom he worked asked Bob if he would like to switch hats and work for the firm. The job would pay less money, but provide excellent legal experience. Bob talked it over with the family, then took the plunge and quit his day job. His wife got a promotion where she worked; they sold some stock to make ends meet, and hoped for the best.

The fourth year at law school was great. Bob was elected president of BLSA, a student organization for African-American law students, which gave him the opportunity to meet interesting speakers, contribute to the improvement of the law school, and develop leadership and organizational skills. His work at the law firm was interesting, and he found it interesting to think that the new engineer in his old job was now his client. Best of all, and despite his busy schedule, Bob was able to see much more of his family, which pleased everyone.

Although Bob never set foot in the career services office or prepared a résumé, he was working on making career choices throughout his law school years. Like Sally and Heather, he made conscious decisions when he approached a crossroad and tried to maximize his objectives.

Serendipity

Of course, these fictionalized accounts do not reflect the exact experiences of any three law school graduates. They do represent some of the planned and unplanned events that happen to all law students. The serendipity of opportunity is always interwoven with aspirations and plans for the future. You may not be able to exercise control over many aspects of your life but where it is possible to make choices, you should. In the face of the obstacles thrown by fate, Heather, Sally, and Bob maintained a sense of direction and positioned themselves to make sound choices for themselves. This should be your objective as well.

How to Use This Book

This book is designed to serve as a hands-on manual for law students who are entering the job market during or after law school. It is designed to serve as a tool to help you get from start to finish in the career choice process. It is not like a novel to be read from cover to cover, or a casebook to be briefed for later regurgitation. It seeks to help you where you need help, so use the parts that help and skip the rest.

The career choice process pictured in Chart 1 may help you to visualize the process you will follow to find a job. The entire model is basically a continued narrowing of alternatives until a final decision is reached, from a starting point where the individual has no idea what the final decision will be.

Chart 1
Munneke's Pyramid—Overview of the Process

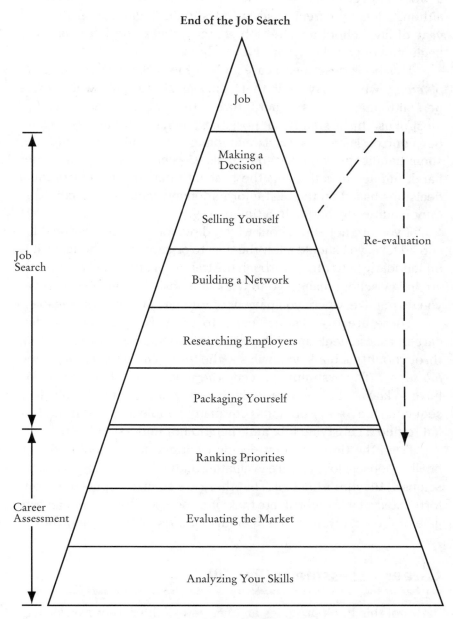

End of the Job Search

Job

Making a Decision

Selling Yourself

Re-evaluation

Building a Network

Researching Employers

Packaging Yourself

Ranking Priorities

Evaluating the Market

Analyzing Your Skills

Job Search

Career Assessment

Beginning of the Career Choice Process

The time frame is flexible. One person may reach the third level by the beginning of the second year in law school. Another may not begin the first level until after graduation. You should allow whatever time is necessary to work through the possibilities, although ideally career assessment should begin during the first year of law school and the job search process no later than the beginning of your last year of law school.

This book describes a career choice model. We avoid the term *planning,* which may infer that some magic formula will allow a person to map out his or her future with a degree of certainty. For most of us, this is simply not possible; much of our fate lies beyond our control. Factors such as economic conditions, luck, and personal handicaps will affect our goals. Career choice, on the other hand, implies ferreting out the best information, making rational decisions based on the best information available, and maximizing opportunities by acting in a timely way.

If you are not sure about which direction your professional life should take, you should allow the time to organize your thoughts. It is undoubtedly better to go through the trauma of uncertainty while you are in law school than to go to work in a position you later discover you do not like, where you have not foreseen what was foreseeable.

There are two distinct parts to the career choice process: career assessment and job search. A fundamental rule is that throughout this book, you will see the terms *career assessment* and *job search*. The first must precede the second. In other words, you have to know what you are looking for if you expect to find it. This sequence may seem obvious, but many people skip the first step, fail to find a satisfying job, and then do not understand why.

From the time you first decide to attend law school until you finally choose a job, you are evaluating, either consciously or unconsciously, the opportunities. That there are so many opportunities is fortunate, yet it is unfortunate that many people either do not investigate or are not aware of the full range of possibilities is unfortunate.

Career Assessment (Part II)

Part II of this book provides an overview of the career assessment you will need to undertake. Each step is covered in greater detail in the chapters that follow. You may spend more or less time on different chapters, depending on your particular needs.

Analyzing Your Skills

Career assessment (Chapter 4) involves analyzing your personal and professional skills, which you should think of as interesting and challenging, rather than painful. Only by beginning with a perfectly honest appraisal of yourself can you make this a valid evaluation.

Every law student is unique, and a key to selling yourself is to tap into your own uniqueness. This involves your work and personal experiences, the education and training you have completed, and the skills that you have amassed before and during law school. If you try to market yourself as a commodity, your task will be immeasurably more difficult than if you define yourself as an individual. Knowing yourself will also help you to make choices about job opportunities that are best suited to your special qualities.

Evaluating the Marketplace

After you have undertaken this self-analysis, which is essentially subjective, you should begin evaluating the job market (Chapter 5), which is more objective. This step, no less than self-evaluation, requires scrupulous honesty. Here, however, you are required to look outward, to view your environment, and to see things the way they are. You must be able to confront the facts honestly and determine the relative importance of them.

Once again, for this analysis to be most effective and helpful, you must consider the positive as well as the negative. Try to balance your weaknesses against your strengths to get an entirely accurate picture. You may find yourself both expanding and narrowing alternatives by obtaining more options while limiting the areas from which you will eventually make your choice. Your market analysis is going to involve not only research on the facts, but the interpretation of those facts, which leads to the next step: ranking priorities.

Synthesizing Interest and Opportunity

By synthesizing the self-analysis and the evaluation, you should be able to generate some options (Chapter 6). If this does not work, you have either not done your research homework or you are not being realistic. Your goal here should be to develop a list of options, ranging from the most desirable situation you could imagine to the bottom line; i.e., what you would find acceptable if worse came to worst. At this point, we are talking about broad categories as opposed to specific positions.

Your job search will involve the pursuit of these options in the order of their priority. In other words, you will focus on the first option first, the second option second, and so forth, through your list. Moreover, as you eliminate options you will need to add new options to the end of the list. Never expend all of your options; there should always be an alternative.

If you have a hard time making up your mind about the appropriate direction for your career, you might need to work on developing decision-making skills. Uncertainty is the element that makes any decision difficult. Even though you can control the decision, you are probably aware that the element of chance influencing the outcome makes it impossible for you to have ultimate control. There will always be a certain amount of risk or chance, but you should try to minimize the degree to which chance affects the outcome.

You should chart a middle course between leaving everything to chance, which could be disastrous, and expecting to eliminate it, which is impossible. In other words, you should know what you want, be well informed of the facts, and be alert for opportunities.

Finding a Job (Part III)

Part III of this book covers the job search, which represents the heart of this guide. There are six steps to the job search:

1. Preparing for the Job Search (Chapters 7–11);
2. Researching potential employers (Chapter 12);
3. Building a network (Chapter 13);
4. Contacting Employers (Chapter 14);
5. Selling yourself (Chapter 15); and
6. Making a decision (Chapter 16).

Of particular note, Chapter 11 addresses the core elements of preparing a good résumé, and Chapter 15 discusses how to sell yourself, including developing good interviewing techniques, securing references, and creating impressive writing samples. How many students would take a final exam cold, with no preparation? Very few. But many students fail to give adequate attention to details prior to beginning the job search, and this is often costly in the long run.

Researching employers, covered in Chapter 12, is hard work for which there is no shortcut. To make a sound decision, you must take affirmative steps to gather relevant information about employers. When your inaction or indecision forecloses an opportunity (for example, letting an application deadline pass), you have forfeited your control of your destiny. Research should be easy for law students, but many forget the same skills they have developed to research a legal problem can be transferred to research on legal employers.

The process of networking found in Chapter 13 is aimed at expanding your opportunities by increasing your contacts with individuals, who may know about career opportunities that would interest you, help you to open doors, and provide support for you. These contacts are your eyes and ears in the world of work. They are your allies in the war against unemployment.

Many students claim that they do not have "contacts" in the legal profession. Networking involves developing new contacts, as well as tapping old ones. It requires work to build a network and effort to maintain it. Yet informal channels of information represent a major source of legal jobs that you should not ignore.

Chapter 14 deals with the intricacies of using your plan to seek specific positions in the priorities you have established. As you start to apply for specific jobs, begin with your first priority. Either you get a job, or you do not. If not, you turn to the next possibility, and so forth through your list. When you exhaust the employers in your highest priority group, then you move on to the second group, and so on.

The final (and often overlooked) step in the process is making a decision, a topic covered in Chapter 16. If you have only one choice, the decision is easy—yes or no. If you have several choices, then you must sort out the factors to reach a final decision that is best for you in the long run. This is easily said, but not so easily accomplished.

Reassessing the Situation

The final chapter in Part III (Chapter 17) examines what to do when even your best-laid plans do not yield the expected results. You might discover in midstream that new skills are required for the position you want. Can you realistically obtain them, or would it be wiser to consider another field? Do the latest statistics show that competition in your chosen area is so fierce as to render it an unrealistic choice for you? What happens when the student (or graduate) goes through the whole job search with no results?

Careful analysis and thorough preparation should help you avoid this situation. However, if it does happen, it is probably best to go back to the beginning and start anew. At this point, you will probably need the help available through the law school career services office. It can be very helpful to talk about your situation with someone who has a broader view of law careers and the current job market.

The Marketplace for Legal Services (Part IV)

Part IV provides a description of the various career paths that law school graduates pursue. The thrust of the first part of the book is to provide a set of tools for making career decisions and undertaking a successful job search. But to what end? What are the career paths that lawyers pursue? How are these paths changing as global economic and social changes redefine the landscape of professional services? What are the myths and the truths in what we read and hear about legal jobs? Are there opportunities outside the realm of traditional law firm employment? Where are the jobs and what do they pay?

Flash-Forward

Movies often use the devices of flashback and flash-forward to strengthen the plot. A flashback takes the viewer back to a time before the linear clock of the film began, to give the viewer more background or develop a character. The flash-forward lets the audience in on events that have not occurred on-screen, which are unknown to the characters in the film. Much of this section has provided a flashback to help you assess your goals with greater clarity. It might also make sense to flash-forward to look into the crystal ball to glimpse where you want your career to take you.

In the end, you can flash-forward to a job that is personally and professionally rewarding. But that is seldom the end of the story. Your career is an unfolding process, rather than a product, and career patterns evolve over time. The average lawyer will make at least five job changes in a legal career, and many lawyers even more. So the flash-forward you seem to see with clarity may have little to do with the flashback on your career fifty years from now.

If you understand this model, the skills and self-awareness you have developed for the job search will help you to make career decisions throughout life, to provide for continued professional development, and to prepare for those unpredictable turns of fate the future may hold for you.

Career Assessment

PART II

Assessing Your Prospects | **2**

A story about the late Supreme Court Justice Oliver Wendell Holmes may have some relevance for law students embarking on the career choice process. One day during his eighty-eighth year, Holmes was traveling by train. When the conductor asked for his ticket, the embarrassed justice could not find it. As Holmes was checking the contents of his pockets, the conductor, who recognized him, assured him there was no problem. "The railroad will trust you to mail your ticket back when you find it," he said. With great irritation, Holmes replied, "My dear man, that is not the problem at all! The problem is not where my ticket is. The problem is: Where am I going?"

Law students, too, are traveling. Many of them do not know where they are going, and will take whatever the world gives them. Others will take matters into their own hands, and take steps to order the choices they make about their future. This process is called career assessment.

"Assessment" does not mean that you can look into a crystal ball and somehow divine where your career is going and how to get there. On the contrary, career assessment is hard work, and the answers are seldom clear. It is rather an approach designed to lead the student to make rational choices about career options. It is also a never-ending process, something you do throughout your adult life.

Self-Assessment

The first step in career assessment involves a subjective analysis of who you are and what you personally think about your likes and dislikes, skills, abilities, interests, needs, values, and goals. In this sense, every law student is unique. Legal education has a tendency to cause students to feel fungible, or to think that they do not have any unique attributes. Anyone who feels this way is giving up too soon.

This self-analysis might well be the most difficult step in the career choice process, as well as one of the most intrinsic to success. Seeing yourself as you really are, not as you were, or could be, or should be, or will be, is not easy. But it is absolutely critical.

If you do not like the image you see, you need to take steps to remedy the situation. Do not rest your decisions, however, on projected self-images that are not accurate. Your self-analysis can help you focus your skills on career objectives in a positive and realistic way. Many law students have not engaged in this sort of introspection before, but an honest self-appraisal is the essential first step.

Career Theory

An understanding of some of the underpinnings of career theory may be useful to the uninitiated reader. Although there are many books on career planning, some of which are discussed in this chapter, the basic theory was probably best set forth by John Holland in *Making Vocational Choices*. Holland argued that individuals tend to like doing things in which they succeed, and that they will succeed in the future in activities similar to those in which they have succeeded in the past. The connecting thread between past, present, and future success is the skill set that helps the person to be successful. It follows, according to Holland, that job dissatisfaction, or "dissonance" as he calls it, is related to the lack of skills necessary to perform work successfully. When we are frustrated in this way, there are three possible responses: 1. We change ourselves (the skills we possess). 2. We change the environment (the skills we utilize). 3. We leave the frustrating environment.

It is essential for you to assess your skills, not just in terms of specific jobs, but also in transferable terms that can be understood in a wide variety of endeavors. For example, a preacher, a politician, a trial lawyer, and an actor may all possess the oral skills of speaking and persuading. And to assess your skills accurately you have to possess a degree of self-knowledge of your personal strengths and weaknesses.

Many law students are surprised—even dismayed—to learn that they must undertake this skills assessment. Did they not, after all, go through the very same thing when they decided to go to law school? Is it not most important just to find a job? Does a busy law student have time to worry about playing silly psychological games? Can one actually plan a career?

Career Decisions

Once you accept the notion that law is not just one career, but encompasses many different careers, it is a short step to the conclusion that you must make choices during law school regarding options available to graduates. You cannot simply wait for the right thing to come along, or postpone critical career decisions until after graduation.

There is a natural impulse to shortcut the process of making career choices, not only because it is uncomfortable to ask hard questions about life choices, but also because most law students do not understand how to manage effectively the career choice process. Just because you made a career choice in deciding to come to law school does not mean that you will not make other choices during law school or after graduation, for that matter.

Another problem many law students face in making career choices is the role that subjectivity, non-rationality, and personal feelings play in the process. Law school teaches students that reason is paramount, and that every decision can and should be made rationally.

Work Values

The law student who deigns to bring personal feelings and subjective judgments to analyses of hypothetical cases is inevitably portrayed as weak-minded by professors. Eventually, most law students learn to sound as if they can analyze questions in a coldly rational way, untainted by emotion. Some even believe this. Unfortunately, it is impossible to divorce personal feelings from career choices, and it is unwise to try because feelings are an important dimension in the process of making career decisions. These feelings often reflect work values: personal attitudes about who we feel comfortable around, the work environment of our employer, the ethics of our peers, the number of hours we are willing to devote to work, and the amount of money we want to make.

Although the analytical skills developed during law school clearly should be viewed as assets in choosing a career, you must maintain a clear perspective on the role of the rule of reason. When hard facts seem to fly in the face of gut feelings, it is sometimes best to follow your feelings. An offer that looks good on paper may be less attractive where subjective feelings point to deep-seated doubts about the long-term satisfaction of working in a particular environment. For more information on work values, see Chapter 4, page 52. Chapter 4 will provide specific suggestions to help you sort out feelings and attitudes, and to get a handle on your professional skills. It will suggest ways to apply the steel-trap logic that law school has inculcated in you, and to use your rationality to avoid letting career choices become a guessing game or a high-stakes crap shoot.

The Ladder

An analogy may be helpful in applying these principles to law careers. Students sometimes believe, or are led to believe, that job opportunities are like a ladder, with practice in a large firm as the top rung, based on some vague notion of prestige, and employment in a nonlegal job as the bottom rung, only slightly more desirable than standing in a breadline or begging on a street corner. In fact,

Chart 2
The Ladder

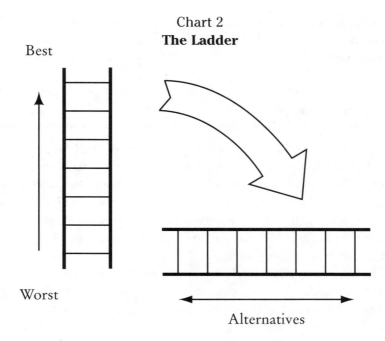

Alternatives

Holland and most career theorists suggest that the ladder should be turned on its side so that various jobs are perceived as options (see Chart 2). Instead of reaching for the top rung and then falling down the ladder until it is possible to grab a rung and hold on, you should view the entire ladder of possibilities and find the right place for you among them.

The important idea in the ladder approach is: What is right for one person is not necessarily right for someone else. "What is right" is partially determined by correlating the skills a job requires and the skills an individual possesses. The closer the match between these two, the greater is the likelihood of finding satisfaction, as well as long-term success, in one's career.

Job dissatisfaction may be partly a natural product of the transition from school to the working world, and is endemic in contemporary civilization. The frustrations of living and working in the twenty-first century are similar in many career fields.

Some of the dissatisfaction, however, may be a product of certain aspects of the practice of law. Furthermore, different kinds of practice have different sources of dissatisfaction as well as different levels of overall satisfaction. The goal of the career choice process is to identify potential frustrations and problems and to avoid them by making sound choices based on the alternatives available.

Skills for Success

Making good career choices can affect long-term career satisfaction, but there are some pragmatic considerations as well. Your résumé, interviewing style, and cover letters will be more powerful if they are based upon and reflect skills and values that have been identified through the career choice process. Your ability to recognize the right job when it comes along is enhanced also by an understanding of these skills.

In her book *Skills for Success,* Adele Scheele contends that the most frequently cited reason given by successful people for their success—being in the right place at the right time—is not so much a product of good fortune as it is a specific ability to identify the right opportunity. This ability is based upon a number of skills, including the skill of knowing what transferable career skills a person can bring to a given job. Scheele forces us to ask how much of the serendipity mentioned in Chapter 1 to describe Heather, Sally, and Bob is pure luck and how much is well-honed skill?

To use another analogy, it is somewhat like entering the New York City subway system without knowing which train to catch. Someone could stand on the platform or ride for hours without reaching the intended destination. Yet, the traveler who knows where she is going can find the right change, the right platform, and the right train to reach her destination.

Too many people approach the career choice process as victims. They take the first train that comes along and go wherever it leads them. If they would only realize that they are in control of their destinies, they could find the right train the first time and avoid much frustration.

Taking the time now to ask and answer questions about job skills and career goals can prevent hours of frustration during the job search, and perhaps years of unhappiness later in life. Too often, busy law students want to skip this part of the process, and get on to serious job hunting. But you are unlikely to bag the job you want if you cannot recognize an opportunity when it comes along.

The exercises presented in Chapter 4 are designed particularly for law students, and are modifications of similar exercises that may be found in many contemporary career planning manuals. They are intentionally simple in recognition of the time limitations many law students face.

Those who wish to pursue this self-evaluation in greater depth may obtain one of the commercial books available. Perhaps the most popular of these is Richard Bolles's *What Color Is Your Parachute?* This perennial bestseller guides its readers through a series of exercises aimed at finding the ideal job.

Its drawback is that in his exuberance, Bolles seems to suggest that one can find the right job simply by following the formula. The failure to achieve that goal may be seen as the fault of the individual for not carrying out Bolles's plan as a true believer would. Also, because the manual is aimed at a general audience, law students will find some parts less helpful than others.

You may be able to find a number of other job-hunting manuals on the market. See the Resource Guide, Appendix A, pages 302–319 for other titles on legal careers. Some of these are aimed at a general audience, and others are targeted to the legal field. Different books emphasize different issues for law students in search of employment. Some are pragmatic; some are touchy feely; some are formulaic. You need to find materials that work for you. This book attempts to cover the important elements of the process on a level and with a tone that law students understand.

Some career planning materials deal in great depth with values clarification, another factor ultimately reflected in career choices. Those readers who are plagued by questions such as, "How do I feel about prosecuting people and sending them to jail?" or "Could I represent a client with whom I am personally in disagreement politically?" may find values clarification useful.

Another approach is to use personal inventories (e.g., the Myers-Briggs Type Indicator, or MBTI) to test how well an employee will fit into a given work environment. These tests have the advantage of relying on a scientific method in their development and validation. When properly employed, they can provide valuable insights about the individuals tested. An increasing number of career counselors and legal employers are using personality tests such as the MBTI in career assessment.

A danger exists that such instruments will be misused by poorly trained administrators or by interpretations that suggest, "If your type is X, you must become a Y." The flaw in the logic is that not only Xs may become Ys, and certainly not all Xs do become Ys. The tests merely show a correlation between Xs and those who have in the past become Ys.

For example, we often picture litigators as erudite, aggressive, and self-confident. Although many litigators fit this mold, many trial lawyers do not. It would be unfortunate if they had chosen to avoid the courtroom because they did not fit the profile on some test.

Like any other analysis, the results of these tests can help you to find areas of practice that you may enjoy, but they cannot make your decisions for you. There may be other reasons leading you to different choices.

If you are a busy law student, you are probably saying to yourself about now, "Enough of this theory already. Let's cut to the chase. What do I need to do?" With that question in mind, let us leave theory to the theoreticians, and get down to business.

The Law School Experience 3

For better or worse, law school leaves an indelible imprint on your psyche, your analytical approach to problems, and your public image. Part of becoming a lawyer involves learning the legal culture: the language, the customs, and the professional ethos. Directly or indirectly, much of the legal education process involves assimilating you into the profession.

Legal Skills

Beyond indoctrination into professional values and the acquisition of substantive knowledge, law school inculcates a number of professional skills. In 1991, the American Bar Association Task Force on Law Schools and the Profession: Narrowing the Gap reported that fundamental lawyering skills were critical to competent practice and that these skills were learned not only during law school, but before and after law school as well. The task force identified the following skills as fundamental to effective lawyering:

- Problem solving
- Legal analysis
- Legal research
- Factual investigation
- Communication
- Counseling
- Negotiation
- Advocacy
- Management
- Ethical sensitivity

The basic principles articulated in the MacCrate Task Force were reinforced in a 2007 report on the status of legal education by the Carnegie Foundation, arguing that law schools should focus more on teaching students the professional skills needed to practice effectively as lawyers. The Socratic method, designed to "teach students to think like lawyers," is not enough to prepare graduates to practice competently. Legal analysis is an important skill, but proficiency as a lawyer involves not one, but an array of skills that you can use in solving problems as a lawyer. At the same time, law school subtly develops other less obvious skills that ultimately may be just as important to success in the legal profession: coping with pressure, meeting deadlines, juggling diverse and sometimes conflicting responsibilities, competing civilly, organizing tasks, managing time, and creating innovative arguments.

Many students are exposed to lawyering skills through clinical education programs, simulation courses, and co-curricular activities such as moot court and law review. For example, students who serve on a law journal develop specialized editorial skills, while students who participate in moot court hone their advocacy skills. Students who work in clinics enhance a number of practice-oriented skills, including client interviewing and counseling, negotiation, instrument drafting, and problem solving. These students may also learn related skills involving office management, time-keeping and time management, and other organizational skills.

It is possible to develop some of these practice-oriented skills in traditional law school classes but, for the most part, there is no substitute for learning by doing. Unfortunately, not every law school student will be exposed to a full range of these experiences. Although there may be a set of fundamental skills that virtually all law students develop to one degree or another, there are certainly other elective skills that essentially make each law student unique.

A positive aspect of this educational divergence is that law graduates truly can market themselves as unique individuals. Legal employers sometimes seem to view law students as interchangeable—they all possess the same knowledge, skill, and inexperience. Although this myth may have some adherents, the better strategy is to think of yourself as someone who possesses a unique set of skills and find ways to distinguish yourself from the crowd.

Personal Skills

A number of personal skills do not appear in any law school catalog. In fact, many students do not even recognize them as skills. While it is probably the case that all law students develop these personal strengths to some degree, different students will develop a different mix of skills.

- ◆ The first skill is persistence or determination. Not surprisingly, skills analysis interviews with law students frequently bring out this personal strength. ("I was the first person in my family to go to law school." "Everything always came easily to me before law school. Suddenly, it was a struggle just to stay in the middle of the class." "I had to work my way through school. I really wanted this.")
- ◆ Another skill is the ability to depersonalize arguments. ("When you said that my argument was stupid, I know you did not mean to say that I am stupid. You meant to say that you disagreed with me and on that much we agree. As for your specious argument that. . . .")

- And, of course, there is the ability to hold your ground under fire. (Professor: "That's your answer?" You: "Yes." Professor: "Did you actually read this case?" You: "Yes." Professor: "If I told you that no court in any American jurisdiction has ever taken your position, what would you say?" You: "I would say that the courts had not really looked at the underlying policy.")

- You have learned to deal with pressure. ("I know you said that if I did not make it home over this weekend, the engagement is off. But I have five hundred pages of reading due for Monday, a brief due at the clinic, and two job interviews on Friday.")

- You have learned an ethos of professionalism. Such concepts as due process, constructive notice, confidentiality, conflicting interest, and burden of proof have become ingrained in your psyche. Certain ideas, such as the notion that you do not have to agree with your client to represent her, and that you do not have to believe in your client's innocence to require the state to make its case, will seem perfectly logical to you. These attitudes are not imparted solely through your professional responsibility course. Rather, they are inculcated through the entire educational process from orientation through graduation.

- You have mastered an entire new language of the law. This specialized vocabulary, with its terms of art and linguistic constructions, will forever provide you with a calculus of communication for your professional life.

- Another set of skills that law school almost always ignores includes personal management: financial management, relationship management, and coping with deadlines. While serving on a law-school academic standards committee, I saw a high correlation between the inability to manage one's personal problems and the inability to perform in law school.

- Increasingly, bar associations, courts, and lawyers are recognizing that this principle applies to practice as well, and it is not uncommon to discover that a lawyer whose law practice is in shambles has a personal life of similar quality.

Whatever else it may be, law school is clearly more than simply learning a set of black letter rules we call substantive law. Too often, students focus on the substantive side of their education (e.g., "I've taken evidence, environmental law, regulated industries, and a seminar on toxic torts.") rather than the underlying skills that set them apart from classmates and those who do not possess a legal education.

Viewed in this light, job hunting involves identifying the situation where your skill set can be applied most effectively. If you can identify your unique pattern of skills, you will always have work and you will find satisfaction in what you do. If you fail to grasp this fundamental principle, you will always be a round peg trying to fit into some square hole, always passing time in some boring job, waiting and hoping for the "right thing" to come along.

Gaining Competence

Most of us readily accept the seeming inconsistency between the notion that when we take the bar examination, we know more law than we have ever known before or will know again, and that we know frightfully little about being a lawyer. Ask any practicing lawyer, "Is a new law school graduate ready to practice law?" The answer will invariably be an emphatic "No!" If we are not competent lawyers when we graduate from law school, how do we attain competence?

Some people begin to learn the nuts and bolts of law practice by working in law offices before and during law school. Others receive an inkling of what to expect through some of the more practical courses in law. Still others may have grown up around legal families where they have learned about the practice of law firsthand.

For the most part, however, we have learned how to become matadors by reading books on bull fighting. And suddenly, we are standing in the middle of the ring.

Although the array of practice skills you develop during law school is formidable, and probably far more extensive than you might have imagined, many career skills cannot be learned before you actually begin to practice law. You can develop some of these skills through part-time and summer work while in law school, but true legal proficiency is a product of experience.

Your law school career services office may help teach career development skills; however, learning how to make career decisions and look for a job involves an entire set of skills that the formal educational process frequently does not address.

In the medical model for education, aspiring doctors go through an internship and residency after medical school. In Canada, through a process known as articling, law graduates must submit to the same kind of on-the-job training. These programs teach novitiates much of the knowledge that is not taught or cannot be taught in a classroom.

In the United States, training is left to legal employers, who often employ a sink-or-swim philosophy. A law school graduate named Alex went to work for the district attorney in a major metropolitan area. When he arrived for work the first day, he found a stack of files sitting on his new desk. When he opened the top file, he noted that he was due in court to prosecute a case at 10 a.m. At 10:21 a.m., he had lost his first case. Many graduates enter law practice only to discover that they are forced to teach themselves how to practice law.

This whole matter is complicated by the fact that there are many ways to practice law. The criminal defense lawyer's practice is not at all like the insurance defense lawyer's. Practice in a small town may be totally unlike working as an associate in a Manhattan megafirm.

Despite all of this, new lawyers master their craft in the first five to seven years after law school. Because the legal profession has not developed efficient mechanisms for providing this post-graduate education, many inexperienced lawyers feel frustrated, incompetent, and confused.

Although studies show that this kind of dissatisfaction tends to diminish over time as the inexperienced lawyer develops competence as a practitioner, many lawyers actually leave the profession during this period. Ironically, despite new lawyers' fears, the vast majority of malpractice awards are against lawyers who have been out of school more than ten years.

Some law students and lawyers develop substance abuse problems. They try to cope with the stress of law school through the use of drugs and alcohol. Over time, a pattern of abuse can develop that will undermine both law school performance and professional growth. Often, individuals who struggle with substance problems engage in a process of denial that is tacitly supported by friends and loved ones. People want to believe that if they can get the job done, it does not matter what they did the night before, but over time the negative effects of drugs and alcohol catch up with them.

If you view competence as a "constantly receding goal," as one ABA Task Force did, you should be able to recognize that your level of performance may not be perfect upon graduation. As you proceed through this book, and as you pursue your legal career in the years to come, keep this in mind about developing professional competence: *A career is more than a series of jobs. It is a collection of unique, interlocking skills that can be brought into play in a variety of different settings.*

The Bar Exam

As if law school finals were not enough, the bar exam stands as one last hurdle you must pass before you are licensed to practice law. Bar examination requirements may be relevant to career decisions in a number of different ways.

- ◆ If you want to practice law in the traditional sense, you must pass the bar in the jurisdiction where you plan to practice. For some positions, such as practicing corporate law or teaching, you may not need to be licensed in the jurisdiction where you work, but you must be licensed in one or more other jurisdictions.

- ◆ Some positions (e.g., hearing examiners in state government) do not include bar passage as a prerequisite to being hired. Even in such areas, however, many law school graduates believe that bar membership is useful to them and, at a minimum, affords the option to go into traditional law practice at some point in time.

◆ The vast majority of all law graduates sit for the bar. In fact, the number of new bar admissions exceeds the number of law school graduates annually. This is because most states allow candidates to sit for the bar more than once, so every year the number of people who graduate from law school and sit for the bar is supplemented by a group of second-, third-, and fourth-time test-takers from prior years. Nationally, most applicants eventually pass at least one bar exam.

◆ The requirements for admission are slightly different in every jurisdiction. If you get a job early, you will be locked into taking the bar and meeting the requirements in that jurisdiction. If you pass the bar in a particular state, your job search, at least as far as law practice jobs are concerned, will be limited to that state.

◆ The passage rate varies considerably from state to state.

◆ Although every state now requires the Multistate Bar Examination (MBE), there are different rules for passing scores and acceptance of an MBE score administered in a different jurisdiction. You should carefully investigate the rules and procedures for taking the bar exam in all jurisdictions where you are considering applying for jobs.

◆ The question is not whether you will pass the bar, but where? Most states offer the bar examination only twice annually, and some (e.g., Delaware, Nevada) only once. Most bar exams are offered at approximately the same time (late July and mid-February). The scheduling problem means that it is logistically difficult to sit for more than two examinations during one examination season. Some states coordinate examination dates so that applicants can take the examination in neighboring jurisdictions. Others afford applicants no such luxury.

◆ Since the United States Supreme Court decision in *Supreme Court of New Hampshire v. Piper,* 470 U.S. 274, 105 S. Ct. 1271, 84 L. Ed. 2d 205 (1985), residency requirements for bar admission have been eliminated for the most part.

Jurisdictions that have attempted to restrict nonresident admission, however, may still present a few snares for the unwary. You may be required to attend a personal interview with the character and fitness committee—a task much easier for the resident than the nonresident. Or you may be required to obtain letters of recommendation from lawyers licensed to practice in the jurisdiction. At least one state (Delaware) requires applicants to serve an apprenticeship before being licensed.

◆ Character may be an issue. A student's youthful brushes with the law or other problems may present complications with the character and fitness committee in some states.

Mobility matters. The ability to move from one jurisdiction to another is also a factor. Some states, through reciprocity arrangements, allow lawyers with experience to be admitted on motion, while other states require experienced lawyers to sit for the full bar examination along with recent law school graduates. Most jurisdictions permit lawyers to appear in court on motion, or *pro hac vice,* in a state where they are not admitted, but there is no such opportunity for transactional lawyers. In many states, the Rules of Professional Conduct provide for lawyers temporary multijurisdictional practice. In these states, as long as a lawyer does not establish a permanent presence in a state where she is not licensed or hold herself out as being licensed in a jurisdiction where she is not, the lawyer will not be subject to discipline from limited incursions across state lines. Alternatively, a lawyer who anticipates establishing a permanent office in a state where she is not licensed should take the bar exam or apply for admission based on reciprocity.

Because of the high degree of career mobility these days, the chances are very good that you will not spend your entire career living and working in one jurisdiction and, even if you do, it is likely that you will have handled cases in several states. Looking down the road a bit, is it possible that you and your family may move? If you acquire a high degree of specialization, is it possible that new and more rewarding opportunities have developed in other areas of the country?

You may never have to face those or similar questions, but this is still a good time to think about potential answers. Many students find it is possible to take more than one bar examination and to qualify for entry into the bar of several states. If you can do so, be one of those students. Bar exams are far easier to take now than later, and taking more than one would be a good hedge for your future. Although you cannot determine the future, it is wise to take preventive measures against factors that could seriously impair your career development.

There is, however, an even more immediate concern: to find out what the exact bar admission requirements are for the state(s) in which you are currently interested. As long as bar admission standards remain under the jurisdiction of the individual states and territories of the United States, it is wise to know exactly what the specific standards are and how they will be interpreted in your own situation in the states where you may wish to practice.

Decisions about when and where to sit for the bar are important ones. They should not be taken lightly. You will save yourself considerable grief if you check out these matters before you make major career decisions.

Many legal jobs are contingent upon bar passage. You cannot afford to fail the bar after a successful educational career and job search. Only a few jurisdictions provide a "diploma privilege" (automatic admission for graduates of state law schools). Many law students do not think about potential problems until it is time for them to graduate and they apply to take the bar. Because information is easily accessible, it makes more sense to deal with the bar exam much earlier in the career planning process than is common.

Making the Best Possible Decisions

The whole job search can be faintly reminiscent of a medieval allegory in which the protagonist sets out on a quest for some noble ideal and encounters unbelievable trials and temptations along the way. Snares and pitfalls abound, false guides lead him astray, and nothing is what it seems to be. The entire journey is like a surrealistic nightmare. But if you are armed with a workable plan, your own modern quest for a job can be quite different.

Many planned and unplanned events punctuate the lives of all law students. Because no one can control every aspect of life, it becomes much more important to act on sound information when the need to make decisions arises.

Many law students express uncertainty about when to undertake various activities in the career choice and job search processes. Lack of sophistication about nuances in the job market and the hiring cycle of legal employers may deprive some students of opportunities that otherwise would be available to them.

Some students simply avoid dealing with career issues because the stress involved in job hunting makes it easy to procrastinate. Perhaps because of the numerous demands placed upon their time, many law students have a tendency to deal only with problems that need immediate attention. These students often look for jobs only when they absolutely, positively have to do it.

If you act on information in a timely manner throughout your law school career, not just when you are approaching graduation, you will maximize your options. The corollary, of course, is that if you fail to act on information in a timely manner, you will reduce your options. It all sounds pretty simple, right?

The truth is that nothing is ever as simple as it seems (just as nothing is ever as complicated as you were led to believe). There are many variables in this equation. You should understand, however, a few basic considerations. Some of these include the law school you attended, the geographic area of the country, the hiring patterns of the specific segments of the job market you are approaching, the timetable, the demands of your spouse or special friend, your outlook on life and long-term career objectives, your individual marketability based on special skills and credentials, and many other factors.

Identifying Your Skills and Values

4

The information you distill from the following exercises can be helpful to your analyzing your career skills. To complete the exercises, you need a new document in Word or other word processing software, and a block of uninterrupted time in a place that permits thinking. Before getting into the exercises, however, there are several caveats:

- ◆ *Tell the truth.* No one else needs to see this, so there is no reason to lie. Absolute, total, brutal honesty is the only way to do the exercises. Anything else will taint the results.
- ◆ *Spend the time to do it right.* The exact time will vary from individual to individual, but there is a limit below which the results will have diminishing usefulness.
- ◆ *Career assessment is ongoing.* This activity is not something to be done once and put aside forever. Career assessment continues throughout life. It may not be necessary to reconsider the results as the job search progresses, but it may be advantageous to rethink the ques-

tions asked here from time to time during your career, particularly at points of choice, transition, or frustration that
inevitably will occur.

◆ *Pre-law career planning is not enough.* The law school classroom experience, clerking, other extracurricular activities,
and learning to "think like a lawyer" make it necessary
to continue career planning already done, using both
the insights gained earlier in the process and those later
discovered.

◆ *It is impossible in one sense to know if a job is satisfying until
you try it.* There are inevitably elements of any work that
must be experienced to be understood. This means that
career planning cannot end with finding a job or graduation
from law school. It is a lifelong activity.

◆ *Career assessment is not the same as career planning.* The
term *planning* seems to suggest that there is a formula that
will get you from here to goal X by following steps 1, 2,
and 3. Things seldom happen according to plan, and many
well-intentioned career planners become frustrated with
the unplanned, and lose confidence in the career choice
process. It is more like following a path through the forest,
making choices at various forks using the best information
available at the time with only a compass as a general guide
for direction, than it is like following a map to drive the
interstate from New York to Chicago.

◆ *Do not procrastinate.* Because making career choices means
facing personal limitations, fears, and skeletons in the closet
(both real and imagined), it is a frightening and anxiety-
producing process. Too many law students cope with this
anxiety by ignoring the problem. This procrastination has
the unfortunate result of foreclosing many opportunities as
time passes. The individual who starts the process during
the first or second year of law school has a greater range
of choices than one who begins after completion of the bar
exam.

◆ *The process may raise more questions than it answers.* Do
not be discouraged if you come away from these exercises
with a sense of confusion. The issues are seldom black

and white. This tension is healthy, and is indicative of awareness. Someone who is absolutely sure of his or her career choices may be someone who has not given them much thought. Anyone recalling the first year of law school knows that when you are sure you know all the answers, you really do not understand; it is only when you feel confused that are you beginning to get close to the answers.

Skills Assessment

The skills assessment exercise that follows is intended to make you think, dream, and dredge up forgotten experiences. More important, by going through his exercise, you will be able to focus with greater clarity on your career goals.

Identifying Skills

Most of us have little experience at identifying skills. Because we seldom identify skills, we cannot articulate them when we need to in the job search process, much less in these exercises. This stumbling block is the single biggest impediment most law students have to effective job hunting.

It can now be revealed: Skills are things one can do. They are actions. Doing is expressed in the English language through transitive or action verbs, such as *analyze, propose, organize,* and *direct.* Thus, articulating skills requires no more than being able to describe actions using the full richness of the English language.

For example, someone who has participated in a moot court competition may have developed the following skills: *speaking, persuading, organizing, researching, responding,* and *listening.* By analyzing an activity in detail, it is possible to break it down into component skills. See Appendix E, page 383–384, for a representative list of skills commonly used by lawyers.

Frequently, it is difficult for law students to make the shift from describing job-specific skills to describing more general job-transferable skills. In other words, when completing these exercises, you will want to take skill descriptions from specific activities and describe them in terms that could be applied to other activities. Furthermore, when applying for a specific job, you will want to take these general terms and describe them in the language of the job.

In the previous example, a moot court participant may be able to identify an array of oral skills. As stated before, however, those same skills may be useful not only in work as a litigator, but also as a minister, politician, salesperson, or actor. In searching for a job, you may not have experience as an associate in a law firm but you may be able to demonstrate that you have done the things that associates do: speaking, persuading, organizing, researching, responding, and listening.

A Skills Identification Exercise

Set aside some time to do this exercise when you will not be interrupted or distracted. An hour should be sufficient for most people. Try to choose a comfortable place with a positive feel. It may be useful to have a dictionary or thesaurus with you to facilitate word choice as an aid during the exercise (as well as throughout the job search). Now you are ready to begin.

- ◆ First, think about the most successful educational experiences, jobs, activities, and relationships you have had over the course of your life. How far back you want to go may be a factor of age, memory, or predilection. Make notes so you will remember these experiences as you proceed.
- ◆ Next, think about what contributed to your success in these enterprises. Your reflections can be as broad or narrow as you like. Add these thoughts to your notes.
- ◆ Now, go back through your experiences and try to extract the concrete skills you used or developed in order to achieve the success you did. Remember to think of skills as *actions*. There is no need to edit your list, so err on the side of inclusivity.
- ◆ When you are comfortable with your skill listings, go back and combine the skills identified in your experience into one list. Note those skills that were connected to several experiences.
- ◆ When you have a single list of verbs, attempt to dissect those described into finer terms by asking what other skills were required to perform the listed skills. Wherever pos-

sible, describe the skills in legal terms, even if you used the skill in a totally nonlegal experience.

◆ Prioritize your list. If a skill appears several times, note the number in parentheses after the skill (e.g., drafting documents).

◆ At this point, you should have a rather lengthy list of skills that you have developed over the course of your life. By itself, the list will help you to prepare your résumé, draft cover letters, complete application forms, answer interview questions, and scrutinize job listings for openings that are right for you.

◆ One more step in this exercise can take your understanding of these skills a little further. Richard Bolles and other writers on the subject of careers have attempted to identify skill groupings. Although their classifications might differ slightly, Bolles's approach is typical. He says that there are six basic skill groups. You can take your list of skills and assign each skill to one of these six groups (most easily on six separate sheets of paper):

- Athletic
- Numerical
- Influencing
- Helping
- Creating
- Investigating

◆ Take a few minutes and think about what this means:

- Do your skills fall into one or two groups, or several?
- Where do you think most law-related skills fall?
- Do you think the answer might be different for different types of practice?
- Do your skills and skill groups seem consistent with your understanding of legal work in the areas of law and practice settings that you are exploring?

◆ Save your edited list(s). You will find a variety of uses for the information you have extracted from your successful experiences:

- Drafting your résumé
- Interviewing employers
- Evaluating job openings to see if there is a good fit for you
- Deciding on a job offer for the same reason

◆ If you are brave and have time, you can repeat this exercise using your failures. Sure, we all have had experiences when things didn't go our way. This is a chance to analyze what went wrong to avoid repeating ourselves—it's better to replicate the good than the bad. Right?

Identifying Values

Another area worth exploring involves work values. Values are subjective attitudes you hold concerning work that will affect your perceptions of any job you take. They reflect how you feel about yourself, your colleagues, and your work environment. When you work at a place where the institution is consistent with your work values, you are likely to feel positively about what you are doing. Conversely, if the organization espouses or reflects values to which you do not subscribe, you are more likely to develop negative attitudes about your work.

Sometimes people who are good at what they do hate their work. If we looked at skills alone, this would not make sense, because we predict that someone who has the skills to do the job will be successful at the job and, if she is successful, she will be satisfied. But if the work does not satisfy her work values, then she will not be happy even though she is competent to handle the work.

Because work values go directly to how you feel about your job, you should try to identify them. To do this in a structured way, create another document and answer these three questions:

◆ In past work settings, are there people you have particularly respected and admired and, if so, what values did they possess that contributed to your admiration?
◆ What principles or values do you want to see in the individuals with whom you will work?
◆ What characteristics among your co-workers would lead you to think seriously about quitting your job?

These considerations are more important than most people think. One toxic co-worker can make life miserable for everyone in the office. A boss whose ethics are more shady than your own can leave your stomach in knots every day when you leave the office. A workaholic amid a group of free spirits is a recipe for disaster. The *Dilbert* cartoon and the television show, *The Office,* pointedly skewer these clashes in work values but, unfortunately, they are much funnier being watched as fictionalized satire than when experienced in real life.

Your answers to these questions should tell you a great deal about your work values. By identifying values that are important, you should be able to look for a work environment that will support those values. It may be worth noting that sometimes the values we espouse in the luxury of reflection are not the same as the values we demonstrate in the crucible of action.

No job is perfect, and sometimes it takes time to establish a supportive atmosphere in a work setting. Many elements of the environment will remain hidden from you until after you go to work because they are difficult to assess during the interview process. Yet if you have an idea about what values are important to you, and look for clues as you interview, you can maximize your chances of making a sound choice in the end.

Pulling It All Together

By this time, you should have amassed considerable information about yourself, and picked up several insights along the way. This process has been designed to help you focus on the specific skills, skill groups and values you have developed in your life, and to winnow salient facts from a variety of sources that you can use in making sound career choices. This information will be invaluable to you at every stage of career planning and the job search. Ask yourself:

- ◆ Are you surprised at the results?
- ◆ Do your skills correlate with your preconceived notions of your strengths and abilities? If not, what accounts for the differences?
- ◆ Are there skills that you feel need to be developed to a greater degree in the future? Which ones?
- ◆ Will your résumé look different as a result of this experience?
- ◆ Will your career plans or job search take a turn?

Most law students find that their perspective on who they are and where they are going shifts—for some, slightly; for others, radically—as a result of skills analysis. There are many so-called experts, such as psychologists and career counselors, who can give and interpret career and vocational interest or aptitude tests. They may be able to help, but they can cost money. Many students can gain sufficient insights for their purposes through this process of regimented self-discovery just described.

Friends, family, and co-workers will all be ready to tell you what you can and ought to do with your talents. Their impressions, while worth noting, do not compare to your own assessment of what you can do. It is very likely that the assessments of those who know you will coincide with your analysis of yourself. If their perceptions of you do not seem to be accurate, you might ask yourself, "Why?" Either they are not getting a clear picture of you from things you tell them or you have not been totally honest with yourself in the evaluation. Either way, you should take note of the incongruity.

For many law students, the most difficult part of the entire process is identifying their skills. While people, in general, have little experience in skills analysis, law students probably have less. If their pre-legal education did not lead them away from subjective inner-directed methods of solving problems, law school undoubtedly did. Despite the fact that skills analysis may make some students uncomfortable, it is not a mystical process that can only be understood by an elect few. Remember these concepts, which are integral to your understanding of your skills:

- As a law student, you possess the innate intelligence and training to think rationally about employment.
- You alone have total responsibility for your life and the direction it takes. And this responsibility is not limited to just becoming competent as a lawyer and achieving success on the job.
- You have to make choices. When the road forks, you have to take one path or theother. Whenever you make a choice, you open up some options and foreclose others; you gain something and you lose something.

◆ Know how you make decisions. The way you get to the answer may be as important as the answer itself.

◆ Act at a time when you have the greatest control over the outcome of your decisions.

◆ Not only should you act to minimize the risk, but you should know what kinds of risks you are willing to take in the job search.

◆ You possess an array of skills that are transferable from one job or career to another. Too often, we think of skills in the vocabulary of one field and fail to see that the same skill might be transferred to a different area.

◆ Your career and life are your responsibility.

As you proceed through this book, the conclusions you reached in this chapter will have several uses. Throughout the process of considering broad career fields, as well as specific jobs, it will be important to compare the skills required by the job with the skills you possess. At this point, having gone through these self-assessment exercises, defining the skills required by the job may still present a formidable problem while defining the skills you have should not.

Evaluating the Job Market

5

One of the most important steps in career assessment involves evaluating the market for new lawyers to determine what is available. Some students may spend less time on this step because they already have a clear idea of what and where they want to practice. On the other hand, realities of the job market may require subsequent modification of initial objectives.

For many law students, taking a broad look at the job market can be a useful or even necessary step in making sound career choices. Surprisingly, a substantial number of law students do not have a good feel for what opportunities exist for lawyers.

There is a great deal of misinformation floating around. Some of it is perpetuated by the news media and legal press. Some of it is passed from student to student at school. Some of it is perpetuated by pre-law advisors, practicing lawyers, and other supposedly informed individuals. As a smart consumer, you will undoubtedly listen to what everyone has to say, but believe only what you can verify yourself.

Another reason to conduct a market analysis is that the market itself is always changing. Before this book is published, some of the information it contains will be out-of-date. Whatever you read or hear should be subject to review to determine whether the information is still valid.

In conducting your market analysis, you will want to investigate five topics:

- *What are the legal needs of the consumers of legal services?* Stated another way, what substantive areas of law or fields where law training is useful will produce career opportunities of interest to you?
- *What are the demographic characteristics of these consumers?* In other words, where do they live and what do we know about them?
- *What types of organizations will be delivering services to these consumers?* More specifically, who will be hiring law graduates at the time you want to go to work?
- *Where are these employers located?* What credentials will employers require of prospective employees?
- *What general economic conditions will affect the marketplace for legal services?* What is the general state of the economy, and the legal economy specifically? Getting down to your situation, what are the financial rewards and prospects for employment?

As a component of career assessment, the market analysis should precede the job search itself. It would be an exercise in futility to establish priorities upon which a job search will be based without looking at the parameters of job availability. You are much more likely to conduct a successful job search campaign if you take a look at the job market opportunities earlier in the process rather than later.

Part IV of this book (beginning on page 211) contains an overview of the marketplace of legal and law-related services. The chapters offer short descriptions of a number of the most common types of career choices. You should view these comments as jumping-off points for your own research rather than the research itself. The remainder of this chapter addresses some basic questions about where you want to work and live that you should ask as you look at the job market. Each of these factors should play an important role in your analysis of the work environment.

Employment Settings

Substantial differences exist in the way you are likely to spend your time on the job in different areas of law practice. This may be relevant to the type of organization where you work. A list of major categories appears in Part IV.

Larger organizations, whether law firms, corporations, or agencies, are likely to be more hierarchical, structured, and institutional than smaller organizations. Organizations may vary widely as to how entrepreneurial they are, as well as how entrepreneurial they expect their employees to be. Interestingly, the largest law firms are relatively small business organizations. Despite the fact that the largest law firms are becoming increasingly large and bureaucratic, the majority of lawyers still practice in the functional equivalent of a "mom and pop" store. Beset by Walmart and mega-box chains, these small businesses struggle to find economic viability in a world that seems to have left them behind.

Different organizations may have different ideas about professional behavior, dress, attitude, and philosophy. They espouse varying views about training and nurturing new employees. And different firms will hold widely varying institutional goals and objectives that inevitably have an impact upon the careers of the people who work for them.

It is not always easy to get a feel for the "personality" of legal employers from the literature, Websites, or statements of official representatives. It is even more difficult to make generalizations about classes of employers.

You should investigate different sources to gain a clear picture of the various job market settings. A conscientious investigation should lead you to some conclusions about the various categories of employment that interest you. In one sense, you are comparing your career skills to the requirements of the market to ascertain where you are most likely to be successful and consequently happy.

Choosing Where to Live

Where you live can be as important to your happiness as where you work. You should look carefully at different localities in terms of the jobs that are available, and the lifestyles that are likely to be supported in that setting. These are some of the key questions:

- How many lawyers practice in the area?
- What do they do?
  - Practice in law firms?
  - Corporations?
  - Government agencies?
- What substantive fields of law are supported by the state and local economy?
- What are the prospects for growth in population?
  - In the business community?
  - In the legal field?
- What opportunities for professional development are you likely to find in these various geographic settings?

Places vary widely in the types of lifestyle they support as well as those they tolerate. Urban, suburban, and rural areas offer unique advantages and present discrete disadvantages. The considerations that go into this analysis are limitless. They can include everything from whether there is a church or community supporting your religious faith to whether you can get to the opera often enough to satisfy your cultural pang.

Increasingly, cities, states, and regions are becoming less unique. You get tacos in Boston and lobster in New Mexico. Shopping malls all seem to have the same stores. Some factors such as climate, ethnic mix, and history may distinguish geographic areas but, on the whole, there are more similarities than differences from place to place today than ever before.

This does not mean that you should not look at a geographic setting; it only means that your investigation may not be an easy one. It may also be the case that some of your preconceptions about places prove to be inaccurate or dated. It is likely also that you will be able to find opportunities in similarly situated cities in different parts of the country. Those who are not tied to a particular geographic location by family, working spouse, or other roots may find greater flexibility than previously imagined.

For some individuals, geographic choice may be the most important element in the career assessment process. Many law students are tied to a particular geographic area. They own a house or other property there. They have a working spouse. They have family and contacts in the community. They have an interest or avocation that can be pursued most easily in a particular geographic area.

Many students select a geographic locale for lifestyle reasons. For the most part, geographic choices should be factored into your priorities. For most of us, geographic choices represent preferences. For some students, the geographic choice may be so critical that it limits the scope of the job search. Such parameters inevitably restrict the available choices, so try to distinguish strong preferences from inflexible conditions.

The role of your law school in geographic selection is often underestimated. Two-thirds or more of the graduates of virtually every law school in the United States go to work within 250 miles of where they went to law school. This is true of so-called national law schools as well as local ones. Graduates of nationally prominent law schools may be able to make a move from coast to coast more easily than their counterparts in new or less widely recognized institutions; even among these schools, however, there is an element of regionalism in the choices of graduates.

Some geocentric decisions may be attributed to convenience and the fact that students develop ties to the area where they live. Some may be attributed to people selecting law schools in areas where they plan to practice. Much of it is the result of gradual accretion; over the years greater numbers of any school's graduates settle in the region where the school is located and this, in turn, expands the opportunities for current graduates.

Metropolitan Areas

The decennial U.S. Census for 2000 identified 286 metropolitan areas in the United States, ranging from New York City (21,199,865) to Enid, Oklahoma (57,813). Fifty metropolitan areas exceed one million in population, and eighty-two exceed 500,000. The Census Bureau includes both Metropolitan Statistical Areas with a single city core (e.g., Atlanta), and Consolidated Metropolitan Statistical Areas with more than one primary city center (e.g., Dallas–Fort Worth). The metropolitan areas include city centers, suburbs, and newly minted exurbs (bedroom communities more than one hour distant from the city center). The ten largest metropolitan areas are:

1. New York (including northern New Jersey, Long Island, southern Connecticut, and parts of Pennsylvania)
2. Los Angeles (including Riverside and Orange counties)
3. Chicago (including Chicago suburbs and parts of Indiana and Wisconsin)
4. Washington–Baltimore (including D.C. and suburban Maryland and Virginia)
5. San Francisco–Oakland–San Jose
6. Philadelphia (including Wilmington, Delaware, and Atlantic City, New Jersey)
7. Boston (including Worcester and Lawrence)
8. Detroit (including Ann Arbor and Flint)
9. Dallas–Fort Worth
10. Houston (including Galveston and Brazoria counties)

The Atlanta, Miami–Fort Lauderdale, Seattle, and Phoenix areas also have over three million inhabitants. What can we say about these fourteen places? First, more than one in three Americans live in one of these areas. Second, many if not all of these areas cross state lines, and all cross county jurisdictional lines. Third, these places are diverse ethnically and culturally. All are growing (most in double digits), and the increases are primarily from ethnically diverse groups. People are traveling farther and farther to go to work, while at the same time employers are moving to suburban locations as well. Finally, a high percentage of lawyers and legal work can be found in these areas.

These metropolitan financial or government centers attract and employ large numbers of lawyers. In all the leading legal markets, the makeup of the bar is diverse as to organization, substantive practice, and demographic composition. These communities are supported by strong local bar associations, multiple law schools, and, in many cases, a dedicated legal press.

These institutions help restore some of the cohesiveness that is lost when the lawyer population becomes so large that bar members can no longer know all of their fellow lawyers. Such cities frequently have a number of law firms containing more lawyers than can be found in most rural counties in their state.

Metropolitan areas with a population of more than 500,000 but less than three million include cities that have significant lawyer populations and substantial legal activity. These cities include state capitals, regional commercial centers, and transportation hubs. Some of the fastest-growing metropolitan areas in the United States (e.g., Denver, Austin, Las Vegas) fall into this group.

The bar in these cities has frequently lost the camaraderie and cohesiveness associated with small-town practice, but may not have developed all the resources and communication services of the largest cities. The largest firms in these cities frequently approximate the size of medium-sized firms in the largest metropolitan areas. Law practice and the bar are frequently less diverse than in the larger legal markets, often reflecting the specific population and the economy of the region.

Almost 200 metropolitan areas fall within a range of population between 50,000 and 500,000. The core cities in these areas are legal centers within a well-defined geographic area. The economy is frequently dominated by one or several clearly identifiable industries, or an extensive agricultural area. Some are state capitals (Santa Fe), or university towns (Iowa City), or both (Madison). Along the Mexican border, cities like McAllen and Laredo, Texas, are growing astronomically with economies that transcend the national boundaries.

In these metropolitan areas, the largest firms usually contain fewer than fifty lawyers, and the bar itself retains some vestiges of a small-town legal community. Most of these cities serve as county seats and as business centers. Frequently, the bulk of legal activity in the county is conducted in the city, if only because the courthouse is there. Generally, there is an extended agricultural economy in the area, as well as local industry.

The 'Burbs

Of the many changes that characterize post-World-War-II America, none is quite as pervasive as the rise of suburbia. Without discussing the sociological aspects of this phenomenon, the demographic patterns are quite clear. Large numbers of residents of many older cities have abandoned the city center for more pastoral habitats.

As newer cities developed, the suburban model became the pre-dominant housing pattern.

In some cases, the suburbs simply assimilated the pre-existing towns and villages. In others, whole new communities blossomed on the sites of farms, ranches, and forests. Shopping malls and commercial strips replaced downtown as the nation's number-one shopping destination. A majority of people born after the end of World War II grew up in the suburban culture, and, in fact, the chances are extremely good that at some point during your professional career you will make the choice to live as a suburbanite.

The suburbs represent a geographical choice for law students in two different ways. First, there is a geographical option for any lawyer who works in a city: to live in the heart of the city or to live in the suburbs. The tradeoff is often between a house with grass and trees and a formidable daily commute to the city, versus the problems and crowds of the urban environment and relatively easy access to work and cultural events.

Most lawyers in these bedroom communities trundle off to the city each day to work, yet a significant number practice in the community where they live. Because suburban communities can vary from small towns to cities of several hundred thousand to vast unincorporated areas, it is difficult to make generalizations about suburban practice. It is in many ways more like small-town than big-city practice. The clients are basically individuals and small businesses. But unlike the small town that may be a county seat or at least have a distinct identity, the suburban town's identity is merged into both that of its parent city and of its sister suburbs.

Suburban cities cannot escape their satellite nature. Not only do many of their citizens work in the city, but city newspapers, television stations, and other media and events dominate the culture. The financial and governmental heart of the metropolitan area is inevitably elsewhere. Nonsuburban towns and cities seem more like microcosms of larger municipalities. The distinction is hardest to make in towns that existed before urban sprawl, especially those on the periphery of the metropolitan area. On the other hand, a definite suburban culture exits, which is neither small-town nor big-city.

The legal business will reflect the particular problems of suburban populations. Courts and administrative agencies are likely to be "downtown." Law offices are more likely to be located in shopping centers and small, detached buildings than in large office buildings. The bar will be less cohesive than the small-town bar, and lawyers themselves are likely to perceive as much identity with the larger community of lawyers as with the local bar associations.

Small Towns and Rural Areas

Despite the predominance of urban practice in the legal profession, it would be a mistake to write off small-town and rural practice. Throughout the United States, hundreds of small towns serve as county seats for nonmetropolitan counties and as the economic centers of robust and dynamic economies. In fact, lawyers live and work in almost every hamlet that constitutes a political entity or operates a court. Other lawyers live outside of any incorporated area on farms, ranches, and mountain retreats.

There is a correlation between population and legal activity. The number of lawyers per capita population tends to decrease as population increases. Thus, the ratio of population to lawyers usually exceeds 1,000:1 in rural county seats, although it may be 100:1 or less in the major cities.

The practice of law is defined by the population and the economy. Certain threads run through small-town law practice almost anywhere in the United States. The largest firm may contain twenty or fewer lawyers. The total number of lawyers in the community often will be less than one hundred.

For lawyers who practice in small towns and rural areas, much of their business involves representing individuals and families. Frequently, many of these clients are linked to farming and ranching in some way or to another local industry, such as fishing, logging, or tourism.

As a rule, everyone knows everyone else. A handshake can still bind a business deal. Grievances are frequently handled informally. Reputations are slowly made and quickly lost. Family ties can be as important as legal expertise in developing a clientele.

Lawyers frequently retain a greater degree of the social standing that is sometimes lost in more anonymous urban centers. Their income is often less than it would be in the large cities, but the cost of living is less, and for many people lifestyle considerations more than compensate for the lack of economic advantages. For these lawyers, going to the county seat may be an excursion. They are frequently on the periphery of the organized bar and may even practice law part-time. Today, modern technology and the media make it possible for more lawyers to practice outside metropolitan areas. Nationally known trial lawyer Jerry Spence, for example, practices from a ranch near Jackson Hole, Wyoming.

Alternative Alternatives

In the modern legal world, an increasing number of legal employers have multiple offices. These might be large firms with offices around the world, large companies with legal department outposts wherever they have work sites, state and federal government agencies, military legal offices, or smaller rural firms seeking to provide services over a wide geographic area. This phenomenon raises the possibility that choosing an employer might not answer all the questions about geographic choice. In the old world of one firm, one office, a choice of firm dictated the geographic choice, and a geographic choice limited the firms one could consider. Today, in many cases, choosing the employer only narrows, but does not eliminate, the geographic options. And it is increasingly possible for someone who gets to a job location and does not like it to move to another location within the same firm, company, or agency.

Narrowing the Options

Before leaving this subject, it may be useful for you to put some flesh on the bare bones that have been presented. Before you start, try to make a list of all the settings you might consider. "Anything" is not a sufficiently narrow response. Combinine the factors, type of organization, type of practice, and type of community, and then list all the combinations you would be willing to consider.

Based on this list, spend some time investigating the job market in these particular settings. Look carefully at your own needs and requirements. Use information interviews and other oral techniques as well as reading to collect your information. This research process can take days to months depending on the number of options investigated, the depth of research, and the amount of time available. You will find, however, that this provides a much clearer picture of the prospects than simply listening to one or two people or reading a single publication. After completing your research, you are ready to establish some priorities and develop a timetable for your job search.

Making geographical choices can be a complex but enlightening venture if based on careful consideration of how you want to live. Unfortunately, many law students make snap decisions about where they want to practice while they agonize over what to practice. The better approach is to funnel information by winnowing undifferentiated facts into organized patterns leading to rational choices. See Chart 3, below.

Chart 3

The Information Funnel

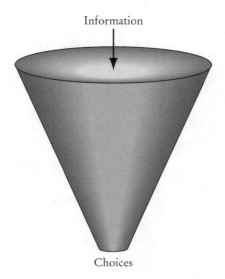

Information

Choices

The choice of a place to practice law may depend on where jobs are available. Some places are glutted with lawyers, giving rise to the view that the job market is tight everywhere. This simply is not true; some areas are very short of lawyers. San Francisco, Boston, and other large cities that are attractive geographically or have a number of law schools, tend to be crowded. Smaller cities with only one law school may have the same problem.

There is no shortage of demographic information for analyzing places to live. There appears to be less information about regional differences in how law is practiced, so you may have to do some research on your own. Local newspapers, information interviews, chambers of commerce brochures, census figures, and other business research data will all prove valuable to you.

Establishing Priorities

6

The final steps in career assessment involve establishing priorities and developing a timetable for the job search. Many law students omit these steps because it seems self-evident to them that after they have looked at their own skills and reviewed the market they can proceed directly to the job hunt.

The importance of ranking priorities is that it gives you focus. It forces you to organize your job search in a manageable and rational way. Similarly, establishing a timetable for the job search early in your law school career relieves the panicky feeling that you must find something—anything—in the last month.

Developing a List of Options

Start your job search with the highest priority and then proceed down the list. It sounds simple, but many law students have problems identifying specific employers during the job search process because they have not prioritized during the career planning process.

It is not necessary to rigidly follow this list of priorities. If a job opportunity comes up that falls under another listed priority while you are still working on the first, you can pursue the job if you want to. The idea is to make the process work for you, not you for it. The paradigm merely calls for you to devote the greater part of your energies to the categories at the top of your list, and pursue other avenues only if your first ones do not pan out.

So, how do you rank priorities? At this point, you should have accumulated quite a bit of information from your self-analysis (Chapter 4) and your evaluation of the job market (Chapter 5). All you have to do is to convert your original list of interests into an ordered list of choices based upon what you have learned about yourself and the market. Your investigation may have uncovered one or two new alternatives. You will also probably want to drop some of the alternatives you had initially considered based upon what you have learned.

At this time, rank your possibilities in a document (see Chart 4). List no fewer than five and no more than ten. The reason for these limitations is to impose a degree of manageability to the list. If the list is too short, you may find yourself unemployed and out of options, an unfortunate combination. If you have too many options, your job search will not seem to have any clear definition. You may find that you have not forced yourself to make choices, but rather merely rearranged a big, unmanageable list.

Maintaining Options

As you go into the job search, you will want to identify specific employers who meet the criteria defined by your ranked list. Begin with your first option and proceed down the list. As you near the end of the list, but before the list is exhausted, you should add additional options. Hopefully, you will not reach this point. It is better to be prepared for the worst-case scenario, however, than to find yourself out of ideas as well as options.

Developing a Timetable

You began the career planning process before you came to law school, but you do not stop when you matriculate. Many students

Chart 4
Ranked Options

Type of Position	Type of Employer	Location	Substantive Area
1.			
2.			
3.			
4.			
5.			
6.			
7.			
8.			
9.			
10.			
11.			
12.			
13.			
14.			
15.			

spend a significant amount of time during the first year of law school going through the steps explained in the last three chapters. They begin the job search during the second year of school and complete it sometime during the third year. If this is the rule, then the rule is the exception.

In reality, the process is much more complicated for most law students. For one reason or another, many law students do not begin the process of career exploration until later in their law school careers, some not until graduation. The closer in time that you are to the date you start work, the more compressed the entire process will be, and the greater the temptation to take shortcuts.

Many law students discover that experiences during law school itself alter the original vision of what they want to do. Career choices made during the first year of law school may not hold up during the third year. For this reason, it is almost always necessary to review your analysis at least annually. In fact, this is something that you should do on a regular basis throughout your legal career. We all change, and our plans should keep step with our identities.

It is not always possible to proceed on a straight line through the career planning process. For many law students, the planning process can be interrupted by diversions into the job search process from early in law school: part-time jobs during the school year, summer jobs, or even full-time jobs taken temporarily so that you can earn enough to complete law school. Thus, it may be necessary to jump forward and deal with elements of the job search (e.g., to look for a job, you have to have a résumé).

In one sense, jobs you obtain during law school represent another facet of the career planning process. You could call this a testing process. As you gain experience in different work settings, you will be able to test your hypothesis about career options in the crucible of the marketplace.

The reality that you may pursue jobs during law school does not alter the fact that career planning is the first step in the process of obtaining employment after graduation. Chart 5 describes a time line that illustrates alternative timetables for the career planning process. You will note the different schedule for day and evening students.

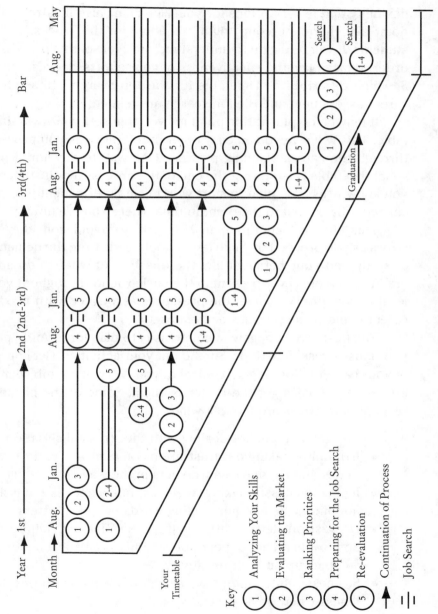

Chart 5
Career Planning Timetable

This chart demonstrates that the longer you wait to begin, the more compressed the time frame will be. This translates into less flexibility and fewer options for you. The chart also illustrates the point that there is no one "right" schedule for the process for all students. It will be useful to understand the cycle of this process in order to maximize the effectiveness of your efforts. See also Chart 6, which describes a "Timetable for the Job Search," to see how career assessment and the job search are related.

It may be helpful at this point for you to insert your own time-table. This will give you an easy point of reference as you proceed through the career planning process. One way to develop a personal timetable is to start at the end of the process. For instance, if you know when you plan to start working at a permanent job, you can work backward to the point in time where you are now.

This simple technique can help you to avoid considerable stress as you proceed through law school. Aside from the demands of study and your personal life, the question of what to do after graduation looms ever-present in the background throughout your legal education. For some, the pressures associated with making career choices can produce acute anxiety.

The best way to negate such stress is to plan for it. Anticipate your most stressful periods. Spread out your activities. Get control of your career before it gets control of you. Very often, job searchers let the process get the better of them. Some of the negative responses to stress are the following:

- ◆ Procrastination: not dealing with the stressful situation
- ◆ Irritability: taking out frustrations on family, friends, classmates and anyone else who gets in the way
- ◆ Ineffectiveness: making careless mistakes, like missing appointments and misspelling words on cover letters
- ◆ Depression: letting little failures become big failures; if applicants do not appear upbeat and optimistic, employers will pick up on their negativity
- ◆ Sickness: quite simply, we are all more prone to physical illness when we are overstressed
- ◆ Psychological problems: when someone's behavior deviates so far from acceptable norms that he functions irrationally, he may engage in conduct that endangers himself or others

Chart 6
Job Search Timetable

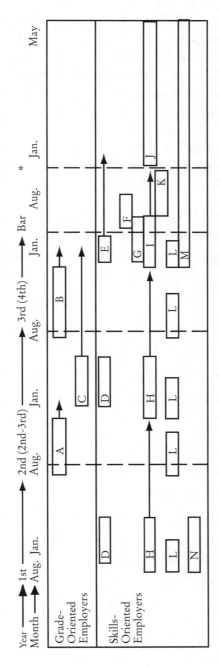

Key

*   *   Bar Results

☐   Box Indicates primary window of opportunity.

↑   Arrow indicates continued limited opportunities.

A   OCI Employers (Summer)

B   OCI Emloyers (Permanent)

C   Judicial Clerkships

D   Non-OCI Government and Public Interest (Summer)

E   Non-OCI Government and Public Interest (Permanent)

F   Government (End of Budget Year)

G   Education, Fellowships, Graduate School

H   Non-OCI Law Firms and Corporations (Summer)

I   Non–OCI Law Firms and Corporations (Permanent)

J   Small Firms (Hiring Only After Bar Results)

K   Solo Practice (Prep.)

L   Part-Time (Local)

M   Nonlegal Business and Miscellaneous

N   1st Year Summer Volunteer

Okay. This sounds pretty dire. If you weren't stressed before reading this depressing news, you are now! The point is that some students react badly to the pressures of the job search, and some more badly than others. Some will encounter serious issues. For the small number of people who have an unusually bad response to job search stress, it is important to seek professional help from a career counselor, a psychologist, or another helping professional.

You should not forget that stress has a positive element, because it motivates you to face challenges and do your best. Stress can clarify issues that seem vague and ill-defined under less pressure. Stress can be molded as an ally in the job search if you manage it well.

Fortunately, most of you will live through all of this quite well, thank you. You may be able to avoid maladaptive behavior like procrastination or a surly mood by recognizing the problem and adjusting your responses accordingly. Almost all of you will find that your mood recovers remarkably once you get a job.

The Job Search

What You Need to Know about the Hiring Process

7

Law students often ask what employers want in a candidate. This question underlies most student concerns about résumés, interviews, preferred courses of study, and the like. Since no two lawyers are alike, and different types of organizations have different hiring practices and needs, it is difficult to generalize about what employers want. The hiring process, however, is not without clues.

Employer Needs

An employer must first be sure that the workload in the office requires additional assistance. This is true for new associates, experienced lawyers, and nonlegal support staff alike. The exception is when the job seeker creates the need by demonstrating a skill set that the employer cannot live without—or believes that to be the case. For example, one might convince an employer that her special qualifications could match unmet needs in the organization. Generally speaking, however, if the employer does not perceive the need to hire someone, the firm will not initiate the hiring process.

Recruitment Costs

Few law students realize the economic costs to a firm of hiring an associate, but employers must evaluate the economic considerations before deciding to hire a new lawyer. One consideration, for example, is where to put a new lawyer. The cost of office space is considerable. In 2008, standard office space in the major metropolitan areas was renting for $30 to over $150 per square foot per year. An area of 100 square feet for a desk and chair will cost a firm $3,000 to $15,000. This figure does not include the cost of furnishing and maintaining the new lawyer's space, or the additional space required for secretarial support.

There may simply not be space available to accommodate an additional person. It is not unheard of for new lawyers to find themselves occupying the library, sharing space with several others, or even working in a basement file-storage area. An employer knows that this is far from ideal, but sometimes the work demands take precedence over the environment.

The new lawyer not only occupies space but also requires support services. Secretaries, legal assistants, and file and billing clerks all take up precious room. It may be possible to absorb a new lawyer into an office without additions to the support staff, but, if any are necessary, an employer must plan for space for these individuals as well.

The list continues. The cost of office equipment such as telephones, PDAs, computers and software, dictating units, and furniture and file cabinets must be included. In 2008, annual overhead costs for a new associate typically equaled or exceeded the cost of salary and benefits for a new lawyer. A simple formula many employers use in estimating the cost of adding an associate to the office is called the rule of thirds. Salary represents one-third of the cost, overhead counts one-third, and one-third of the expense is eaten up in partner training and review time.

No matter what the size of the law office may be, the decision to add an associate will also involve recruiting costs. In larger firms, the cost to recruit one associate may exceed $150,000. In smaller firms that do not run formal recruitment programs, the cost will be less, but it is still a substantial investment.

To put this into perspective, if a large firm needs to hire twenty new lawyers at $150,000 per hire in direct and indirect costs, the program will cost $3 million just to get the associates in the door. The major part of this expense is from partner and associate time involved in interviewing. The costs of training the new hires, including lost time spent overseeing and reviewing their work, and writing off time spent by the new lawyers that cannot be billed to clients, may exceed the recruitment costs of such a program.

Even the smallest office, planning to add only one associate, faces a substantial investment of time and money in the recruitment process. Every minute of reading résumés, making phone calls, writing letters, and interviewing candidates is time away from client work. It may seem more convenient for you that the employer come to your campus, but if the number of people from your school interviewing with an employer is small, it may be much more cost-effective for the employer to interview at the law office.

Another consideration is the per capita cost of hiring a new lawyer. If a five hundred-lawyer firm adding twenty lawyers invests $150,000 per person hired, that cost divided by all the lawyers on staff equals $6,000 per hire. If it costs a sole practitioner $25,000 to recruit one associate, the money must come out of the solo's own wallet. In practical terms, this means that small firms are less likely than large ones to use campus interviews, summer clerkship programs, or high starting salaries as a recruiting strategy.

A final consideration is the cost of losing an associate. If you and the firm decide to part company, the loss is more easily absorbed by a large firm, which generally anticipates a certain turnover among associates. But for the small firm, losing someone after spending time and money on recruiting and training can be disastrous. There is pressure to make the right decision the first time. At the same time, the small firm may lack the resources to conduct a thorough recruiting program to find the right person.

Your best strategy is to let the small firm know you want to work for them. Be willing to assume some of your own interviewing costs, and expect to make less money when you start. Work really hard during the first year of employment—it is even more critical to do this in the small firm than in the large firm.

Economics of Hiring

In addition to recruiting costs and overhead costs, many other economic factors go into the decision to hire a new lawyer. Learning a few basic principles of law firm management will help you understand the very different hiring patterns for different employers:

◆ First, hiring is an economic decision for a law firm. If you as a new lawyer do not carry your weight, your stay with your employer may be brief.

◆ Second, it is easier for a large firm to predict its needs in advance, recruit effectively, and bear the cost of training new associates than it is for a small firm or sole practitioner.

◆ Third, understanding the economics of law firm hiring will give you an advantage in the interviewing process, whether it be on campus or in the law office.

The fees charged to clients in a private law office determine its income, and hiring decisions are inextricably linked to this reality. Law firm income directly impacts compensation levels that legal employers offer.

In most firms, all the lawyers in the office who work on a client's case keep time records. Each lawyer will have an assigned dollar rate, which the client will be charged. Charges are also recorded for legal assistants and secretarial work, photocopying, telephone calls, travel time, court time, and so on. Normally, the client will be sent an itemized bill on a monthly basis for all of the charges incurred.

How the hourly billing charges for lawyers are calculated is of critical importance to you. Partner rates are based on such factors as who developed the business, who did the work, and the degree of expertise required. Associate rates are based on quite different factors and these are more important for your consideration.

Hourly rates for associates, determined by the number of years they have been admitted to the bar, usually will be fairly uniform for associates at the same level within an office. Figured into the hourly rate is the associate's salary, share of overhead, employee benefits, and other costs that cannot be charged directly to a client.

To keep track of time spent on various client matters, each law firm employee keeps detailed time records, usually expressed in six-minute units or 0.1 hour. Phone calls, photocopying charges, and similar expenses are also noted. Many associates are unpleasantly surprised to find that the law office expects nore than 1,700 annual billable hours from them. Some firms actually require associates to bill over 2,000 hours each year.

Those 2,000 billable hours may not seem extreme if you assume that you will work just forty hours a week for fifty weeks a year in order to meet that criterion. Unfortunately, much of your time will not be billable. A beginning lawyer may take twenty-four hours to draft a contract, for example, while an experienced associate could have completed the matter in eight hours. The client cannot be charged for the additional sixteen needed by the new lawyer to complete the work or the time spent by a partner or senior associate redrafting the contract if the beginning lawyer's work was deficient.

Associates cannot bill time spent on administrative tasks, training, evaluation, or talking informally to colleagues. In actuality, many associates discover that they can bill little more than one-half of the time spent in the office to client matters. Thus, to bill forty hours to clients each week, an associate may spend seventy to eighty hours in the office or twelve to thirteen hours per day, six days per week.

Note that even firms that do not bill on an hourly basis often require the use of time records in order to track the cost of providing services and the profitability of work in hourly terms. Studies have indicated that lawyers who keep time records earn substantially more income than those who do not, so the practice has become well-entrenched in the private practice of law.

What does this have to do with hiring? The average law practice grows at a typical rate, such as 5 percent per year. A sole practitioner who bills 1,300 hours per year to clients (solos typically cannot bill as many hours to clients as lawyers in firms because the solos cannot delegate as many administrative tasks) will only have 65 new billable hours of work in a year. A firm of ten lawyers who bill 1,500 hours each will have 750 new hours, and a firm of one hundred, 7,500 hours. The projected number of new billable hours will determine how many new lawyers can be hired in a given year. The bottom line, however, is that the firm has to have enough work to keep its new hires busy.

From your viewpoint, you are unlikely to bill any hours to a client during your first day with a firm. During your first year, you may bill less than 1,000 hours, and the costs of hiring, training, and supporting may exceed by far the income you bring into the firm. As time passes you will become more productive, and at some point you will produce as much as you cost the firm to keep you. After another period, your income (for the firm) will recoup the losses from your first few months. Then there will be a period of clear profit for the firm before you are made partner and begin to "share in the pie."

Thus, a ten-lawyer firm with its 750 growth hours may or may not be able to hire you. The hundred-lawyer firm will be able to hire you and seven or eight classmates. The sole practitioner with only 65 new hours, however, can only hire you if she has a phenomenal growth year or takes the money out of her personal income to pay your salary.

As a rule, firms of ten lawyers or more can predict their hiring needs, and the larger they are, the greater the precision. Smaller firms usually cannot project hiring requirements a year or more in advance. Remember: if a firm offers you a job in November of your last year of law school, you will not be sworn in as a lawyer until the following November. Thus, smaller firms are destined to be more sporadic in their hiring, and to seek to fill positions closer to the time when they need the help.

Corporate and Government Budgets

Corporate or government employers face a situation substantially different from that found in the private practice of law. A budget for a corporate legal department or government agency is established considerably in advance of the year it is to cover. The degree of involvement of the general counsel in the budgeting process varies from organization to organization. Each employer must cover the cost of any new additions to the staff within the budget guidelines. Although there may be procedures available for supplementary appropriations in emergency situations, these funds frequently are not disbursed liberally.

The corporate legal department or government agency must incorporate its budget for new staff into the total organizational budget. Over the past decade, many companies have tried to improve their financial picture by cutting costs, often by downsizing or eliminating departments. In the case of legal departments, although it is more cost-effective to retain in-house counsel than to hire outside counsel, there is often considerable pressure to reduce legal costs by discouraging litigation in favor of nonadversarial dispute resolution systems.

Large organizations must consider the needs of a variety of units when they contemplate expansion. This means that the general counsel is not free to add lawyers to the staff, or offer higher salaries, in isolation. The lawyers in a company are just one of the costs of doing business, and like other costs they need to be contained and managed in the eyes of top executives.

Work Assignment

Assigning cases in a law firm is a delicate balancing act. The client obviously prefers a senior partner to be visible. While having an associate do the work is more economical for the firm, a partner or senior associate must review the new lawyer's work until the office has complete confidence in the beginning associate's work.

Another factor in the selection of an associate to work on a particular project is the lawyer's expertise. For example, an associate assigned to an environmental case will acquire a good deal of knowledge about the issues involved. When a similar case arises in the office, it will be more economical to assign the case to the same associate to make use of the knowledge already gained.

This process of gaining expertise by accretion produces de facto specialists in the law. New lawyers should be cognizant about how work assignments will affect their present value to the firm as well as long-term marketability. Although some large firms rotate new associates through a number of departments before assigning them to one, most large firms and many smaller firms do not. In these firms, your first assignment may well decide the course of your career.

Productivity

Abraham Lincoln said, "A lawyer's time is his stock in trade." Productivity or the amount of work accomplished in one hour is a major concern to the employers of new lawyers. Compensation rates for new lawyers today are much higher than those in the past and current rates are, in turn, reflected in the fees charged to clients. An employer cannot be satisfied simply because a goal of 1,700 billable hours was attained by an associate. At what rate was the work produced? What revenue was realized from the work? What was the caliber of the work product? To what degree was a learning process involved? How efficiently were information sources tapped?

The productivity concept, which came out of experience in industry, has subtly but radically changed the evaluation of the work of lawyers. Some law students find it distressing to think that such pedestrian concerns as productivity and profitability seem paramount to service ideals in a professional setting. Unfortunately, this aspect of practice is unavoidable. Productivity also exercises an important influence on many employment decisions.

For example, an older law school graduate who has developed special skills in a nonlegal area is still an unskilled lawyer at the beginning of practice, and will require training and experience to become productive. It is difficult, if not impossible, for an employer to offer such a lawyer the same kind of salary he or she earned in the nonlegal position. On the other hand, if an individual's pre-legal skills have direct application to the law firm's practice, the associate's learning curve will be accelerated and productivity increased. In some cases, therefore, the law student with more work experience may have an advantage. For example, a degree in engineering or hard science may help a lawyer in an intellectual property practice, or a CPA certificate may help a lawyer in the tax field.

Although a special background may permit rapid growth and lead quickly to the compensation levels of more experienced lawyers, there is still a possibility of economic hardship for the individual in transition from another field to law. That is probably why many experienced people use their legal education to enhance their positions in their current fields of expertise rather than starting all over again as a new lawyer.

Hiring a Lawyer vs. a Legal Assistant

The question of productivity also is important in an area that has troubled law students for the last several decades: the imagined competition with legal assistants for available positions. Actually, in the mind of the employer, the choice of a candidate involves an evaluation of current productivity as related to future productivity.

An employer who hires a legal assistant hires someone who will perform a limited number of specific duties over a substantial period of time. On the other hand, if the choice is made to hire a law graduate, the employer anticipates that the graduate will develop skills and assume an ever-increasing range of legal responsibilities. A law graduate can perform the duties of a legal assistant, but a legal assistant can never perform all the duties implied by the term *lawyer*. Some lawyers began their careers as legal assistants or secretaries. Others performed legal assistant duties during clerkships during law school. These lawyers may possess some advantages over inexperienced law students as well as other legal assistants who never go to law school. In truth, law clerks and legal assistants, as well as many legal secretaries, perform routine legal work that does not require the expertise of a licensed attorney.

Summer Associate Programs

Summer associate programs are commonly used as a recruitment device by larger organizations to recruit new associates. Smaller firms frequently hire law students as clerks, part-time during the school year or full-time for the summer. In either case, such arrangements allow the student an opportunity to see firsthand how a law office operates, the interaction of office personalities, the degree of organization, and many other factors. In turn, the employer can see the student in action on a day-to-day basis and better assess the individual's abilities than in a single interview. Thus, everyone can avoid the problems and miseries that can occur because of a hiring mistake based on too-little contact. See pages 108–113 for more information on these opportunities.

If it is impossible to obtain a clerkship or summer associate experience because you are otherwise employed full-time, consider whether you can demonstrate your qualifications to a potential employer through volunteer work, piecemeal research, or a law school externship programs. The idea is to create situations where the employer can observe your work directly.

Who Decides?

Unlike corporations where personnel managers are permanent fixtures, the hiring partner or a hiring committee in a law firm is appointed by the senior management to serve for only a limited period of time. Thus, it may be difficult, if not impossible, for the graduate to determine where the hiring decision finally rests.

In some cases, associates are part of the hiring committee. For larger firms, the recruitment administrator will be included in the hiring process. And in many small firms, the hiring decision is actually a group effort.

Difficult as it may seem to sort out, you should strive to identify the individuals who will be deciding your fate. Questions about salary and benefits, as well as other factors to be negotiated, are best directed to those responsible for hiring decisions.

Conclusion

In deciding whether to hire and whom to hire, employers look at basic issues such as the work that needs to be done, both now and in the future, available space and support services, the costs of recruiting and training, and potential for productivity of the new employee(s). During the interview process and while working, you should be sensitive to these business aspects of practicing law. Your employer may not expect a new lawyer to know much about the economics of law practice, but will appreciate your willingness to learn.

Getting Started

8

A job search can be lonely if for no other reason than that you are putting yourself on the line. The situation is made lonelier still when you are seeking your first legal position and are surrounded by peers with whom you compete for jobs. There are allies out there, but you must take the trouble to develop them.

Much of this book addresses practical considerations and pragmatic problems about planning a career and finding a job. Implicit in much of this advice is a fundamental psychology: If you can identify what you want, you possess the tools to attain it.

Perhaps a more reflective look at this "psychology" for success will help to place the career choice process in perspective. Too many self-help books ring untrue. They seem to suggest that you can talk yourself into success. Or they imply that there is a secret formula that when imparted to the uninitiated will allow them to achieve happiness and success.

Too often, these works read like the high school cheerleading squad exhorting the football team to win. Self-help writers feed on the American dream that if you want something enough, you can have it. The converse, of course, is that if you fail to achieve your goal, the reason is because you did not want it enough.

Attitude Matters

There is no doubt that a positive mental attitude is absolutely critical to success in any job search. Employers are not impressed by the "hat-in-hand approach" of a candidate who says in effect, "I know nothing, but if you teach me, I might be a good lawyer some day." Of course, you do not know everything there is to know about practicing law when you graduate law school. Employers understand that. You do not need to remind them how little you know.

What you must do instead is tell them what you have to offer. This simple, fundamental necessity is, in many cases, the biggest hurdle separating the job seeker from the job. Why? Because many people do not learn how to identify and present their qualifications to others. Self-knowledge and personal marketing skills are important. Returning to our football team analogy, these skills are the running, tackling, and blocking that we need to have to reach our goal.

Chapter 4 of this book discusses the need to identify the skills you bring to the job. These skills are defined by your past achievements. Your future accomplishments will utilize old skills as well as new ones you develop as you grow. It is important to take the time to develop a professional identity. With that knowledge, you can recognize and place yourself in situations where your particular talents can most effectively be utilized.

This book provides a formula to help you figure out who you want to be and how to get there. There is nothing mystical about this formula. This book does not say that if you fail to proceed step by step, you will not find a job or happiness. What it does offer is a logical approach to a fundamental problem that we all face: deciding what to do with our lives.

The psychology of winning, as presented here, is more than just desire. It is a positive presentation of your skills based upon careful analysis. The confidence you take to the job search should be based upon preparation, not hype. The difference between winning and losing an oral argument is often preparation, and preparation also provides a psychological edge when you stand up to speak. Good BS without preparation is just BS. Anyone who has been through eight weeks of law school knows this. Why should it be any different when you look for a job?

Another underlying concept throughout much of this book is self-determination. Too many people are willing to give up their self-respect by handing over the power to make decisions about their lives to others. We come into this world alone, and go out alone. When we make fundamental career decisions no one else can be inside our heads. A host of individuals and forces can influence and contribute to these decisions, but no one else can make them.

This book assumes that you are willing to take responsibility for your life and make decisions that serve your personal best interests. Many of the "don'ts" described throughout this book relate to various devises used by job seekers to abdicate this basic responsibility. Only when you can be your own woman or man can you exercise this existential right. For many, it is simply a matter of making the decision. For others, the task may be complicated by emotional baggage from outside the legal environment. For those people, personal counseling may be a necessary part of this process.

Mindset for Success

It may seem trite to say that you must maintain a positive attitude if you are to be successful in the job search. Books have been written about the importance of positive thinking in attaining personal goals. Although it would be simplistic and unrealistic to suggest that one can attain success simply by willing it, the history of humankind is replete with stories of people who achieve seemingly impossible objectives through the strength of their personal will.

What separates the achievers from the dreamers? Surely, the panhandler on the street once had dreams, just like the successful person. But is it enough to say that one was a quitter and one was not? Is it enough to say that one got the breaks and one did not? Or to say that in the final analysis one had talent and one did not? The intellectual traps of social Darwinism, metaphysical predestination, and existential nihilism all suggest that events shape our destinies, and that personal decisions are meaningless in the course of our lives.

If you accept the notion that you are not in control of your life, then you will probably not be in control of your life. If you want to say that society, blind luck, God, or some other mysterious force pulls the strings in your life, you minimize the importance of personal decisions.

You must take control. You must decide that your decisions make a difference in what happens to you. You must accept the significance of your responsibility for your own career. Saying this does not mean that luck does not have a role in what happens to you, nor does it preclude a relationship with God, whatever your concept of a Supreme Being may be. It certainly does not suggest that your family, cultural inheritance, societal norms, or personal talents and limitations have no bearing upon what happens to you.

Events and forces outside your control do affect your life. Much of what happens, however, lies within your own control. Too many people give away too much in this sphere. They abdicate choices that are theirs to make.

It is no mean feat to assert control over decisions that are not intrinsically dictated by external forces. It is easy to go with the flow, and difficult to take charge. Frequently, we run up against brick walls and get knocked down in our efforts to scale them. There is a distinction between an insurmountable barrier and a challenge that can be overcome.

The fact that you are in law school attests to your ability to overcome obstacles in your life. Law school will give new meaning to the word challenge. From the law school you attend, to your class rank, to your extracurricular activities, to your work experience, everything and everyone will seem to conspire to stand between you and the job you want. You must adopt a mind set for success.

To devolve this discussion from the esoteric to the practical, look at some ways that you can achieve a positive attitude:

- *Pick your friends wisely.* Surround yourself with people who are realistic, but supportive. Why spend time with pessimists, doomsayers, and negative thinkers? You can choose your friends, so pick ones who are upbeat and positive.

- *Eat right and exercise.* There is a definite correlation between a positive self-image and a healthy lifestyle. Law school tends to push you away from physical activity, good dietary habits, and reasonable sleep patterns. Trust me on this one: You will feel better about yourself if you get plenty of sleep, eat something besides fast food, and work out regularly.

- *Reward yourself.* Because much of the career assessment and job search processes involve setting and achieving goals, you can enhance your performance by imposing some simple conditioning on yourself. Set up a base schedule of rewards for accomplishing objectives. Give yourself small rewards for small accomplishments and big rewards for major ones. Let yourself be happy when you succeed. Pavlov would be proud of you.

- *Meditate.* Many law students blanch at the idea of meditating, but meditation is simply a period each day when you clear your mind of the thoughts and pressures that normally clutter it. It is important to find a peaceful setting uninterrupted by telephone calls, noise, and other people. For many law students, such as those who are also working mothers, finding time alone is almost impossible, but if you can take just fifteen minutes each day to clear out the mental clutter, your attitude will improve markedly.

- *Plan ahead.* This book is a blueprint for planning. By following the logical steps presented here, you can provide yourself a methodology with a track record of success. If you know that you are doing all you can to maximize your opportunities and further your career, you can approach this process with confidence and vigor.

Don't Paint Yourself into a Corner

The importance of using options as a technique for maintaining a good mental attitude in the job search cannot be overemphasized. The concept is simple: Always give yourself an alternative.

Desperation is an insidious thing. It starts with those little seeds of fear we all have that no one will ever hire us. It sprouts into panic when our initial plans fail to materialize. It can blossom into full-blown depression when we perceive that there are no viable options open to us. When that happens, we are likely to say, "I'll accept any job." And when we do, it often turns out to be a mistake. If you can avoid painting yourself into a corner, you are much more likely to sustain the positive attitude you will need to accomplish your goals in the job search.

Finding Help 9

The career services office at your law school is not the only place to get assistance in the job search. Personal contacts and other sources may be just as helpful. The career services office is for many students, however, the focal point of a career search.

Your Career Services Office

Teaching law students about the variety of legal careers and employment prospects in these careers is integral to the career services program of the law school. Certain job hunting skills can and should be taught in the law schools. Students who embark on a legal education generally have a reasonable expectation that they will be able to find employment in the field for which their education has prepared them. The career services office at your law school is committed to this goal.

There are two caveats: First, every law school is different, and it follows that every career services office will be different to meet the needs of its particular student body, administrative requirements, and employment pattern for graduates. It is difficult,

97

therefore, to make any absolute statements. Second, the ultimate responsibility for getting hired must fall on the student, not the career services office. The office is a resource and service center that can and should support your efforts, but when you get to the interview room, there is only you and the interviewer.

The American Bar Association requires that the law school should provide adequate staff space and resources in view of the size and program of the school to maintain an active career counseling service to assist its graduates to make sound career choices and obtain employment. A good career services program should include the following elements:

- ◆ The law school should have specific personnel responsible for administering the school's career services program. Administrative responsibility for career services should be in the hands of a person trained in law, counseling, or a profession related to career development. If a faculty member assumes responsibility for career services, this person should be granted a reduced teaching load.
- ◆ The law school should have specific space set aside for career services activities, including a resource area, interview rooms, administrative space, and counseling areas that assure privacy. In addition, the privacy of student records should be protected.

Interviews conducted under the auspices of the law school should adhere to the principles and standards promulgated by the National Association for Law Placement prohibiting various forms of discrimination and other behavior (see Appendix B).

- ◆ The school should conduct educational programs on legal career options, résumé preparation, interviewing, and other job-hunting skills as needed. Career education should be taught as an integral part of the educational process.
- ◆ The career services office should assist students seeking part-time work not to exceed twenty hours per week and summer positions, as well as permanent employment.
- ◆ The law school should participate in the annual employment and salary surveys of the National Association for

Law Placement and maintain information on employment patterns of its graduates in an area readily accessible to students. The school may also conduct internal surveys for the benefit of its students and graduates.

◆ The law school should provide individual career counseling for students. Ideally there should be at least one fulltime equivalent counselor or advisor for every 750 full-time equivalent students enrolled in the school. In cases where a trained counselor is not on staff at the career services office itself, career advice may be provided by faculty members, student services of the parent institution, or in cooperation with bar or alumni associations.

◆ The law school should provide continuing services to alumni of the school as well. Services extended to students should be granted to recent graduates until they have obtained permanent employment after graduation.

Because the career services office is the place where the academic and real worlds meet, you should find out what services it offers. At most schools, the office contains a wealth of information about legal and law-related careers. It will answer these questions: What types of positions do most of your school's graduates accept? What are the current salary levels being offered to graduates of your school? Are there new materials available on careers? Are alumni lists available to those who seek positions outside the usual placement pattern of the school? Where can you find the materials about careers in law?

The office also receives information about specific job opportunities. Some, but certainly not all, will be in connection with on-campus interviewing.

Get acquainted with your career services director. Don't pick the busiest time of the year, such as the fall recruiting season, and don't wait until your senior year to do it. Set up an appointment to sit down and discuss your professional goals.

Give the director an opportunity to share with you his or her experiences gleaned from aiding in the career plans of many, many others. In turn, you will have the advantage of becoming something more than a number on an application form to the director. That can be of tremendous help as you begin to narrow your search. By engaging the career services staff, you can increase the network of its storehouse of expertise.

Keep in touch with your career services office after graduation. Many openings do not develop until you have been admitted to the bar. If you already have a job, information on the position you have accepted and the compensation you are receiving will be helpful to graduates coming after you.

The career services office plays a major role in the life of law students. Sometimes students express frustration that the office only serves the top 10 percent of the class or only serves the needs of large corporate law firms. What these students see is a reflection of the competitive job market they face and the aggressive hiring practices of some employers. Their experience with individuals who work in career services is generally much more positive.

Personal Contacts

Many students who enter law school do not personally know any lawyers. If you are in this situation, you will want to develop a network of professional mentors. Your objective is not to develop specific job opportunities, though that frequently occurs, but to develop a better understanding and knowledge of what it actually means to practice law. Here are some specific suggestions to help you develop more personal contacts:

- ◆ If you do not know any lawyers, perhaps you have friends in the business community who regularly use lawyers' services. They might be willing to ask lawyers they use to talk to you about the profession.
- ◆ Go to court. Observe the procedures and the interaction of members of the bar involved in trial work. Try to define what it means to be a professional person earning a living by practicing law, as opposed to a student learning about the law.
- ◆ Join bar associations and committees. The American Bar Association offers student memberships, as do many state

and local associations. In addition, many offer the opportunity for enrollment in a section devoted to a substantive area of practice.

◆ Take advantage of CLE programs that allow you to mingle informally with attendees. Your law school provides many such opportunities, such as lectures, competitions, receptions, and career services panels. Local bar associations also offer CLE programs that are open to law students. If a chance is offered for student participation, take it. It will mean extra responsibility, but it will also increase your chances of knowing lawyers with whom you may be professionally associated later.

◆ Subscribe to bar periodicals and online services. Note the names of the bar leaders and their views on the legal issues of the day. Keep a file of articles and news notes that are tied to specific lawyers.

◆ Even better, correspond with lawyers who write for or are mentioned in these information sources.

◆ Talk to your professors. Not only are they in a position to know your work as a student, but they also are professionally or personally acquainted with many members of the bar. Their opportunity for comparative analysis of employers and opportunities can make them invaluable guides for you.

With all of these contacts, seek to develop an understanding of the practicing bar. Such contacts also give you a chance to ask each lawyer one important question: "Knowing what you know now, what career course would you recommend to a lawyer just entering the profession?" Keep track of your contacts and the context for later reference (see Chapter 13 on Networking).

Someday, you will have ten years of experience behind you. You will know and understand things that can be perceived only through such experience. But by meeting and talking with lawyers now, you have the chance to develop your own plans based upon the experience of those who have gone before you. The better you understand the profession you are about to enter, the better your chances for a successful job search.

Other Resources

There are other resources available to you outside the ordinary circles of the legal profession. Many students, particularly those considering alternative careers, overlook these contacts.

What follows is not a comprehensive description of all possible resources, but rather some possibilities for students who are imaginative enough to develop their own ideas. Do not hesitate to be creative in coming up with ideas for job hunting. Group and team research efforts have been successfully employed by some students. You may be successful because you are able to come up with an angle that no one else has considered before.

- ◆ *The Internet:* So much information is available to law students about legal employers, job opportunities, and contacts that it may seem overwhelming. Appendix A includes a list of Internet resources, but you will want to develop your own sources based on your personal needs.
- ◆ *Libraries:* In some cases, traditional libraries may have resources you can use, which are not available online. Do not limit yourself to the law library at your law school, but use public and university libraries as well. Many universities have offices that conduct research into business and population trends, and many private research organizations also conduct such research. Information available through these organizations can save you hours of digging.
- ◆ *Other career services offices:* Remember that the undergraduate career services offices at many universities can help you with general information. Many law schools provide reciprocity of services with offices at other schools.
- ◆ *Newsletters and newspapers:* Information abounds in both the legal and general press. In many fields of law, specialized periodicals provide a steady flow of information to insiders. Online services, Web sites, blogs, and discussion groups can be enormously useful. Many cities and states also provide information in the form of brochures, newsletters, and Web sites. Although some of these services may require a subscription fee or membership in an affiliated

organization, the job information is often worth the investment. The classified ads of most bar journals and legal newspapers also list openings for positions.

- ◆ *Agencies:* Many state and local governments, in addition to the federal government, provide employment services. While the effectiveness of these agencies may vary from place to place, the diligent student will want to cover all bases. Also, if you are unemployed, find out whether you are entitled to unemployment benefits.

See the Resources Guide of this book (Appendix A) for a more detailed list of resources for the job hunt. You should recognize, however, that a comprehensive list of information resources would be impossible to compile, in part because we dwell in a sea of information, and in part because the sources are changing all the time as new tools emerge and others disappear. As you conduct your job search, some resources will be considerably more helpful than others, and you will inevitably craft your research efforts to meet your specific job search strategy. Regardless of your career plans, however, your investigation will be more valuable if you are both creative and thorough.

Investing in Yourself 10

Your decision to go to law school represents a significant investment of time, money, and energy. Another part of this investment is the cost of whatever you would have been doing with your life if you had not gone to law school. Let's say that you attend a private law school as a full-time student. Your direct costs of tuition, books, and other school-related expenses might amount to $25,000 per year, or $75,000. If you gave up a job paying $40,000 per year or $120,000, your legal education represents an investment of almost $200,000. Like any other investment, you hope that your investment in law school—and in yourself—pays off.

You have many allies in your quest to assure a good return on your investment but, in the final analysis, your future rests squarely and inescapably in your own hands. To achieve your career goals, you must make a major commitment of time, effort, and in a limited way, money. You have invested a great deal in your legal education.Be ready to go the extra mile to make it worth your while.

What Do You Have to Offer?

The sooner you have some idea of the course you would like your career to take, the sooner you can point your education and work experience in that direction. Some fields of law put greater emphasis on research and work experience; others stress high academic achievement.

In all cases, planning is important. Be sure you have completed the exercise in Chapter 4 so that you really know the product you are selling: yourself. It may mean the difference between successfully working toward a goal, or settling for what's left over. This chapter focuses on specific ways that you can enhance the investment in yourself.

Academics

Law school grades are a factor taken into consideration by most legal employers. Emphasis on grades may vary from slight to heavy, depending on the employer. For many law students, grades are the elephant in the room that nobody wants to talk about.

Employers recognize this situation as well. Their difficulty lies in trying to establish some standards of measurement that will permit them to make value judgments comparing one candidate to another. Employers rely heavily on grades as a basis for what they hope is a reasonably rational judgment about your potential.

Equal employment opportunity laws have underscored the importance of this issue by making it necessary to make objective, rather than subjective, evaluations regarding individuals being considered for employment. When you are in law school, grades may be one of the few bases for distinguishing one student from another. Interestingly, as the years go by, importance of law school grades is minimized as you acquire a track record, which can be evaluated independently of your transcript.

To make the most out of your academic situation, you need to address this topic candidly and directly. You need to put it into its proper perspective. The following suggestions are intended to provide some useful guidance in dealing with this sticky issue:

- Remember that grades are not the only factor an employer considers. Each year, many students sell themselves to employers who would not have hired them on the basis of their grades. Likewise, some students with outstanding grades have difficulty finding jobs for reasons that totally escape them.

- Don't blame your troubles on your grades. You should not be blind to the importance of academic performance in law school, but you should not use grades as an excuse (nor should you use grades as a crutch if they are good). You do not need to say, "I would have done a lot better if that SOB Professor X hadn't been out to get me." If you sound like you think your grades reflect some sort of innate inferiority, you will turn off even the employers who do not place total reliance on law school grades in their hiring decisions.

- Be frank when you discuss your grades, no matter what they are, and avoid sounding defensive when talking to potential employers. If you sound evasive when you talk about grades, employers will assume that you have something to hide (perhaps more than you actually do).

- Be positive and show that you have skills that the employer needs. If an employer is not persuaded by what you say about yourself, you have to be able to believe that it is his loss and not yours.

- Grades may represent an ability to work hard and write well in a highly competitive environment, and your own experiences outside the classroom may demonstrate the same qualities, but they represent only a fraction of the skills you will need to be a successful practitioner.

- If your grades are not spectacular, seek to gain other experiences and let employers know that you have other positive work habits: You get along with others. You are a self-starter. You have integrity.

- Look at employers' past hiring patterns. None of us likes to get shot down, so we all play the odds in deciding whether to "go for it." It is important to know what kind of a risk-taker you are. Or, put another way, how stringent would an employer's requirements have to be before you simply would not apply for a job?

Think of yourself as arguing a case (your own), and having to meet a certain burden of proof (some may have more of a burden than others). Law students learn the art of advocacy. This is the time to put it to work for your own cause:

- What kind of argument will be persuasive?
- How well do you build the evidence?
- How can you convince someone that you are more than a number?
- How can you wow them with your personality?
- How can you demonstrate your interest in this particular job?
- How do you convey such intangible aspects of yourself as your interests, your integrity, your maturity, or your determination?

It is, of course, easier to tell someone how to do this than to face the prospect personally. But what is the alternative? Too often, fear of rejection, failure, or anxiety caused by uncertainty about the future, lead law students to procrastinate to avoid facing the situation. Many people postpone dealing with these stressful issues until all their options have been foreclosed. You can ill-afford to stick your head in the sand and wait for things to happen *to* you.

Summer Jobs

Many students work during the summer months to earn money for school, to gain valuable experience in law-related work, or simply to get away from school. Summer opportunities with legal employers are generally greater for students who have completed two years of law school than those who have finished only one. Many post-first-year students work for free in law offices just to get experience. Obviously, getting paid beats working for free, but experience is valuable regardless of the compensation.

Most medium- to large-sized law firms, and many agencies and corporations conduct formal summer clerkship programs. These are usually well organized and high paying. They afford the opportunity for a permanent job. The bulk of the recruiting for these clerkships is done in the fall through on-campus interviews and job listings.

Many small firms or agencies also hire law clerks for the summer, even though there is no organized clerkship program. The pay is often lower, and the employer is probably more interested in work than in recruiting permanent employees, although permanent associations do result from such clerkships.

Many of these clerkships are listed on a bulletin board or Web board at the law school, or through outside organizations like local bar associations. Students often locate the employers themselves, and many even convince employers who previously have not hired law clerks of the need to do so.

Some students elect to work at nonlegal jobs to earn money. These often pay better than many legal jobs, although the experiential value may be diminished. Career services offices on your campus outside the law school often have information on jobs in their fields. Other openings can be located through classified ads, job Web sites, and personal contacts.

Because the competition for summer legal work can be intense, some students opt to take a semester off and work full time during either the fall or spring semester. Others switch to an evening program and work full time after the first year. Both approaches give students a chance to work in a legal setting and gain useful experience.

Summer school represents another alternative for many students who hope to finish law school early or to lighten a course load. To get a different viewpoint or to be near home, some students take courses at other law schools. Many schools also offer summer school programs abroad, which allow students to travel as well as receive course credit for law work.

You should begin to make your summer plans early in the academic year. By the end of March, many summer jobs are filled, and there are not enough to go around. Although some jobs always come through the career services office after finals in spring, you are likely to be less than satisfied with your options if you wait until the last minutes.

Part-Time Jobs

Law school career services offices usually post part-time job listings for law clerk positions, as well as nonlegal work. Many students do not wait for job notices but write or call local lawyers personally, or talk to friends who are currently working as clerks. Many of these jobs are passed from clerk to clerk informally. It is common for many firms near a law school to select permanent associates exclusively from the ranks of their law clerks.

A word of caution: Outside work can have a detrimental effect on your academic performance. The American Bar Association requires law schools to limit full-time students to twenty hours of work outside school, and urges first-year students not to work until November 1, and from interviewing for internships until December 1. If you avoid working during the first year, you will have made a sound decision. If you must work, talk to an academic advisor or counselor to get suggestions on how to manage your load.

Think about it: A full-time student who takes fifteen credits, spends an equal amount of time preparing for class (some would say this is a threshold level), and performs twenty hours of work is putting in a fifty-hour week. An evening student taking ten hours, studying ten, and working forty is tied into a sixty-hour week. In short, the value of the outside work must be weighed against the sacrifice in terms of education and personal life.

Clinics, Internships, and Externships

All law schools offer clinical education experiences, as well as internships and externships in law offices outside the law school. These programs provide an opportunity to gain hands-on practical experience not possible in traditional courses. The concept of learning by doing, long recognized in the medical field, has been slow to catch on in legal education. Today, however, there are more live-client experiences than ever before.

If you have taken advantage of one or more of these programs, take some time to think about communicating to others what you have learned to do.

- ◆ Potential legal employers will want to hear about your experiences. How well you convey your proficiency can go far in building a positive reaction with an interviewer.

- Be cognizant of confidentiality. If you talk about cases, be careful to protect the identity of clients. If an employer perceives you as loose-lipped, it may quash your chances of getting a job offer.
- Many clinics operate in areas related to poverty law, so it will be incumbent upon you to explain how these experiences might be transferable to other areas of practice.
- Your clinical supervisor can be one of your best references, so take time to develop a good relationship.

Writing and Law Review/Journal

Another credential that you can show to employers is writing experience. Many students gain writing and editing experience on one of their school's law reviews. Undoubtedly, law-review experience can add panache to an otherwise ordinary résumé. Many schools have two or more journals and there may be an unwritten pecking order of prestige related to comparative selectivity. Because law review experience tends to enhance your marketability, you should pursue law review membership if you have the opportunity to do so. Aside from the boost to your credentials, the experiences of research, writing, editing (and being edited), working as a part of a team, and managing such a publication inculcate a variety of useful skills for the practice of law.

For those who do not have the opportunity to write for a law review, it is nevertheless important to develop your skills as a writer. At some law schools, unfortunately, it is possible to graduate with no legal writing experience after the first year. Considering the important role that legal research and writing play in virtually every type of lawyering, it is unfortunate when a law school does not require more. And considering the number of prospective employers who want to see writing samples of students they interview, it is tragic that many candidates can produce nothing but a first-year moot court brief.

You can do something about this problem. Opportunities for writing are varied: "paper" seminars and courses, essay contests, advanced moot-court competitions, research assistance for a professor, and part-time or summer jobs.

Push yourself to compose the best possible work product. Subject your writing to editorial review by others. Spend some time every week doing research and writing in school or in a summer job, and you will have plenty of samples to show prospective employers. When you plan to use written work from a job or judicial clerkship as a writing sample, however, be sure you obtain permission from your judge or supervising lawyer before you release the document.

Nonlegal Jobs

Almost every law student has worked in a nonlegal position before or during law school, some in high-level professional jobs and others in menial service jobs. Whether a family business or an easy way to make pocket change, nonlegal jobs represent alternative opportunities to develop skills that will be useful in the practice of law. Too many law students ignore, minimize, or downplay the degree to which nonlegal jobs gave them skills they will use as lawyers. Potential employers may fall into this trap as well. As you should have seen with the Skills Assessment Exercise in Chapter 4, pages 50–52, professional skills can be derived from any number of sources. What we have to do is to recognize what we have gained from these experiences outside the law and communicate to others how we can utilize what we have learned in the legal context.

Education and Experience

Many students who did not pause after undergraduate school before starting their legal education find themselves with little or no work experience to complement their schooling. Conversely, students who have been out of school for some time complain that their years away from academia leave them out-of-sync with legal education and legal employers.

Even during school, students must frequently balance the costs and benefits of pursuing purely educational objectives (i.e., grades) against developing experiential skills through extracurricular activities (e.g., moot court) or work (e.g., clerking part-time for a law firm).

There are no easy answers to this dilemma, partly because the solution may vary according to the various career paths law graduates pursue, and partly because the answer will vary from individual to individual. It is probably overly simplistic to say that one should attain the most experience possible without sacrificing academic objectives.

It is just as important to weigh the advantages and disadvantages of academic work choices during law school as it is to engage in effective career planning generally. Although you may not be able to do anything about some parts of this equation, like how much and what kind of experience you acquired prior to law school, you do have control over decisions you make during law school.

Choices about how to balance your education and work experience inevitably must be made in light of broader career planning considerations. In other words, what you should do now depends on where you want to go later. With the exception of some highly focused individuals, law students generally do not integrate long-term goals into short-term plans.

The earlier in your law school career that you begin to engage in career planning, the greater opportunity you will have to apply your insights in that process to academic planning during school. Additionally, your assessment of your skills and marketability may lead you to pursue different avenues during school than you would have otherwise.

Debt Load

One material factor in the job search equation for many law students today is debt load. If your parents were not wealthy, if you did not get a full scholarship, if you were not supported by a working spouse, if you did not work night and day to pay tuition, then you probably have student loans to pay off.

The cost of legal education on top of college (and sometimes graduate school) can be staggering. Students who have loans from several levels of college, graduate, and professional schools may owe more than $150,000 when they are done. It is not unusual for law school graduates to owe $100,000 from law school alone. Such students begin practice with a cash-flow problem.

Unfortunately, loan repayment must begin when school is over. Defaulting on these student loans is not likely to make a strong impression on the bar admissions authorities, so the prospect of carrying a built-in financial obligation with you into the real world can be an unwanted burden.

In practical terms, a heavy debt load often can limit the career choices available to students. Graduates looking at student loan payments may be forced to forego certain lower-paying alternatives (e.g., public-interest law) in favor of higher paying positions because of these obligations. In 2007, a new federal law permitted graduates who accept public service jobs to obtain loan forgiveness or consolidation, but this relief may not be available to all graduates (see College Cost Reduction Act of 2007). The reality is that choices you make during and even before law school may have consequences for the options available to you after graduation. It may be necessary to grab the money and run by taking the highest paying job available.

If you face this problem, it will be necessary to incorporate your financial obligations into the analysis of your career plans. You should discuss the possibilities not only with your financial aid officer, but your career counselor as well.

Initiate a plan that keeps borrowing to a minimum. It may make sense to go to law school part-time while working during the day, eschew law-related jobs during law school for higher-paying nonlegal positions, actively seek scholarship or fellowship money, investigate work-study possibilities through your school, and pursue loan programs that permit deferment or repayment adjustment.

To deal with economic problems, you must be honest with yourself concerning your needs. Determine whether there is any degree of flexibility you might be able to show to obtain a particularly desired position. Your career services office can supply valuable information about the range of compensation currently being offered to graduates of your school, and it should be those figures upon which you base your financial analysis of potential income as related to your need.

Dual-Career Families

The 2000 Census reported that one of the most significant demographics in the American workplace was the dual-wage-earner family. Lawyers are no exception. The chances are very good that you and your spouse or significant other will both work. In two-career families, it is necessary to look at the career opportunities for both partners.

The opportunities for one partner may not be as good as those for the other in communities where they seek employment. One partner may need to deal with licensing requirements to relocate to an area where the other has found employment. One partner may need to commute long distances if neither spouse has a portable practice. Dealing with these issues can be problematic if the partners do not talk candidly about the situation. Only by talking openly and honestly can a couple reach a result that is mutually satisfactory.

If your partner is also a lawyer, there is an additional dimension to the general problem. For many years, law firms have had an unwritten but very real rule that they would not employ lawyers married to other lawyers to avoid potential conflicts of interest. Couples were left with either agreeing that one of them would not engage in private practice, or working together in their own firm.

This practice has declined in many areas, but in many smaller communities, however, the old bias dies hard. If a law firm hires one-half of a lawyer couple, the other is forced to seek employment in a corporation or government office. This attitude can be particularly insidious if the spouse forced into corporate or government work is more often the woman.

Other Considerations

Oddly, the very breadth of choices offered by the legal profession can be a limitation because it is a physical impossibility for you to fully explore all the potential career options. But you can examine the vast array of possibilities, and pick and choose those for future examination that appear most likely to provide career satisfaction.

One area of limitation is your own law school. This is far from an absolute limitation—merely a relative one. It arises from the employment market served by an individual school. That market is defined both by geography and by the type of office the school's graduates most frequently enter.

For example, it is not surprising that graduates of law schools in the Washington, D.C., area tend to be heavily concentrated in the federal government. Or that graduates of the Indiana University School of Law often find work with the firms in that state. If you are not sure about the type of market your law school serves, ask your career services officer to show you employment reports for your school for the last five years.

This marketplace limitation is not purely arbitrary. Consider the role of the employer in determining that market. The preference of alumni for hiring graduates of their own law school has long been noted. There are some very sound reasons for this preference

First, having attended a particular law school, a prospective employer is fully aware of the school's standards, the caliber of its academic program, and the suitability of that training for the client market served by the firm. Second, the employer may personally know many of the professors of the law school and will therefore feel comfortable in calling and talking to them concerning an applicant's educational qualifications. The employer may even ask for a gut reaction regarding the applicant's ability to fit comfortably into the employing organization. Favorable comments from professors can be of immeasurable help in a job search, particularly if the graduate is not one of the top-ranking students but has demonstrated positive qualities of personality and character that may not be highlighted in a formal résumé. Additionally, the employer may have had an opportunity to get to know you personally, having met you through law school alumni activities and functions.

On the other hand, what if your career goals lie outside the particular area served most frequently by your school? Here, your imagination and aggressiveness in developing position resources will be your best ally. Arm yourself with literature that will demonstrate the quality of your school, and be ready to provide references to professors with whom the prospective employer may talk freely. Lists of alumni now located outside your school's regular market may also be obtained through the career services office or the alumni office as an aid to direct contact.

Another possible limitation will be your undergraduate or nonlegal experience. For instance, in the field of patent law, if you do not have undergraduate training in a scientific or technological field, you will find it extremely difficult to find a job. On the other hand, if you have an engineering or science degree, employers may want to pigeonhole you as a patent lawyer.

In most situations, however, undergraduate training and nonlegal experience serve more as an advantage in the job search. Undergraduate work or an advanced degree in accounting, or experience in tax work will definitely receive priority consideration by prospective employers in the field. It behooves anyone with special training or experience to analyze the job market for potential employers who may fully utilize these skills, in addition to your legal training.

Your Résumé 11

Successful job hunting requires a set of skills, which, once learned, can be used repeatedly throughout your career. Writing a résumé is an exercise in self-assessment and organization necessary for success at any level. Composing a persuasive and impressive cover letter is a good practice for all those times in the future when you will be required to present yourself or an idea in a letter. And the job interview is, of course, only the beginning of many such encounters. The current job seeker may become the future employer, the lawyer interviewing (or being interviewed by) a prospective client, or once again a job seeker hoping to move on to a better position.

Preparing a Résumé

A recent cartoon shows a portly gentleman seated in the office of a lawyer-search consultant. The caption reads, "My résumé, sir, is what you see sitting before you!"

Since most of us are unlikely to be hired simply on the basis of our compelling presence, it is generally useful to have a résumé. The employer who will be evaluating your qualifications needs to have a résumé. The résumé tells the employer who is a likely candidate for the position and who is not.

In this respect, the résumé is a baited hook. It tells the prospective interviewer enough about the candidate to pique the interviewer's interest, leading the interviewer to think, "I would really like to meet this person."

The résumé also provides a framework for the interview. A great deal of time can be wasted in a twenty-minute interview if the employer knows nothing about the applicant beforehand and the applicant has to answer many tedious questions about grades, experience, and other basic qualifications. Under these circumstances, the applicant might become confused about names of employers, dates, or other details, and lose valuable time in which he or she could be asking questions about the firm or corporation. With a good résumé, the employer can review the applicant's qualifications in advance and use the interview time to clear up important details and get some sense of what the applicant is like as a person.

The following step-by-step description explains how to create an effective résumé that will make employers want to meet you. Do not shortchange yourself by plugging your data into someone's boilerplate form.

Do Your Homework

Your résumé should help focus on your goals and objectives. While compiling your résumé, you will be forced to evaluate your goals, your skills and abilities, and your limitations. You will also have to consider what is available in the job market: given your career and geographical preferences. See Part II of this book for more information.

◆ Do not make the mistake of thinking that all this self-analysis can wait until later. Your résumé should be aimed at the kinds of employers you hope to work for if it is to be effective. Compiling a general résumé and firing it off to hundreds of employers in hopes that one of them will respond is reminiscent of the famous line, "I shot an arrow into the air; it fell to earth I know not where!" You do not shoot an arrow randomly into the air if you want to hit a target—you aim it. It is perfectly acceptable to aim several different résumés at several different career targets.

◆ As you prepare your résumé, ask yourself: Who will you be interviewing? Who does the interviewer represent? What information will the employer want to know about you? What personal characteristics and aptitudes do you possess that would be most attractive to an employer? What accomplishments should you stress in applying for this kind of employment? Your answers to these questions will determine the structure of your résumé.

◆ What do you want to do? At this point, a certain amount of self-knowledge and a good deal of thought are needed, but the investment of time and energy will be well worthwhile if the result is an effective résumé.

List Your Qualifications

When you have identified your employment objective(s), you are ready to start working on the résumé itself.

◆ First, jot down a brief statement or statements of your objectives. Although not usually listed in printed legal résumés, the objectives will help you focus as you put the résumé together.

◆ Next, record in outline form everything you think might be relevant to these objectives, including your educational background, work experience, and other relevant factors.

◆ Start with the present (law school) and move backward to college. Include all honors, activities, and publications, as well as your grade point average. Do not include high-school experience unless your high-school record contains something especially relevant. One student, for example, had attended the same prestigious private high school as a partner in the firm to which he was applying. While his other qualifications were excellent, you can be sure that mentioning his high school in his résumé did not harm his chances. Another student might have had some special achievement or honor in high school that would have direct bearing on the type of job she was seeking.

- Except in very unusual cases, it is not necessary to go back to year one to give the employer relevant information.
- Next, summarize in outline form your entire work history, including names of employers, dates, and general statements of the most important duties for each job. Make a note of significant skills developed on each job. Again, list everything you can remember.

Edit or Expand Your List

After listing the information usually included in résumés, you should now edit ruthlessly.

- If you are a second- or third-year student, or a graduate with some work experience, your task may be to cut irrelevant material from your list. Leave out undergraduate activities if they have little bearing on what you want to do.
- If you have had summer or part-time clerking experience, do not bother including the construction job you had in your junior year of college, or the summer you waited tables in a resort.
- If you are a first-year law student hoping for a summer or part-time clerkship, your problem may lie in not having enough on your résumé to make much of an impression. In this case, expand your list.
- Include college activities and important papers and projects. Include titles of law school courses taken or in progress to show that you have some familiarity with the work you will be doing. Describe work experiences that show you to be hard-working and dependable. Add any references that would mean something to the employer.

Shape and Arrange Your Qualifications

Once you have a rough list of items to be included in your résumé, it is time to shape and arrange those items in the pattern that will be most effective. In some ways, it is very difficult to give general advice about writing a résumé because each person's résumé should be a unique representation of a unique individual.

◆ To present yourself as such a unique individual to prospective employers, your résumé—your proxy—must stand out. Employers tend to view students as generic or fungible. You, on the other hand, must establish yourself as a gem or, at least, a diamond in the rough.

◆ Academic honors provide immediate identifiers. There are, however, others. Look at your list again.

◆ What have you done or accomplished that distinguishes you from most of your classmates? Work those accomplishments into your résumé in the appropriate sections.

Heading—Start with the Facts

Your résumé has to start somewhere and the heading is the first thing a reader (employer) will see, so include your basic contact information up front.

◆ The standard approach is to begin the résumé with your name, street address, e-mail, and telephone number(s). These should be prominently presented at the beginning of the résumé to make it easy for employers to contact you.

◆ If your current address is temporary, provide a permanent mailing address, such as that of a family member. If necessary, rent a post office box. You need a good, easily accessible address.

◆ Supply a telephone number, preferably with voice mail, where you can be reached easily so an employer can make an appointment for an interview quickly and conveniently. Make sure your message sounds professional and helpful. If there is someone who is willing and able to accept appointments for you, you are in luck.

◆ Most law students and employers have access to e-mail, and it may prove easier to make connections online than by snail mail or phone. Some employers, however, may prefer the old-fashioned means of communication, so be prepared to utilize hard-copy letters or the telephone, as well as e-mail.

◆ If you have access to a fax number, you may want to list it.

◆ The operative theme here is availability. An employer who is moved to action by your résumé should be able to pick up a phone and arrange an appointment immediately. An employer who cannot reach you at a time when interest is high may be less inclined to call back on another occasion.

Education

Where you have gone to school and what you have done in school is usually the first major category in your résumé, because it is often the area of greatest interest to employers. As you gain experience in practice, your work history will eventually become more important than your education. A few simple steps will assure that you present your educational background in the most positive way.

◆ There are several ways of presenting your academic performance. You can include your grade point average (most employers expect to see it), or list the courses in which you did particularly well.

◆ You may want to group courses according to area of concentration to show expertise, or chronologically to show improvement. Some students prefer to make grade and class standing information available only in the interview. Many employers assume that if your grades are not on your résumé, they are not very good.

◆ Check with your career services office to find out your law school's policy on grade representation. Many schools require grades and class standing to be communicated in a particular way.

◆ Activities and honors usually should be listed as well, but they can be included in a separate category to showcase them.

◆ List your college or university, the date and type of degree you received, and all pertinent honors and activities. Again, the way you arrange the material will influence the message you communicate about yourself. Try to be more selective about pre-legal entries rather than law school entries.

◆ If you attended graduate schools or special programs, you will want to list those as well. Some older students who have attained several academic degrees may need to leave out or summarize some of their educational experiences to conserve space.

The way you classify your academic record and activities will depend on how you can best highlight your strong points. Chart 7 depicts a matrix with which you can group entries by educational level (legal and pre-legal) or by content (academics and activities). Although most résumés divide entries along a legal/pre-legal demarcation, there is no magic in that arrangement, and you should present entries in the way that makes you look best.

Chart 7
Education Matrix

	Honors	Activities
Legal		
Prelegal		

Experience

Education is certainly important, but legal employers frequently look for new lawyers who will "hit the ground running." These employers may be as interested—or more interested—in what you have done, as they are in what grade you received in Con Law. In fact, if your grades are not at the very top of your class, then you may need to demonstrate that you have relevant experience to enhance your marketability as a candidate. To this end, the following observations may provide helpful:

- ◆ Concentrate on legal work by listing these experiences first and in greater detail, with the present or most recent job listed first.
- ◆ You should include the name of your employer, dates of employment, and a brief description (using action verbs; see Appendix E) of your most important responsibilities. Try to focus more on the content of your work than on the timing of your employment.
- ◆ If you were chairperson of a committee, helped with a political campaign, lobbied, or volunteered in some other capacity, then you acquired valuable skills, and this information should be included, especially if your other work experience is limited.
- ◆ For nonlegal work experiences, try to focus on those aspects of the job that built skills that could be useful in your work as a lawyer.

Chart 8 illustrates a matrix based upon experience. As with the education matrix in Chart 7, the experience matrix is divided between legal and nonlegal positions, as well as employment and

Chart 8
Experience Matrix

	Employment	Pro Bono
Legal		
Prelegal		

pro bono (volunteer) experiences. The point is that you can present your experience differently, depending on what is most likely to impress the employer you want to hire you.

Publications

Publications, if you have them, can appear in the context in which they were written (under education or experience) or, if there are several, can be listed in a category by themselves. You may include unpublished writing samples in this category as well, as long as you are sensitive to confidentiality of real clients named in documents, and the intellectual property rights of other owners. In addition to listing publications on their résumé, many students prepare to make electronic or hard copies available to employers upon request.

Personal Information

Disclosing personal information can be problematic. Although employers are restricted by law as to the kinds of personal questions they can ask you, personal experiences can help you break the ice, build a connection in an interview, and help you to be remembered afterward. If you include such information, it is usually best listed at the end of the résumé. Consider the following points as you decide whether and how to include the information:

- ◆ Personal information tells briefly who you are and what you are like. It is unlikely that a single list could serve to describe all the possibilities to incorporate in this section. What you include here will depend on the image you want to present.
- ◆ Employers cannot legally ask your date of birth, marital status, whether you have children, or other similar personal information that might be used to discriminate against women or minorities. Sharing personal information with employers is up to you. In some cases, you may make an employer uncomfortable by raising such issues (e.g., marital status).
- ◆ If you include personal information, you may want to list things like place of birth, nationality (if born outside the United States), special skills, languages, geographical

preferences, hobbies or travel (if pertinent or especially interesting), and when you will be available for the job.

◆ Information about your health, height, and weight might be relevant if you were going to work on a construction project or entering a beauty contest, but not for most law-related jobs. Also irrelevant (and often negative in impact) are the name and occupation of your spouse, the names and ages of your children, your religious beliefs, political persuasion, and self-laudatory statements (e.g., "highly motivated").

◆ Anything that is likely to create a negative impact is best omitted. Say "single" instead of "divorced" if you feel you must reveal your marital status. You do not need to mention the ages (or even existence) of children, particularly if they are very young and you are a single parent. If you have a noticeable health problem or handicap, do not mention it in your résumé, but be prepared to explain in your interview that your problem would in no way affect your work performance.

References

It would be unusual for an employer to fail to conduct due diligence in making a hiring decision by contacting references. This being the case, here are a few things to remember:

◆ Most employers will want to contact your references directly. The names of references may be included on the résumé if you need to fill up the page or if the names will be recognized by employers. Legal employers may not ask for references if you do not list them, so the commonly used "References available upon request" may let employers know that you have references, but fail to motivate evaluators to contact the references.

◆ In lieu of using valuable space on your résumé, prepare a separate reference sheet listing names and telephone numbers (as employers are much more likely to call references than to write to them). Three to five references, not relatives or counselors (such as ministers), are usually enough.

Try to use at least one law professor and make sure your references know that you will be listing them. Make sure your name and contact information appear on the reference list because it might be utilized separately from the résumé.

♦ Although the common practice is to the contrary, some students include professional preferences or a job objective, indicating areas in which they have particular interest and or experience. Here is a good place to bring in special qualifications even if they are nonlegal in nature. Beware of listing preferences if you have not decided to specialize in the areas you list, because doing so will probably typecast you. The same advice applies to inclusion of an "objective" statement, which is popular in many business résumés.

Lay It Out, Type It, and Review It

You can design your résumé in a word-processing program such as Word or WordPerfect. If you have access to graphic design software, you might be able to produce a more sophisticated looking product. You may also be able to purchase résumé-preparation software or templates to help you. The bottom line, however, is that regardless of how you do it, you need to take the raw data you have developed and create a written document you can use. You may also want to consider the following.

♦ You may want to prepare different versions of your basic résumé for different purposes or even for specific applications. You should always revise your résumé when changes in your situation take place.

♦ Single-page résumés are definitely preferred by legal employers looking at law students. This may be difficult for older students with a long job history, but you should try.

♦ Remember that you can fit more on a page by using a smaller type size or scalable fonts, but do not select type so small that it is hard to read.

♦ Use an 8-1/2-by-11-inch format, not legal size. An oversized résumé is unwieldy and gets dog-eared in the employer's briefcase and files.

First Draft

When you finally have a draft document, evaluate both its content and appearance. Use this checklist to make sure your design is on target:

- ◆ It should be clearly organized and neat.
- ◆ Your name and heading should stand out and the text should be placed in pleasing proportions on the page.
- ◆ Make sure that you have clearly emphasized your strong points.
- ◆ Ask yourself, "Does this résumé present the image of myself that I want to communicate to potential employers?"
- ◆ Make sure that you incorporate the skills you identified in Chapter 4. As you describe your activities and experiences, utilize action verbs to convey a sense of accomplishment.
- ◆ Describe your pre-legal and nonlegal skills in a way that looks credible in a legal context.
- ◆ Did you make effective use of white space, type sizes, and boldface or italics?
- ◆ Did you omit unnecessary facts and direct the information specifically to the employers you want to reach?

Have someone else objectively evaluate your résumé: your career services office counselor, a fellow student, a professor, or a lawyer. Everyone has a different opinion about what will make the best résumé. In truth, there is no perfect model. In the end, you must decide what pleases you.

Revise and Improve Your Draft

You may be satisfied with your first draft, but it is more likely that you will go through several drafts before you are ready for prime time. Do whatever it takes to get it right. If your résumé fails you at the outset, you will never get a chance to sell yourself in an interview.

- ◆ Any résumé older than three months is probably out-of-date. As a job seeker, you should regularly update your résumé as your credentials evolve.
- ◆ You also may want to modify your résumé to reflect changes in tactics or direction.

Proofread

After the résumé is typed, proofread it very carefully for errors. It is really quite amazing how many résumés are sent out with obvious typos in them, and it is impossible to guess how many jobs have been lost for lack of proofreading. Use the word processor's spell-checking feature to ensure all words are spelled correctly, but remember that spell checkers can make mistakes as well (e.g., "there" and "their" both look correct to the spell checker). Also ask someone to proofread it. A second pair of eyes may prove better than the spell checker for certain errors.

One other thing to look for is content that inadvertently raises negative connotations about you, or expresses an idea in a politically incorrect way, or just seems awkward when you read it. Fix these flaws before your résumé goes out the door.

Make Copies

When you are satisfied that you have a final draft, you are ready to distribute your masterpiece. You can use hard copies or electronic copies.

- ◆ Hard copies:
  - ◆ Be sure to use a laser-quality printer so that the letters are crisp and dark and will reproduce well.
  - ◆ Variety on the page is desirable; some items can be in bold or italic, for instance, but be sure that the main body is typed in an easily readable font.
  - ◆ Make sure to use high-quality bond paper as well, not the standard printer paper you used for your drafts.
- ◆ E-copies:
  - ◆ You may be sending your résumé as an attachment to an electronic or e-mail application. You can use the saved version of your résumé in your word processor, in a universal text file if you have no graphics issues, in a PDF or ZIP file, or in one of a variety of other format options. Some Internet Service Providers (ISPs) have trouble reading certain kinds of files, so you may need to save your résumé in several formats.

Examples

Let's take a look at some examples of résumés for the hypothetical students profiled on pages 11–16: Heather Meadows, Sally Fielding, and Bob Downing. Their résumés are included here as Charts 9 through 11. These examples illustrate how three students with three different backgrounds might compile an effective résumé. All three have targeted their résumés for a desired audience. Information has been carefully selected and grouped for effective presentation. All three résumés look clean, are easily accessible to the reader, and are likely to be well within the comfort range of most legal employers. Note how the style of a résumé might have to change for a nonlegal or nontraditional job, see Munneke, Henslee, and Wayne, *Nonlegal Careers for Lawyers,* ABA (2006).

Heather (Chart 9) is graduating from Columbia, one of the top law schools in the United States, with an impressive undergraduate background as well. She has done all the traditional things to get a job through Columbia's on-campus interview program. The fact that she is interviewing the fall or her last year in law school is a signal that she either has not accepted or did not receive a permanent offer from her summer associate job. Interestingly, Heather has used her publications and interests to set herself apart from all other similarly qualified competing candidates.

Sally (Chart 10) went to Xon Law School in Miami, Florida. Xon is a good law school, but it is small and not very well known outside of Florida. She always jokes that it's *not* the oil company! Although her background is not as chi-chi as Heather's, Sally has strong work experiences and foreign language skills that may come in handy in a multicultural metropolis like Miami.

Bob (Chart 11) went to Pace Law School, a young institution that offers an evening program and attracts a variety of corporate types to its Westchester location. Bob worked as an engineer for a water district after college, and then came to law school, quitting his day job before his final year of law school. His background and interests both point to the field of patent law, where he hopes to work after graduation.

Chart 9

HEATHER MEADOWS
560 West 120th Street, #13R
New York, NY 10027
(646) 123-3214
hl155@columbia.edu

EDUCATION

COLUMBIA UNIVERSITY SCHOOL OF LAW, New York, NY
J.D. Expected, May 2009
Activities: *Columbia Law Review,* Staff Member
Teaching Assistant, Contracts

UNIVERSITY OF CHICAGO, Chicago, IL
M.A. in International Studies, June 2006
Activities: Latin American Students Association
Research Assistant: International Relations Seminar

BROWN UNIVERSITY, Providence, RI
B.A. in Political Science, May 2005
Honors: Phi Beta Kappa
 Elected to the Honor Society for Political Science
Activities: Debate Team, President, winner national finals
 President, Student Senate

PUBLICATIONS

"Restructuring Securities Law to Promote Equity in Investments,"
Columbia Law Review, January 2008

EXPERIENCE

SKADDEN, ARPS, SLATE, MEAGHER & FLOM, New York, NY
Summer Associate, Summer 2008
Conducted research and prepared memoranda on litigation, mass torts, international arbitration, project finance and commercial property law issues. Participated in litigation and trial advocacy workshops. Attended client meetings and participated in firm pro bono activities involving immigration review issues.

HON. JOHN E. RULE
UNITED STATES COURT OF FEDERAL CLAIMS, Washington, D.C.
Legal Intern, Summer 2007
Researched and wrote memoranda regarding tax and intellectual property issues.
Attended court proceedings.

CALIFORNIA HIGH SCHOOL, San Diego, CA
English Teacher, 2006
Taught classics in an inner city public high school. Organized Special Olympics participation for families of high school students.

LANGUAGES

Fluent Spanish; moderate fluency French; beginner fluency Chinese

INTERESTS

Marathon running; writing short stories; international travel (visited 15 countries)

Chart 10

SALLY FIELDING

230 Avenue of the Americas, #8G
Miami, FL 33199
(305) 564-1234
jj@xon.edu

EDUCATION
Xon School of Law, Miami, FL
J.D. expected May 2009
> Activities: Society of Immigrants and Refugees Rights, Chair
> Courtroom Advocacy Program – Participant

State University, Holliday, NY
Bachelor of Arts in English, May 2006
Minor in History
> Activities: Task Force on School Governance, Co-Chair
> Student Counsel – Representative
> Baseball Intramural Team - Pitcher

EXPERIENCE
Donnelly, Buchman & Aprea, Miami, FL
Summer Associate, Summer 2008
Surveyed state court opinions to advise attorneys on litigation strategy. Researched real estate and trust issues regarding a family inheritance. Reviewed updates and lease agreements for local condominium law. Wrote a memorandum relative to water damage revisions in residential home insurance policies. Attended and assisted with deposition regarding a tort action.

Onner & Silver, LLP, Miami, FL
Legal Assistant, Summer 2007
Drafted complaints, pleadings, motions, settlement demand letters and discovery requests including interrogatories and requests for production. Researched case law pertaining to employment, civil rights, and ERISA. Interviewed clients, coordinated witnesses, abstracted depositions, organized and prepared demonstrative exhibits.

Florida State Legislature, Miami, FL
Aide to Representative Barnes Noble, Summer 200
Reviewed draft legislation regarding the regulation of assisted living centers. Composed press releases and wrote correspondence for constituent requests.

LANGUAGES
Fluent French and Portuguese

INTERESTS
Squash; web game design; wine tasting

Chart 11

Robert Downing

222 Meadows Road,White Plains, NY 10954
(914) 555-4444 *rdowning@law.pace.edu*

EDUCATION

PACE UNIVERSITY SCHOOL OF LAW, White Plains, NY
Juris Doctor and Environmental Law Certificate expected May 2009
GPA: 3.43   **Class Rank:**   Top 20%
Honors: Dean's List (all semesters)
              The Andrew Block Scholarship Recipient, 2008
Activities: Black Law Students Association, President (2008-2009)
              Environmental Law Society, Secretary (2005-present)

LEHIGH UNIVERSITY, Bethlehem, PA
Master of Science in Chemical Engineering, *cum laude,* received May 1997
GPA: 3.84

MANHATTAN COLLEGE, Riverdale, NY
Bachelor of Science in Chemical Engineering received May 1991
GPA: 3.91
Minor: French
Activities: Delta Delta Kappa Fraternity; French Club, President (1990)

LEGAL EXPERIENCE

SMITH, MADD, COW & HOWE, LLP, New York, NY
Law Clerk, June 2007 – Present
Perform legal research for small environmental law firm. Draft complaints, motions, liens and legal memoranda. Participate in settlement and negotiation conferences. Respond to requests for documents. Assist in the preparation of depositions. Interview and provide legal and scientific information to clients. Designated as direct contact for clients on matters involving engineering issues. Successfully drafted a motion for summary judgment resulting in a favorable award to client.

OTHER EXPERIENCE

COUNTY WATER DISTRICT, Yonkers, NY
Engineer Manager, September 1994 – May 2007
Performed advanced design, project and management responsibilities that entailed designing, writing, bidding and overseeing rehabilitation contracts in excess of $900,000. Supervised staff of five Engineer Assistants and interns.
Engineer Assistant, January 1991 – August 1994
Performed all water reviews. Inspected, reviewed and coordinated the construction of a water main facility for the village of Hartsdale.

LICENSES

Professional Engineer, New York, February 1995

MEMBERSHIPS

New York State Bar Association
American Society of Chemical Engineers
New York Water Environment Association
American Intellectual Property Law Association

Applications and Transcripts

In addition to a personal résumé, many job applicants will need to produce other documents as a part of the application process, including transcripts and application forms. Not all employers will expect you to produce all of these documents, but you should be prepared to do so, if necessary.

All law schools will distribute official transcripts when requested to do so by students. Federal law prohibits the institution from releasing such information without your permission. Thus, employers cannot obtain a transcript without your written authorization.

Many corporations and government agencies routinely ask for transcripts, although few law firms do. As cases of résumé fraud increase, however, this may change. Handing an unofficial copy to the interviewer is insufficient. Instead, you will be asked to sign a release before, during, or after the interview.

Take special note of the requirements for individual application forms, which are, in a sense, a variation of the résumé. If you are planning to apply for a federal government position, obtain Form 171 (See Appendix E and www.usemb.nl/sf171.htm) from your local post office because virtually every federal office requires this form to be filed to be eligible for consideration. Make one original and copy it for each separate application, but sign each form separately.

Many state and local governments also require a form. If you are seeking a state or local government position, inquire about this possibility before an interview or, if possible, even before submitting your résumé.

Writing Samples

Some employers ask applicants for a sample of their writing (see earlier discussion in Chapter10 , pages 111–112). A substantial number of firms and most judges want to evaluate your research and writing skills directly, rather than indirectly through professors or references. Accordingly, you should always carry with you a copy of a writing sample to hand over if requested. Don't routinely send out a writing sample with every cover letter and résumé.

Students sometimes ask, "What should I use for a writing sample?" Generally, the answer is to use your best work. If you are not sure, have someone else read the possibilities.

For most third- and fourth-year students, their best work probably came after the first year of law school. For second-year students, this may not be the case. You should do everything you can to produce written work during law school, not only because of the importance of writing skills in law practice but also because of the relevance of writing samples to the evaluation process.

Letters of Recommendation

The topic of references has already been addressed (see discussion, pages 128–129). An additional aspect of this question is the use of letters of recommendation provided to employers by job applicants. As a rule, legal employers are not impressed with reproduced letters of reference. Somehow, they know that you would not give them a letter that said, "I would never recommend Ms. Smith for a job!"

Even unsolicited letters sent directly by your references to employers may be viewed as annoyances. Your best strategy is to make the names, addresses, and phone numbers of your references available when asked, so that those employers who are interested can contact your references directly. On the other hand, some employers may require all applicants to submit letters of recommendation. You may also have a special reason for using a personalized letter from one of your references. For instance, a professor you have done research work for may have been the law school roommate of the managing partner of the firm where you are dying to work. In such case, a personal letter (or even e-mail) might be the perfect touch. Use your discretion.

A Final Note

Remember who you are interviewing. Who does the interviewer represent? What will employers want to know about you? Your résumé should facilitate the interview process, introducing personal characteristics and skills most attractive to an employer. It should highlight the accomplishments to be stressed in applying for a job. A certain amount of self-knowledge and a good deal of thought are needed to present the best possible picture, but if it will be well worth your time if you manage to succeed in this effort.

Researching the Employer **12**

Finding a job involves a lot more effort than merely showing up for an interview on time. Before you arrive at the interview, you must conduct considerable preliminary behind-the-scenes investigation. Taking shortcuts will only leave you with less control of the situation and fewer good possibilities to pursue. Researching the employer is one area where you may be tempted to take shortcuts. Resist this temptation. A key to successful job hunting is learning enough about prospective employers to be able to demonstrate why they need you. To accomplish this objective you must do your homework.

Research can be tedious, and this type of research is no exception, but getting good information that you can use is vital to a successful job search. Your three-year investment in law school, however, deserves a planned and thorough effort to find the best employer and working situation possible.

Applying to employers at random or going into an interview cold is as sensible as buying an expensive pair of shoes without trying them on. Your job will be a major part of your life for the next several years, and the first step in a career that may span forty years or more. The amount of time you spend learning about prospective employers may make the difference in your long-term happiness in life.

Building an Employer Database

The basic rule for building an employer database is to find out as much about each organization as possible. As you go through the process of digging up information, remember these fundamental questions:

- What type of person does the employer need?
- What skills will the employer be looking for to meet its needs?
- How do your particular skills meet these needs?

It is important to know how you will fit into the organization but, more important, it is critical for you to bring value to the table. Employers do not hire people out of charity or generosity, but because the decision-makers in the organization believe that the person they are hiring possesses the potential to create net value for them. Thus, the key to effective employer research is to identify a nexus between what they need and what you have to offer. Here is some of the specific information you need to discover about each employer:

- What is the work environment like?
- What are the backgrounds, exponential background, accomplishments, and interests of members of the firm?
- Who are the clients and what are their legal needs?
- How does the organization obtain clients?
- What services does the firm provide for these clients?
- How many employees work for the organization?

This program may sound like a lot of work, but if you break down your efforts into small, manageable segments, you can accomplish it much more effectively. For example, writing a hundred personalized letters at one sitting is a Herculean task, but you can manage writing five letters a week (one letter each day).

You can find many information resources in your law school career services office or law library. You can locate materials online that are not available in the law school, or in the university or public libraries. You can conduct information interviews with a variety of individuals who possess information about potential employers, including professors, classmates, and other personal contacts (see Chapter 13, Building a Network, for more information).

The Internet is the most fertile source of employer information, and you can conduct research from wherever you have access. Some students may have Internet access at work, but employer policies vary on personal use of the Internet, so you should check this out before you take advantage of your employer's resources.

You probably have a laptop, iPod, or Blackberry, but you also may be able to use a desktop home computer if you need more room to spread out. If your computer is more than two years old, you may want to consider upgrading either the entire system or outdated components.

In addition to Internet access, you should have a plan for organizing the data you collect. One approach is to print out everything you find and organize the papers in notebooks. Alternatively, it might make more sense to save data in an organized file management structure using folders and subfolders, saving your work. You can also create a database or spreadsheet to manage and access information (see Chart 12 for an example of how a spreadsheet can be organized).

The database outline in Chart 12 helps you to track your contacts with prospective employers, along with other information about the organizations you are considering. Looking at the question of information from a different perspective, many students wonder what information they should know about employers they are considering. Apart from the general admonition that the more you know the better armed you will be, there are some key facts that you should keep at your fingertips:

Chart 12
Model Spreadsheet or Database

Name of Employer: _____

Address: _____

City: _____

State: _____

Zip: _____

Phone: _____-_____-_____

Hiring Partner: _____

E-mail or Phone: _____

Recruitment Administrator: _____

E-Mail or Phone: _____

Personal Contact: _____

E-Mail or Phone: _____

Number of Lawyers Employed: _____

Number of Offices: _____

Locations: _____

Type of Organization:* _____

Substantive concentrations: _____

Application: _____/_____/_____

Interview 1: _____/_____/_____

Interview 2: _____/_____/_____

Offer: _____/_____/_____

Accepted: _____/_____/_____

Reject: _____/_____/_____

Salary: _____

Notes: _____

_____

_____

_____

_____

_____

_____

*Categories and Sub-categories of Organization:

P=Private Practice (s=small, m=medium, l=large, v=very large)

C=Corporation (g=general counsel/legal department, n=nonlegal)

G=Government (f=federal, s=state, l=local)

J=Judicial Clerkships (f=federal, s=state, l=local, a=judicial administration)

M=Military/Armed Forces (j=JAGC, m=other military)

N=NGO/Non-Government Organization

A=Private Association

L=Legal Services/Public Interest

E=Education (l=law teaching, t=other teaching, a=administration)

O=Miscellaneous or Other

- Name of the employer, including spelling of name partners' names
- Address, including relevant branch offices)
- Names of your contacts at the firm (grads from your school, people you have met)
- E-mail address and telephone number for each contact
- Name of the person responsible for hiring within a particular firm. If not clearly denoted in the employer's hiring literature, you may need to select the senior partner, a partner whose bar affiliations indicate a strong practice interest in the area of specialization to which you are drawn, an alumnus of your law school, or another person you believe should receive employment inquiries.
- Job openings, including job titles, salary information, and responsibilities
- Job requirements (the unwritten job description of what you will really be expected to do, such as travel, billable hour requirements, and routine work)
- Application and offer deadlines (especially if they differ from NALP Guidelines)
- Application requirements (e.g., transcript, writing sample, proof of citizenship)
- Personal observations/insights

In a corporation, government law department, or similar organization, the general counsel usually assumes the same role as senior partner in a law firm, and frequently has direct hiring responsibility. If there are other individuals listed to whom your inquiry more logically might be directed, however, note the name and the reason for selection. For almost any employer, a phone call can provide the appropriate name to which your letter should be addressed.

Because your job search should not be restricted to advertised openings alone, you should seek to find potential openings using other sources. You can utilize legal and alumni directories, as well as telephone books from cities across the country. You can contact various organizations that provide legal job search assistance. Finally, if you want to know which firms and corporations have shown an interest in graduates of your law school, thumb through the résumés of employers who interview at your school.

Many interesting ideas for researching employers can be gleamed from career books, such as Richard Bolles's *What Color Is Your Parachute?* These books contain step-by-step instructions for job seekers and cover a variety of topics, including the art of conducting information interviews and gathering facts. In the final analysis, most job search books contain much of the same information, so reading one book—this one—will probably be enough.

Deciphering Employer Information

Many law firms and corporations, particularly larger ones that conduct on-campus interviews, produce employer résumés, brochures, and other print information. More common, you can turn for information to law firm Web sites. Most firms that have formal recruitment programs and many that do not provide information Web sites. Reading this information can be tedious and repetitive, full of platitudes and catch phrases. The trick for you is to cull useful tidbits from the chaff of verbiage you read.

The employer's information can be slick and professional, or simple and unsophisticated. Although you might be tempted to draw conclusions by the glitziness of the presentation, remember: All that glitters is not gold. Regardless of form, these marketing pieces may tend to obscure rather than to clarify the employers' picture for you.

It is possible, however, to find meaningful information if you know where to look and how to systematize your findings. As you read the employer's literature, try to answer the important questions described above.

In addition, some of the unanswered questions may prove to be illuminating as well, and give you ammunition for the interview. The whole interview process should be aimed at collecting and utilizing information in order to be able to make sound decisions.

Employers frequently try to paint a favorable picture of the organization. At the same time, the information typically falls into a number of distinct categories, including the following:

- History and background of the firm, agency, or corporation

- Organization and structure of the office
- Employer's philosophy of practicing law
- Major clients/industries
- Primary areas of practice
- Hiring standards or requirements
- Hiring needs for the upcoming year
- Description of summer clerkship program
- Starting salaries, benefits, and salary potential
- Intangible benefits
- *Pro bono* and public service activities
- Training and professional development
- Networking opportunities with lawyers working for the employer
- Advantages of living in the city or community where the employer is located
- Other factors which make this employer unique

Many legal employers participating in fall on-campus interviews complete a NALP Form. Not only is it much easier to compare one organization to another using the NALP Form rather than a firm résumé, brochure, or Web site, it is easier to track changes in an organization from year to year. NALP Forms contain a wealth of information from areas of practice, to hiring patterns, to salary structure. NALP Forms are published in the hard copy *National Directory of Legal Employers* and electronically on Westlaw (http://nalp.org or westlaw.com).

Smaller firms and other organizations that do not recruit on-campus may not complete NALP Forms or produce other literature to guide you. For these employers, finding relevant information may be quite challenging. Law students are trained to ferret out facts and case law when they conduct legal research, and the same skill can help them discover facts about legal employers. Conducting online searches in electronic databases can uncover a wealth of helpful information, including:

- What reported cases lawyers in the firm have argued
- What newspaper and magazine articles have mentioned lawyers in the firm
- What books and articles lawyers in the firm have written

Even after you read an organization's literature or NALP Form, you may still have unanswered questions. For example, where can you find out about working conditions, reputation, and the treatment of new lawyers? For the answers to these questions you may have to read between the lines.

Directories

A number of directories compiled by bar associations and commercial publishers provide information about legal employers. If you learn how to use the *Martindale-Hubbell Law Directory,* state legal directories, *Standard & Poor's Register of Corporations,* the *U.S. Government Manual,* and other specialized directories, you can supplement the information that employers provide about themselves. Even telephone directories include comprehensive lists of law firms, agencies and companies.

The Federal Yellow Book series is available through most law school career services offices. These directories provide easy access to a wide array of employers in particular categories. The local telephone book or Yellow Pages of any community will always include a section on lawyers or attorneys. Many of these resources are also available online.

Martindale-Hubbell

The *Martindale-Hubbell Law Directory* (also available at http://www.martindale.com) is the most comprehensive and oldest legal directory in the United States. Although many firms are not listed in the law firm section of the directory, because they must pay for these "ads," virtually all lawyers who have been licensed to practice in any jurisdiction appear in the free individual section. *Martindale* arranges its listings in alphabetical order by state. In each of the printed directory volumes there are four main sections:

◆ The first lists all licensed attorneys in the states included in that volume. The information here is abbreviated and coded according to a key found on the inside cover of each volume. In this section you can discover when a lawyer was born, his or her date of bar admittance, firm and status within the firm, undergraduate and law degrees, and the firm's competence and ethics rating (e.g., *av*). No telephone numbers are listed, but the addresses of solo practitioners are included.

◆ The second section contains detailed descriptions of law firms with more extensive biographies of each lawyer in the firm. Here you will find many firms with more than five lawyers, but since only those firms that have paid for space are listed in this section, many firms are not listed. This section includes full addresses and telephone numbers of firms, biographies of members, areas of specialization, and representative clients. Look for graduates of your law school among members, and check members' professional affiliations to see what their interests are. This is one way to find out before the interview whether the firm will really be interested in you, and you in them. You should also pay attention to the firm's listed areas of practice, but do not be misled by generalizations. Terms like "general civil practice," "real estate," "probate," and "trials and appeals" could apply to most firms, and so do not tell you much about a particular firm. On the other hand, the terms "insurance" and "defense" seldom appear in the same listing with "negligence" and "worker's compensation," and terms like "criminal," "tax," and "public housing" give you a very good idea of the kind of work you might do if you worked for that firm. The list of representative clients is also a good source of information, but bear in mind that probably only businesses, corporations, and banking institutions will be listed. A small-town lawyer or one who represents only individuals would probably not list representative clients.

◆ The third section includes information on legal support services and suppliers of products for lawyers. Ostensibly a service to the bar, this section appears to be more of a means of raising advertising revenue than anything else.

◆ A fourth section of *Martindale* contains a directory of corporate law departments, a directory of Canadian and international lawyers, and digests of Canadian, international, and American laws by state, the District of Columbia, Puerto Rico, and the Virgin Islands. Anyone interviewing with out-of-state firms can review these digests to gain a quick snapshot of the law in relevant jurisdictions in case legal questions arise during an interview.

If you are using the *Martindale-Hubbell* Web site (http://www .martindale.com), the potential for managing information increases exponentially, because you can construct complex searches covering a number of different variables to identify lawyers or firms that meet your profile. The information is not presented in a linear format (i.e. Volumes I-IV), so you can device different points of access to suit your own needs.

American Lawyer

American Lawyer, a news magazine for and about lawyers, and a variety of related publications regularly collect and publish surveys and other data about law firms and other employers (e.g., the Am Law 100 list of the largest U.S. law firms). These lists are commonly used by students to organize and analyze data about potential employers.

State Legal Directories

If you do not find all you want to know in *Martindale-Hubbell,* try the state legal directory for the jurisdictions where you are applying for jobs. Many of these directories are published by the Legal Directories Publishing Company, Inc., or by the state bar association. The state directories, like *Martindale-Hubbell,* include individual lawyer listings, paid law firm listings, and other ancillary information.

State legal directories also incorporate other useful information, such as the staffs of various federal, state, and local government departments and agencies, the courts, and both U.S. and state legislators. If there is a judiciary section, it will contain biographies of judges within the state.

Corporate Directories

If corporate law is your main interest, your most valuable tool may be the *Standard & Poor's Register of Corporations (S&P). S&P*

includes a list of corporations by name, showing their addresses and telephone numbers, officers, accountants, banks, and law firms used, revenue for the past year, number of employees, products, and other information. Check to see if the company has a corporate counsel in-house, or if it engages a particular outside firm for its legal affairs. *S&P* also lists directors and executives of corporations, with biographical information and home addresses. The hard-copy version of the directory indexes this information in order to make it easier to find.

In addition to *S&P,* you may find useful information in *Dun & Bradstreet, Fortune 500,* and the annual reports of various companies. Much of this information is available in both print and online formats. Business-school career services offices often collect considerably more information on companies than law school career services offices do, so it might make sense to visit the office that services the business school of either your law school or undergraduate school.

In addition, students may want to search more information considering the fact that the corporate marketplace for jobs dwarfs the legal marketplace.

- ◆ Morningstar
- ◆ *The Wall Street Journal*
- ◆ *New York Times Business Journal*
- ◆ Business school libraries
- ◆ Reserves research centers
- ◆ Public libraries (business/financial sections)

As is the case with legal directories, many corporate directories are available in both print and online versions, and some are published exclusively in electronic format. University business schools and public libraries often have more information on corporations and other business organizations than law schools, so as a law student you may need to explore outside the law school box to locate these resources.

Government Directories

For information on federal government agencies, try the *U.S. Government Manual,* which will tell you the names of officials and agency staff members. Many federal and state agencies publish internal directories as well, and information about government offices is incorporated in virtually all local telephone directories.

Another fine source of information about employers in Washington, D.C., is the Congressional Quarterly's *Washington Information Directory*. This directory carries thousands of information sources in government and private associations on the following topics: economy, energy, health, consumer protection, education, employment, housing, justice, transportation, minorities, communications, defense, science, international affairs, environment, and women.

A third resource for government and public sector jobs is the *Federal Yellow Book* series. Not to be confused with the Yellow Pages, the *Yellow Books* contain contact information for a variety of government agencies, NGOs, political action groups, and other organizations operating "inside the beltway." In recent years, these titles have expanded beyond the confines of Washington, D.C., where they started, to governmental entities throughout the country.

If a job with state government appeals to you, check the library reference department to see if a guide to state agencies has been published in your state or in the state in which you hope to live. Some guides of this nature contain information on the structure and functions of every state agency, but may not tell you anything about the staffs of the agencies. For names of individuals to contact, you will need to go back to the state legal directory.

Online Databases

In addition to the Lexis, Westlaw, and Martindale-Hubbell databases, there are literally hundreds of specialized databases and directories available online through commercial networks. The resources section of this book contains a more extensive list of information sources about legal employers, including many Web sites. You should keep in mind, however, that the nature of research is to discover information that is not widely accessible. If you can take advantage of search engines such as Yahoo, Lycos, or Google, the scope of your research is limited only by your inventiveness.

Web Sites and Blogs

In recent years, a variety of other information sources has appeared. Blogs written by interest commentators and Web sites created by firms, companies, agencies, consultants, news services, and commercial job resources all contribute to increasing the volume of information available to law student job applicants. Some of this information is valuable, some useless, some of it is factual, some pure conjecture, some of it accurate, some . . . well, you get the picture. Appendix A (page 285) includes information about many of these resources, but this is a constantly changing landscape, so creativity in conducting research is a premium.

Building a Network 13

The term *networking* is sometimes overused and often misunderstood. Some people think that networking merely means using contacts to find jobs. Others dismiss it as psychobabble, a campy way to mystify something that is very simple. Both these perceptions contain grains of truth, but miss the big picture.

Networking does involve using personal contacts in the job search process. And the basic idea is quite simple: Everyone has a network. Some people are born with family connections, and other people build their ties through life experiences, but all of us develop personal and professional contacts over the years.

Not everyone understands how to leverage contacts. Ideally, you should manage your contacts in an organized way. This involves not only creating a network, but maintaining and utilizing it as well. Networking should not be something that you do just when you need a job, but rather as an ongoing activity.

Creating Your Network

Everyone has contacts. While some folks may start out with more than others or do a better job of making contacts, anyone can build a network. The first step in the process is to make a list of all the people you know well enough to call on the phone and not have to explain who you are.

This list can include relatives, friends, college and law school acquaintances, lawyers, business associates, social and political contacts, and other people you have gotten to know along the path of life. They do not have to be people you see every day, nor do they have to be lawyers. It is a common mistake to assume that only lawyers have information about legal jobs.

Keep a record of as much information as possible on all these people: addresses, phone numbers, employers, birthdays, and other useful facts. The best way to save this information is to utilize some kind of database. Microsoft Outlook and other personal information manager (PIM) programs are set up to collect and categorize contact information. Palm and similar personal desktop assistants (PDAs) also provide an easy-to-use contact manager that you can hold in your hand. You could create your own database, but why bother when the technology is already available, and inexpensive as well? Some people even use old-fashioned Daytimers or index-card systems. The point is that you need to do something to organize this information so that it is easy to retrieve when you need it.

Expanding Your Network

The second step in building your network involves expanding it. As time passes, you will encounter more individuals who will become a part of your network. This process of accretion occurs naturally, but your biggest difficulty will be following up on initial contacts to establish them as part of the network. Social custom seems to dictate that a one-time meeting is just that. It takes follow-up to create an ongoing relationship. If you are willing to take the initiative, you will be surprised how quickly your network grows. Here are some specific suggestions to follow:

- Do not wait for chance meetings. Go out and find people who can help you professionally, with whom you share some common intellectual, philosophical, or professional ground.
- Pursue contacts you have developed through informational interviewing.
- Go to CLE programs, bar association meetings, law school events, and community activities.
- Do volunteer work and become active in professional and social organizations.
- Let people know who you are, what you are doing, and what your interests are.
- If you are looking for a job, you will find that more opportunities are developed from résumés mailed to your network than to unsolicited employer lists.
- Try to meet personally with as many people in your network as possible. Let them know your plans and expectations.

These are just a few ideas, but you should be able to think of others. For those who are not as naturally gregarious and outgoing, this aspect of networking can be the most challenging part of the process. If you are shy or reticent, you may need to work hard to force yourself to be more assertive, and to find ways to meet people under circumstances where you are most comfortable. Whatever you do, however, do not wait for contacts to find you.

Maintaining Your Network

While you are always building your network, you must take time to maintain it. This means not only updating information about people, but also communicating with people on a regular basis. Even if you are not looking for a job, keep in touch with your contacts so that they do not think you only call when you want something.

You can develop your network by giving something to your contacts: information. Send them clippings, articles, and comments about issues that you know will interest them. If you fine-tune the network, you will discover that contacts with some individuals will be more regular than with others.

You should try to communicate at least annually with everyone on your list. You can use holiday greeting cards for this purpose, although most of us do not usually think of holiday information-sharing as a time to massage our broader network. Some lawyers have extended the concept of the holiday letter to a permanent, regular, professional newsletter.

Try to keep up with this maintenance work. If you procrastinate, you may find that eventually you forget the information you need to update your contact list. In order to do a good job of maintaining your network, you need to spend some time contacting your network virtually every day. You can use phones, mail, e-mail, fax, and personal meetings (e.g., lunches). This may seem to be a formidable task at first, especially given the crunch of day-to-day activities. If you get in the habit of taking a little bit of time each day when you answer mail and make phone calls to contact a couple of people from your network, the process will become second nature to you if you think about how people you know could use information that comes across your desk.

Revise your list regularly. Indicate people you can contact directly, and contact them. Try to track down as many of the missing links as possible. Chart 13 will help you to develop your list of contacts. Do you know where these people are? Do they know where you are? What legal skills would these contacts be most interested in knowing about? What legal employers are these contacts likely to know?

Utilizing Your Network

If you have built and maintained a good network, utilizing it in the job search will be easy. It is important to articulate what you are looking for, so do not be afraid to tell people what you want.

If your current employer is not aware of your interest in leaving, you will obviously have to be more discreet and ask those you talk with to maintain confidence. There is a tradeoff here. The more people you talk to, the more your job-hunting plans become common knowledge. In a small legal community, this does not take long! On the other hand, the more people who know about your plans, the more likely you are to come up with solid opportunities.

Visit as many people as you can in person, call others, and send everyone a résumé. This does not have to be done all at once.

Chart 13
Networking Checklist

A. Five friends from childhood through high school:

1. _____
2. _____
3. _____
4. _____
5. _____

B. Five friends from college through law school:

1. _____
2. _____
3. _____
4. _____
5. _____

C. Five teachers or professors:

1. _____
2. _____
3. _____
4. _____
5. _____

D. Five work supervisors or business associates:

1. _____
2. _____
3. _____
4. _____
5. _____

E. Five lawyers or professional contacts:

1. _____
2. _____
3. _____
4. _____
5. _____

If you assume that a job search will take six months and that you will work on it every day, you can gather a tremendous amount of information during the course of your search.

Do not be disappointed when some people let you down. Inevitably, some of your contacts will promise to get you an interview with Ms. X at X, Y & Z or to give you names of firms with openings, but fail to deliver. Do not hold it against them; this is just the nature of the process. It is just as likely that someone from whom you expected no help at all will come through for you. So, in the end, things balance out.

Do not forget to follow up. Keep records of your contacts with people and get back to them periodically as your job search continues. If they do not hear from you, they may assume that you have found something and that you are no longer in need of their help.

When you do land a job, let these contacts know so they do not continue to work on your behalf when it is not necessary to do so. Everyone's time is valuable, so it will benefit you to respect the time of your network contacts.

As a final note, the heart of your network may well come from law school contacts: your graduating class, professors, and graduates who preceded you. You belong to a very small club. You can help each other. Talk to each other; support each other. The career services office, the dean's office, and the alumni office at your school are all committed to increasing the level of communication among graduates of the institution. You can further this aim simply by building, maintaining, and utilizing your own network.

Remember that networking is an activity that you must pursue tirelessly. You must make a point of keeping in touch with people, and not merely calling when you need something. On the other hand, you should expect to help out your contacts when they call, as they will when they know the lines of communication are open.

In this light, utilizing your network means considerably more than keeping a list of contacts for job search purposes. These are the people you may turn to throughout your professional career for advice on everything from a specific case to discussing more personal thoughts and concerns. College and law school afford you opportunities to build both close friendships and casual ones. Once you enter the working world, however, such opportunities diminish considerably.

Job Hunting Nuts and Bolts   **14**

Much of the literature in the career planning field fails to offer alternatives to traditional job hunting techniques. Even experienced career counselors seldom suggest really creative approaches to the process. But the truth is that not everyone will succeed following the traditional paths.

Not everyone went to Harvard. Not everyone made law review. Not everyone has a parent who will hire him no matter how poorly he did in school. In other words, something should be said for the benefit of the other 90 percent.

What problems do you face when you begin your job search without an instant network of relatives or preexisting contacts? For you, the task is to create contacts on your own. You have to work harder, longer, and smarter than your more fortunate classmates.

One of the most difficult problems a job seeker has to face is how to make contacts with prospective employers when he or she has no certain knowledge about what jobs are available. In such a situation, the individual must find the opening, or in some cases, even create the demand.

This method of job hunting variously known as "pounding the pavement" or "beating the bushes" can be frustrating and dehumanizing. The percentages drop as soon as you go from jobs you know are available to those you think might be available. Still, much of the headache can be avoided by following a few simple rules:

- *Plan carefully.* If you have some idea about what you want, some priorities, and some system for your search, you will have overcome the major hurdle. Too many people start looking first, and ask questions later. This not only cuts down on efficiency, but also increases the likelihood of accepting a personally dissatisfying position. Your research and evaluation before you ever start to look for a job should be painstaking and thorough.

- *Persevere.* Recognize the fact that you may not meet with instant success. Prepare contingency plans and keep looking. Retrace your steps from time to time, especially in areas with large lawyer populations. Whenever you get a lead from one source, follow it up. In fact, you should attempt to find leads even when your discussions with employers are otherwise unproductive.

- *Pick and choose.* Blanket applications usually are not the best way to apply for jobs. Carefully drawn personal letters to employers are usually more effective.

- *Pull all your strings.* Crass as it may sound, always try the easiest route. Ask for help from family, friends, or acquaintances who are practicing lawyers. If you have an icebreaker, or a recommendation, do not hesitate to use it.

- *Pool your resources.* Working cooperatively may seem alien to many law students for whom law study has been a singular activity. The idea of teamwork in job hunting, however, is no more revolutionary than study groups in your first year. Using a team approach, you and one or more other persons interested in the same type of practice go to a city together, but interview separately, avoiding overlap.

By comparing notes at the end of an interviewing day, the amount of territory you can cover will be multiplied. It is essential that you lay the ground rules beforehand, and start out with an attitude of cooperation.

It is important to use your creativity in all of these efforts. The greatest asset you can have in job hunting is a creative and fertile imagination. These suggestions do not exhaust the job hunting possibilities. If all forty-thousand annual law graduates looked for jobs in exactly the same places, the competition would be intense. If you can find avenues that others have not thought to pursue, you will have a distinct advantage.

Applying Long-Distance

Most law graduates enter practice in the state or area where they went to law school. For graduates leaving the area after graduation, contacts with outside lawyers may seem limited. Actually, the limitations only depend upon the amount of time and effort you are willing to spend. Applying long-distance will require more research because you must base your decisions upon where you would like to live as well as with whom you could work. The following comments suggest ways you can go about researching, finding, and applying for such positions:

- ◆ *Research desirable areas to live.* Get newspapers and magazines from different cities. Write to the Chamber of Commerce. Check out local Web sites. Find out about the economic, political, and environmental conditions in the area, and then ask yourself if these conditions will be agreeable to you.
- ◆ *Contact local bar associations.* A state bar will have addresses of local bar associations and their officers. Many times these people can help.
- ◆ *Read the bar journals.* Almost every state has a bar journal, and many of these have a placement section.
- ◆ *Research some more!* Try to find out who the legal employers are and how you can find potential openings. Even if you have lived in the area before, you have probably never looked for a legal job there. Check your career services office files. Check *Martindale-Hubbell* to locate other graduates from your law school or your undergraduate alma mater. Watch the current job listings at your school.

- *Establish personal contacts* (see Chapter 25). Even if you do not have contacts within the legal community, you might know someone who does. Check groups with professional interests similar to yours, and if you have an interview that does not result in a job, always ask for other possible leads.
- *Use letters of introduction.* Some students have firm ideas about where to begin looking for a job upon graduation, but have no idea how to begin looking. When they arrive at their destination, they discover that a strange city can be an imposing obstacle to even the most daring individual. Many career services offices will provide a letter of introduction to career services offices at other schools in the area requesting that they provide names of persons who might offer employment or help you to get some feel for the local employment market.
- *Go there.* Everything is easier when you visit a place personally. Despite the cost, an interviewing trip will demonstrate your interest. Many students make the ultimate commitment: Move to the area, take the bar exam, and keep looking until they find a job.
- *Apply for temporary jobs.* It is easier to look for jobs if you live in an area than to try to do it long-distance. Also consider positions like judicial clerkships to get you there.

Where Are the Lawyers?

Lawyers often attend conventions, conferences, and institutes that focus on their specialty. If you are interested in a particular area of practice, go where the lawyers are. Many CLE conferences are offered free or at reduced rates for law students. This approach may require you to be assertive in meeting people and arranging interviews or can offer informal opportunities to talk during breaks or discussion groups. Join state, local, and specialty bar associations—most have student membership plans. Many of these groups also have substantive committees that you can join, and the lawyers on the committees are likely to welcome an energetic law student to help them with their work. You may even be able to identify events or watering holes frequented by lawyers and meet local practitioners informally. Remember: You will never meet your future employer sitting at home.

Pitfalls for the Unwary

Although this book urges you to assert your individuality, assess your talents and interests, and take control of the job search process, there are those who give you advice to the contrary. Three particular approaches to the job search deserve attention because of their ineffectiveness. These are the hat-in-hand approach, mass mailings, and putting all your eggs in one basket.

- ◆ *Hat-in-hand:* This approach begins with a mental attitude that you will be lucky to find a job, any job. If you have to take what you can get, there is little reason to devote much attention to what you have to offer. In the end, you will probably find a job based upon a fit between your skills and the employer's needs. The hat-in-hand approach, however, can divert your attention to many openings for which there is no fit and little prospect of getting hired. A hat-in-hand mentality also tends to cause you to undersell yourself. Rather than starting with the best possibilities and working down a priority list as this book suggests, the hat-in-hand approach leaves you at the bottom of your list.
- ◆ *Mass mailings:* Sometimes a corollary of the hat-in-hand approach, mass mailings represent an attempt to get a job by playing a numbers game. In commercial advertising, a direct-mail ad campaign may go out to thousands of recipients. Most of these will not respond, but a small, predictable percentage that do will make the campaign profitable. A response rate of 0.5 percent is considered good, so two hundred letters might result in one interview; four hundred might result in two or three. It is not just a question of financing such a campaign, but rather who will respond to a mass mailing.
- ◆ *All your eggs in one basket:* Some law students want one job so much that they pursue only that position. Some students count on a part-time job developing into permanent

employment. Others have received assurances that a job will be available for them when they graduate.

Not a year passes when virtually every career services director in the country encounters at least one desperate graduate whose plans have fallen asunder. Do not be caught in this situation. Even if you have a strong possibility for employment, check out others. Maintain alternatives in case your first choice falls through.

Timetable for the Job Search

The job search is made more difficult by the fact that the timetable for job applications is a complicated one. In fact, there are many different timetables for the job search. This is because different types of legal employment may require you to contact employers, interview, and make decisions at different points in time.

These scheduling anomalies can catch the inattentive law student by surprise. If you overlook critical dates, you may foreclose many job opportunities. Chart 5 on page 73 provides an overview for many of the critical dates in the job search process. You should use this chart in structuring your own personal job search. In addition, the following generalizations pertain to specific job markets.

- ◆ *Large firms and corporations:* Large firms, corporations, and other employers that participate in the fall on-campus recruitment process at law schools typically do most of their hiring through campus interviews. This is true whether the firm visits your campus or not. They interview for summer clerks during the second year of law school, make offers to clerks at the end of the summer, and interview third-year students for positions only if they do not fill all openings from the ranks of summer clerks.
  - This process takes place each fall and the dates are established by the particular schedule set up by your law school career services office.
  - NALP guidelines concerning the acceptance of offers by employers participating in fall on-campus interviews influence the timing of interviews, office visits and offers, so be aware of these principles.

- If you want to get a job with an employer that recruits through campus interviews, you must keep this timetable in mind, even if you do not go through the interviews themselves.

◆ *Small firms:* Small firms tend to hire new lawyers when they need them. Frequently when they need someone is yesterday, so the firm will require candidates to have taken and passed the bar exam. Other small firms recruit almost exclusively from the ranks of part-time (as opposed to summer) law clerks. Thus, there is no magic time frame for small firm hiring, other than sometime early in the first year of law school until several months after graduation.

◆ *Clerkships:* See Chapter 21, page 248 for a more detailed overview of the clerkship hiring timetable. In the broader context, however, you should be aware that post-graduate federal judicial clerkship interviews take place within the same general time frame as on-campus interviews for summer associate positions at larger law firms. Some but not all state clerkship hiring may extend into the summer or fall after your second year. Your school may also have special procedures for applying to judges for clerkships, and should you miss this window, your chances of getting hired are diminished considerably. Clerkships for state judges generally lag behind federal clerkships. Consult the court in the jurisdiction where you will be applying.

◆ *Government agencies:* Government agencies are often influenced by budget cycles that run for a year, beginning in September or on some other annual date. Even agencies that try to recruit through on-campus interviews do not know how many openings they will have until the following spring or summer. The armed services, Foreign Service, FBI, as well as graduate law programs have their own application deadlines and beginning dates for training and educational programs. Check with your career services office for more information. It is important to look for application deadlines and hiring patterns whenever you conduct research on legal employers. Be sure to note this information on your employer database.

◆ *Other employers:* It is difficult to make generalizations
about all the different types of employers outside the traditional employers that hire the majority of law graduates.
If you are looking for work in a specific industry, there may
be timetables and procedures unique to employers in that
industry. For business opportunities in general, the pattern
is likely to be based on need at a particular point in time, as
is the case with small firm. If you are exploring possibilities
off the beaten path (at least for law students) you may have
to search a little more to find the appropriate path(s) for
those fields of employment.

How Long Will It Take?

Many students ask how long the job search should take. Of course,
the answer depends on many factors. Assuming that you have
done all the necessary background research, prepared a résumé,
and committed time to the job search, you should plan on several
weeks of sending out applications. This assumes that you will be
doing things other than looking for a job, and that you will not send
out all your applications at once. You will be following up on old
applications as you send out newer ones.

As a rule of thumb, you should expect to hear from employers
about two weeks after you send your letter, less for e-mail applications. If you have not heard anything after four weeks you might
want to follow up with a second letter or phone call. If you have
not heard anything within six weeks, you probably will not. Unfortunately, some employers lack the staff or simply the courtesy to
respond to students who contact them.

If your initial efforts are not successful, this stage of the job
search will continue. Weeks can easily turn into months. As a rule,
if you have actively pursued legal employers for three or four
months without a positive response, you should probably go back
to the drawing board. Your career counselor may be able to pin-
point problems that are hampering your success.

When an employer becomes interested in you, the next step is to
schedule a screening interview. It normally takes two to four weeks to
contact you, schedule the interview, and conduct the interview. Even

when the law school career services office serves as a facilitator for the interview scheduling, there is some delay between the time you first sign up for interviews, and when the interviews are held.

Because you may be talking to a number of employers on different dates, this stage of the process normally lasts for several weeks. Most law students find that there is a natural limit to the number of interviews they can endure when not pressed to do so by necessity. If they begin to receive positive responses to their first interviews, many law students cease contacting new employers until their initial interviewing is completed.

After the screening interview, you can expect to wait two to three weeks before hearing from the employer. The time frame may be extended if the employer conducts a national search with many applicants or reduced if the search is limited to two or three individuals. Allowing another two to three weeks for employers to make decisions, you should expect to have offers in hand within three to four months after you started the process. So if you plan on going through fall on-campus interviews, the process will start in mid-summer and you should be finished by mid-November.

After you receive one or more offers you should have some time to make a decision. Since employers want you to decide as soon as possible, most students want to extend the time frame to maximize their options. With respect to on-campus interviews, NALP suggests that employer offers to graduates not previously employed by them and to summer clerks be held open for 45 days, or December 30, whichever comes first, and to graduating students previously employed by them until November 15 (see Appendix B). Some employers expect an answer on the spot. (Federal judges are famous for this.) Although these matters are generally subject to negotiation, a sense of fair play and reasonableness on the part of both employers and candidates should put limits on the time frame for making decisions.

You may find yourself cut out of the process at a number of different points. If you have not taken the time to initiate new applications before older ones are rejected, you may find yourself at some point back to square one facing another three or four months of job search. It is probably fair to say that your job search will not go as well as your wildest hopes, but will go better than your gravest fears. A job search of three to six months is not unusual; one extending beyond nine months is atypical.

The timetable for part-time job searches, because of the temporary nature of the employment and the quick turnaround of the openings, is generally abbreviated. And a job search for a highly technical or specialized position may last a year or more.

For the substantial number of law students who go through the on-campus interview program at their school to find a permanent job, the process takes a good portion of the fall during the second and third years of law school (third and fourth for evening students). Although it is possible to skip second-year interviews and look for a permanent job during your final fall in law school, a majority of positions offered through on-campus interview programs are the result of summer clerkships obtained during the second year.

In order to get a sense of your own timing, work backward from the time you hope to begin work on a new job through the various parts of the career planning and job search processes, and identify benchmark dates for critical interim steps (e.g., when you need to revise your résumé or send out letters). Then insert these dates in your personal calendar, including reminders enough in advance of the critical date to do whatever you need to do by your self-imposed deadlines. If you use a PDA or PIM, creating these dates and reminders will be much easier than trying to do it by hand. Do not create a timetable that is so tight you will never follow it. Be realistic and come up with a schedule with which you can and will live.

Conclusion

Different legal jobs as well as law-related jobs can be expected to follow different cycles. Small firm hiring does not follow any cycle at all. Your research into potential employers should include the timing of the application process. If getting a job requires being in the right place at the right time, you can significantly enhance your chances by figuring out when the right place and right time will occur.

Selling Yourself 15

The statement "you are unique" may not strike you as particularly profound. Of course you are unique; you have been told so since childhood. Your many accomplishments set you apart from the crowd.

Unfortunately, many law students lose their confidence in their own uniqueness as soon as they begin to look for a job. They act as though they are fungible. They talk as though they have no special skills. Part of the reason lies in the law school experience itself, while another part relates to the job search process. These two elements can combine to undermine your ability to sell yourself to employers.

Law school is a little bit like marine boot camp. The course of study strips away your old identity and replaces it with a new one as a lawyer. For better or worse, you will never be a nonlawyer again. During your first year, you learn that you are almost never right. By your senior year, you discover that despite years of studying legal theory and black letter law, you know little about practicing law. Unlike previous school experiences, you can put everything you have into a course and still not get the highest grade.

The job search process is tough on the ego, also. Whether or not this is your first experience looking for a real job, it does not take long to discover the debilitating effects of job hunting. You may find it extremely difficult to feel unique in the face of this adversity. Many law students have encountered little adversity in their careers, so the job search can bring a rude awakening.

What can you do to maintain a strong sense of individuality?

- First, the better you understand your own skills, interests, and values, the easier it will be to articulate to employers that you are not just another grain of sand on the beach. Focus on your skills in relation to the job you seek rather than to the skills of your classmates.
- Second, keep in mind that this is not a new battle. Throughout your life you have confronted pressure to be ordinary, and the fact that you are where you are suggests that you have resisted. Resist again.
- Third, always identify a nexus between what you have to offer and what you believe an employer wants.
- Fourth, keep in mind that you only have to score once in this game to win. The wildcatter only has to strike one gusher to make up for all the dry wells, and you only need one job despite the fact you may apply for many more. Maintain that wildcatter mentality.

In order to market yourself, you must know the product you are selling. You need to know its strengths as well as weaknesses, its appeal to potential consumers, and its value in the marketplace. Whether you perceive this product to be one of a kind or one of forty-thousand identical items produced in the current model year can have a significant impact on your ability to sell the product in the marketplace.

Identifying Employers

Just as you are unique, each employer is unique. Sometimes that truth is lost in the mass of employer lists and placement information. Your goal as an applicant is to identify an employer who needs someone like you.

This does not mean that you cannot apply for more than one position at a time. It does mean that you should learn enough about each employer to whom you apply to be able to articulate why that employer needs to hire you. This becomes almost impossible to do with a mass-mailing campaign.

Your school's fall on-campus interview program represents the largest single group of employers you can hope to manage at one time. The more carefully you dissect employer information, the more readily you will be able to make informed choices about interview selection. This preselection or self-screening process on your part, whether you are interviewing on campus or going out on your own, will enhance your chances of being selected for an interview, being hired, and being happy after you go to work.

Earlier chapters of this book deal with techniques for researching employers. If you have followed the advice there, you should have a significant compendium about employers at your disposal. As you narrow your leads from classes of employers to specific organizations, you should seek increasingly detailed information about potential employers prior to the interview.

Some of the information will be in written form, prepared by the employer or compiled by some other source. You can learn much by talking with your network sources beforehand. A great deal of information can be obtained orally and then confirmed or amplified during the interview process. You will be eliciting oral information from the interviewer. When you can anticipate the interviewer's answers about the organization, your level of sophistication will be perceived as interest in the job, whereas lack of knowledge is often perceived as disinterest by interviewers.

Talk to professors, students who have clerked for the employer, judges, other lawyers, and even clients before the interview. Not all of these people will be helpful, but some will, and they will give you the information you need. When you talk to contacts, know exactly what you want to find out and get right to the point. Try not to telegraph the answers you want to hear when you ask questions (e.g., "Isn't X, Y & Z a good firm?"). Unless it is obvious or necessary, do not specify that you will be applying for a job with the organization. Just say that you are curious or conducting research.

At this point, legal employers may be horrified at the prospect of thousands of law students calling everyone under the sun for background checks on them, but in reality few law students will take this advice. They will not have the time, consider it too intrusive, or simply believe that the return will not justify their efforts. Those of you who do dig beneath the surface will gain a decided advantage in the job search. You will be better prepared for interviews and can also use your research to eliminate many prospective employers, or at least lower them on your priority list.

You do not need reams of information on each prospective employer. If you can articulate in a paragraph or less what makes this employer unique, you will generally have all the information you need to know. The best way to gather answers to your questions about an employer is through an information interview. This can be a formal appointment, a chance meeting, or a phone conversation during the preemployment process to gather information.

In his book *What Color Is Your Parachute?,* author Richard Bolles talks about information interviewing at an early stage in the career planning process. He suggests that you go to the person in the organization who ultimately will have the power to hire you, for the purpose of gathering information even before you apply. Then, when you come back to apply for a job, you will already have the information you need to sell yourself and know your interviewer.

Even if you do not conduct, as Bolles suggests, a surreptitious pre-interview, many information interviews can lead to real interviews and jobs. Whether you are going directly to the organization or meeting with someone else, keep in mind these rules (which apply to job interviews as well):

- ◆ Dress neatly.
- ◆ Be prompt.
- ◆ Treat secretaries and receptionists with the same degree of respect and consideration that you do the person you are interviewing.
- ◆ Establish rapport.
- ◆ Explain your purpose.
- ◆ Question effectively.
- ◆ Listen actively.
- ◆ Keep in mind what you want to learn and pursue that information assertively.

- ◆ If the interviewee does not have or know the information you require, ask for additional leads.
- ◆ Leave a business card or résumé, since sometimes people will have an idea after the interview and want to contact you.
- ◆ Take notes during the interview, or as soon as you leave, because this information will fade quickly.
- ◆ Send a follow-up note or thank-you letter if appropriate.

After the information interview, log your contacts into your database, along with any salient notes. Many of the individuals you meet can become part of your own network (see Chapter 13). Even if these individuals are not in a position to offer you a job, you can build upon these contacts for future reference, far beyond the employment process.

Contacting Employers

Once you have written your résumé and researched potential employers, you are ready to contact your target. You may be sending your résumé to employers you interview through your career services office or in response to specific job notices. You may also want to use your résumé to solicit interviews with employers whose type of practice interests you and who are located in an area in which you would like to live.

In many cases, even when applying electronically, a cover letter is a necessity. If your letter specifically targets the organization's needs, it can greatly enhance your chances of being hired.

Mass mailings to law firms, on the other hand, can be a costly and time-consuming task with little result. As related previously, direct-mail advertisers know that a response rate of one for every one hundred letters is unusually good. The approach you take and the language with which you state your interest can determine whether your letter comes to rest on the hiring partner's desk or in the trash can. You must use the letter to convey your interest in the type of practice a firm, corporation, or agency engages in, and your desire to become part of such a practice.

Your letter (see Chart 14) should describe how your skills and interest complement the firm's goals. It should reflect a little of your personality while getting its message across clearly and succinctly. Neatness, punctuation, and spelling are important. An error can eliminate your chances to be hired, especially if your letter is the only impression an employer has of you.

Several approaches can keep communications open. You may ask for an interview directly. You may even suggest a time. You may tell the employer that you plan to visit the office "unless it is inconvenient." It all depends on how assertive you want to be.

Do not neglect, however, to say something about a future meeting, as you are unlikely to get a job on the strength of your résumé alone. Highlight one particularly strong point from your résumé in your letter, but do not restate the résumé in prose. In one sense, your cover letter should persuade the interviewer to turn the page to read your résumé. Together, the cover letter and résumé should pique the reader's interest enough to get you in the door.

A follow-up letter or phone call may be useful to assure that you are not forgotten. You walk a thin line between assertiveness and pushiness, so use your discretion. See Chart 14 for an example of a letter of application. Remember: This is merely a suggested approach. You must write letters in your own words if you want them to truly represent you and your interests.

Word processing allows you to personalize letters quickly and easily, although most students simply use a word-processing program to merge addresses with a boilerplate body. The problem with computer-generated letters is that they look and sound impersonal. Not surprisingly, many law firms react to such applications the way you do to junk mail. The more personalized your letter sounds, the better the odds. The length of each letter is not nearly as important as its content, but as a rule, keep the letter short and direct.

If you have maintained a database of potential employers, you are now ready to begin contacting them. If not, you will have to do some research (see Chapter 12).

As Chart 14 indicates, the first paragraph of your letter should indicate why you are contacting a particular firm or organization. Your primary reason will usually be the nature of its work as evidenced by its clients, professional affiliations, and the like.

Chart 14
Letter of Application Outline

Your name
Your address
City and state
Date of writing

Name of person addressed
Organization
Address
City, State Zip

Dear _____:

First paragraph: Tell why you are writing, name the position for which you are applying and tell how you heard of the opening.

Second paragraph: State why you are interested in working for this employer, and specify your interests in this type of work. If you have had experience, be sure to point out what particular achievements you have accomplished in this field or type of work.

Third paragraph: Refer to the attached personal data sheet or résumé which gives a summary of your qualifications as well as a photograph, or to whatever media you are using to illustrate your training, interests, and experience.

Fourth paragraph: Have an appropriate closing to pave the way for the interview by enclosing a return envelope, by asking for an application blank, by giving your phone number, or by offering some similar suggestion for an immediate and favorable reply.

Yours very truly,

_____

But perhaps a speech or a position taken by a member of the firm struck a responsive chord in your own view of the profession and its goals. Or you may have been referred by someone to the organization or established your own contacts in the firm.

Regardless of what your reasons are, be sure the first paragraph of your letter describes them. This first paragraph is important because you are asking a busy lawyer to take the time to review your application. It should indicate that you have taken the trouble to become acquainted with the firm and that you know enough about the organization to believe it might be interested in you. The fact that you have done this kind of research indicates that you are serious about seeking a position, and is also subtly flattering to the organization. If you send your résumé to an alumnus(a) of your own school, you should still indicate why you chose that particular firm or organization, and ask that your letter be passed along to the individual responsible for hiring decisions.

The second paragraph of the letter should expand on your reason for contacting the firm by pointing out some part of your background or experience that you feel might be relevant to the firm's needs. Generally, you will refer to your résumé at this point in the letter (e.g., "As my enclosed résumé indicates . . ."). There may be other background information not shown on your résumé that would be important to employers. For example, if you contact a firm with a large number of Spanish-speaking clients, you could mention that you have studied Spanish for eight years or speak Spanish at home.

The third paragraph should indicate how to contact you and arrange for an interview. Be as specific as possible. If you will be in the law firm's community during a certain period of time, state when, and, if possible, give a local address and telephone number to reach you during that period. Repeat addresses and telephone numbers from your résumé to encourage action. Employers understand that you cannot sit by the phone twenty-four hours a day. The following statements are entirely appropriate:

- "I will be in class most of the time, but I have arranged for an answering service to accept appointments for me."
- "I will call your office to confirm the time you find most convenient."

◆ "The person answering the phone has a complete schedule of my time commitments and will be glad to arrange a convenient time for you to meet with me."

If you have been farsighted enough to arrange an interview schedule to meet the employer's convenience, that thoughtfulness will not go unnoticed. Remember that most lawyers are busy people (and the fact that they are looking to hire someone may punctuate this fact), so respect their time and schedule.

The appearance of your cover letter is just as important as the content. With desktop publishing software, you can create your own letterhead at a fraction of the cost of printing. Keep the appearance neat and conservative, using quality stationery in white or cream. Proofread everything. A single typographical error can be the kiss of death for your application.

As you send out your letters and résumés, note the dates in your contact database. As you receive replies, note the dates and the nature of the responses as well. If you do not hear from an employer within a reasonable time, send a follow-up letter or make a phone call. If you are not sure what is reasonable, consult your career services director or some other knowledgeable person. If your application will be under consideration for several months or longer, periodic communications from you may help keep your application fresh, but try not to become a pest.

Interviewing Employers

Is there a magic formula that guarantees a successful job interview? An elixir to cure knocking knees, sweaty palms, and a blank mind? Unfortunately, the answer is no. Interviews involve a complex interaction between the people involved, reflecting the various values, needs, and personality traits of each. By arming yourself with knowledge of the employer's needs and preferences, as well as your own strengths and weaknesses, you will have a better idea how to conduct the interview and what questions to ask.

A successful interview is not necessarily one that results in a job offer. It is, instead, one that allows both the employer and the potential employee to discover what the other wants, what goals are important, what working conditions are most desirable—in short, to gain an honest impression of whether or not a working situation would be mutually satisfactory.

This is not easy to discover in the limited time available in the interview situation, and to avoid any misconceptions, both parties should be entirely honest. An important rule is to be yourself. Otherwise, you might find yourself in an uncomfortable employment situation.

The primary goal of any interviewee should be to become more aware of the dynamics of the interview situation, and thereby to control it. An interview can be any face-to-face meeting between an employer and potential employee to discuss the employment possibilities of the latter with the former. The dynamics of the interview are the interactions, both verbal and nonverbal, between the interview participants. They will constitute each party's basis for evaluating the interview.

In order to control the interview, you must recognize which aspects of your background to emphasize, and establish specific objectives to accomplish during the interview. Because of time limitations inherent in the interview situation, it is important to select and control the information you give the interviewer.

The primary area under your direct control is the attitude with which you approach the interview—your mindset. Imagine yourself as an investor approaching a prospective banker. You have funds to invest, and the banker has services to offer. In such a setting, the banker will naturally have questions regarding the amount you wish to deposit, the percentage of return that you expect, and the length of time the bank would have use of your funds.

You, in turn, would want to know the advantages and disadvantages of the various forms of investment the bank has to offer, the degree of safety of your funds, and the types of services you would receive. What should result is a businesslike exchange of information aimed at reaching a mutually satisfactory arrangement. If this could not be achieved, you would then proceed to consult with other bankers along the same line. The typical interview lasts twenty to thirty minutes and consists of a greeting, a discussion, and a closing.

For most legal jobs, you will encounter between one and three interviewers in each interview, although you may go through many interviews in the course of an interview day. But remember: an interview may not be a formal one in the office or at school; it may occur during a chance meeting at some other place.

One thing that should be avoided at all costs is tardiness. You should be on-time or a few minutes early whether the interview is at the law school or at the employer's place of business.

A conservative, neat appearance is generally advisable. In both dress and demeanor you can come on too strong just as easily as not strong enough. It might be necessary to purchase a new interviewing wardrobe to project a professional image. The expense may be considerable, but you should think of it as an investment.

Once your attire has been selected, you can then concentrate on the most important aspect of preparing for an interview—knowing the employer. Review your database on the particular prospective employer.

You may also want to see other sources of information, like a corporation's annual report. Your career services office may have a complete description of a law firm on file for you to consult. A government agency may publish a brochure that describes in detail the work of the agency including the work of its legal department. Too much information is better than not enough.

As you review the information you have collected, formulate the questions you would like to ask regarding the organization and its opportunities for you. Jot them down. Include the names of people to whom you may be speaking. Oral introductions can be hard to recall, but once you see a name in writing, remembering it is much easier.

While the interviewer is sizing you up during the greeting phase of the interview, you should be aware of your reaction to the interviewer as well. Researchers have found that people develop strong and often lasting impressions about the appearance, attitudes, values, and abilities of other people within the first few minutes after meeting them. If you feel an initial dislike or uneasiness about someone, move more slowly into the interview and attempt to ascertain why you feel that way with direct or indirect questions. If a first impression is favorable, adopt a more informal stance, or approach the interview itself more aggressively.

Good eye contact, a firm handshake, a memory for names, and a big smile are helpful, but too many people get so wrapped up in carrying out these functional activities that they lose all spontaneity, as well as the ability to think quickly. They may come across as shallow and rigid. It is more important to be relaxed and natural at the start of the interview than to perform some kind of ritual.

The types of questions asked in an interview situation often address what kind of law practice interests you, what substantive knowledge you possess, and other goal-related questions. Not only will the employer want to gain an accurate impression of your goals at this point, but you will have an excellent opportunity to discover whether the employer is doing the kind of work you would find challenging and enjoyable.

Honesty is vital at this stage of the interview, or you are likely to create an image of yourself that you would not be comfortable living with should you eventually go to work for the employer. For example, if you indicate that you are interested in doing research, this is probably what you will be doing if you are offered a job.

The potential employer may evidence some interest in your past employment experience, academic qualifications, and interests. You are, for the most part, in control of the direction the questioning takes at this point, since you have drafted your résumé and it reflects those points you want to discuss. It is important, both in the résumé and in the interview itself, always to stress those facts about yourself that you consider outstanding—those that in some way separate you from the other interviewees. If you are honest and straightforward, you are much more likely to discover an employment situation in which you have the freedom to be yourself and do the things that you enjoy.

Interviewing Styles

An interviewee who is alert enough to ascertain the interviewer's approach to the process can "key" on the interviewer in phrasing answers to questions. Differences in personality account for some differences in interviewing style. Although the following synopsis is an oversimplification, it may be useful to think about interviewers in terms of a number of distinct interviewer types:

- *The Collector:* Some interviewers may be interested only in collecting information such as where you went to school, activities, and areas of principal interest.
- *The Shrink:* Others might take a more psychological approach, questioning you about areas such as attitude toward school, goals, aspirations, and conceptions of various issues.
- *The Conversationalist:* Some seem more interested in merely talking or in gaining an overall impression of you through less direct questions. With this type of interviewer, it is often important to keep the discussion from straying too far from information about the job itself or your particular qualifications.
- *The Professor:* Still other interviewers ask rapid-fire questions about legal issues. It is important to avoid yes or no answers, and do not be intimidated. Remember that this is no worse than law school.
- *The Dud:* In a bad interview, the student and employer are just unable to communicate.
- *The Ego Deflator:* This interviewer prematurely rejects you without asking any questions or telling you anything, but you know when you walk out that you will not get the job.
- *The Interrogator:* This interviewer will press you quite hard on difficult questions, sometimes of a personal nature, or does something to test your reactions (e.g., drawing an X through your résumé before you sit down). This technique, known as the stress interview, is common in the business school setting. If something like this happens to you, do not lose your cool or you lose all control of the situation.
- *The Violator:* This Neanderthal shows definite signs of unethical or discriminatory conduct. Do not hesitate to terminate the interview and take appropriate action. For more information on how to handle discriminatory interview tactics, see the NALP guidelines in Appendix B and consult with your career services officer.

Normally the interviewer concludes the interview, but you should take the initiative if the interview appears to be running overtime. It is possible that the interviewer is hoping that you will stop talking, but is reluctant to cut you off. A timely exit can be as important as any part of the interview. Do not leave without determining how, when, and where you can expect further communications concerning your potential employment.

Once you have left the interview, immediately make notes for your database, including the names of the individuals who interviewed you and the date. That will prevent the embarrassment of forgetting someone's name should you meet again, professionally or personally.

As soon as possible after your interview, write an acknowledgment letter. Such a letter is not only a thank you for the time and courtesy of the individuals with whom you have spoken, but more importantly, it is also an opportunity to repeat your special qualifications and to note any areas in which there appeared to be a true meeting of minds. If there were any decisions reached regarding future contact, restate these as well.

The acknowledgment letter is also a way to notify the office that you have a continuing interest in the position. Unfortunately, this courtesy is not extended frequently enough. The exception to this rule involves fall on-campus interviews, where employers interview hundreds of candidates in a short period of time. In that situation, acknowledgment letters may be viewed as superfluous, so use your discretion.

Employers consistently mention several common negative factors among law students they interview. These include:

◆ Apparent lack of interest in the job by the student: This may seem strange since the student is applying for the position. However, the comment may reflect that the student is shopping around, is unclear about his or her career aspirations, or is simply not well-informed about the employer.

◆ Apprehensiveness about the interview: Use simple stress-reduction techniques if this is a problem. It is perhaps little consolation to say that everyone has butterflies before an interview. Dress comfortably, sit down somewhere if you have to wait, and relax your mind. Talking to someone else may also be helpful in easing the tension. Take two or three deep breaths just before going into the interview room to lower your blood pressure and calm your nerves.

◆ Inability to explain why he or she should be hired

◆ Evasiveness in answering interviewer questions

◆ Failure to raise interesting questions or demonstrate a spark during the interview

Everyone goes through interviews and everyone faces the same stresses. When interviews do not go well, it is difficult not to let it get you down. It is important, however, to always put your best foot forward, no matter how you feel. Like an actor in a Broadway play, the show must go on every night, no matter what happened the night before or at home during the day.

The Office Visit

The office visit is always important, whether it is a follow-up to an on-campus interview or a first meeting. Because the office visit is usually longer than a screening interview, you often get an opportunity to see a law office in action. It is often much more difficult, however, to keep up a front for both you and the interviewer(s), so make a conscious effort to stay calm. Before you leave, try to get some commitment regarding your possibilities for employment and if it is clear that you will not receive a letter, seek new leads from those you interviewed. It is possible that they were impressed with you but just can't make you an offer.

If you manage to get one or more invitations for office visits, here are a few things to keep in mind:

◆ Be observant. What is the general tone of the office? What are the individual personalities? What do the relationships between individuals appear to be? If you are sensitive only to the impression you are seeking to make, you miss valuable opportunities to assess the office in ways that no amount of research can provide.

◆ Get your facts straight. When and for how long do they want to see you? How do they handle reimbursement of expenses? Are spouses or "significant others" invited? Who arranges travel and hotel rooms? Many students find themselves in a bind because they do not ask about these things and the firm does not say anything either. Generally speaking, big firms reimburse; small firms do not. If you are visiting more than one employer in an area, you should suggest that they split expenses (and never ask for multiple reimbursement). Also, if an employer invites you to visit an out-of-town office, it is customary that your expenses are paid. If you suggest the meeting, this is not the case.

◆ Get directions and a good map. Do not get lost and miss an hour of your interview. If you plan to interview with more than one employer, plan your movement from one to the next to avoid being late.

◆ If you have gotten this far you have probably already done your homework, but do more. Reread the firm or agency résumé. Find out if there are other students being invited for office visits, and what the firm's hiring patterns have been in the past. Check carefully the composition of the firm for age, schools attended, and practice areas. Look to *Martindale-Hubbell* to find out such things as the ages of the partners and associates, the law schools that they have attended, where they are originally from, and the type of clients they handle. Ask other students or professors who may know the firm to share their thoughts with you.

◆ Read the local newspapers (most likely available online) and regional magazines to get an idea of what the community is like and what current issues concern its citizens. Married students will need to assess whether the area will appeal to their family. If your spouse accompanies you, he or she may need to spend the time looking for a job, checking out the housing market, or visiting schools.

◆ You may also get some substantive legal questions, so be prepared. Since you are more likely to get questions about an area you know than something totally off-the-wall, reread your law review note or other research mentioned in the résumé.

◆ Office visits vary considerably from employer to employer. Not all office visits last a full day, but almost all are grueling. A recruitment administrator may take you from lawyer to lawyer, you may be led to the next interview by your last interviewer, or you may be sent from office to office on your own. You can expect to see as few as three lawyers in a half-day interview, or as many as fifteen in a full day, individually or in groups.

◆ At some point during the day, frequently at the beginning or end, you will be given a tour of the facilities. Be observant and ask questions during this guided tour.

◆ Ask about office operations, such as timekeeping and billing systems, secretarial and paralegal assistance ratios, structure of the office and assignment of new lawyers, technology and other office equipment systems, library size and checkout system, filing system, and office space allocation and configuration. Do not be timid about asking challenging questions.

◆ Do not write off the younger lawyers you visit: Many employers rely heavily on them for input into hiring decisions.

◆ Each appointment should be considered a separate interview, so give each one your best. Your campus interview was just the first hurdle. You must pass muster in each of these subsequent interviews to get an offer. Ask similar questions of everyone you meet in order to better get a "flavor" for the firm. Study individual personalities when meeting with lawyers on a one-to-one basis. It may be helpful to ask interviewers what they do each day.

◆ Entertainment, very often with associates or younger lawyers, is intended to put you at ease, so enjoy yourself—just do not spill the vichyssoise in your lap. Evening entertainment is less frequent and ranges from stuffy to sporty. It is more likely to include partners or senior lawyers and spouses.

◆ No matter how many people you see, treat each interview as if it is your first and most important one. During on-campus interviews, the recruiter may be tired while the candidate is fresh. This dynamic is reversed in the office interview, so make sure that you remain alert. For example, do not stay out late the night before your interview. And during the office interview, ask for time to freshen up, if it is not offered.

◆ Remember the same principles of effective interviewing that got you to the office visit: Be yourself, emphasize what you can offer, and control the situation. Add to this a little stamina, and you are on your way.

Another area of particular interest to students is how a firm goes about making a hiring decision. Again, this often depends upon the size of the firm. In a large firm, a committee may be responsible for hiring decisions, even though other lawyers have input into the process. In a smaller firm everyone is involved. You generally must receive a unanimous confirmation. As a result, there may be two or three office visits to find out early whether or not everyone feels they can work with you. Large firms are more likely to screen out candidates at an earlier stage of the process than small firms where hiring decisions involve all or most of the lawyers. Large firms also tend to play a numbers game with offers. Small firms on the other hand often make only one offer at a time. These differences are reflected in different approaches to the interview process generally.

Answering Tough Questions

Certain lines of questioning may prove very uncomfortable for many candidates. Two critical topics, salary and benefits, must be addressed at some point. If the interviewer brings up the topic it may indicate that the firm plans on tendering you an offer, since, as a general rule, they will not discuss salary with those students who do not interest them. You should not raise the issue during the initial interview. Wait until you are sure the employer is interested in you before getting into sensitive subject matter.

Although many interviewers may have little power to negotiate, they should be able to give some indication of whether or not your expectations are reasonable. Be sure you know both the range of starting salaries in your geographical area and the salary range for the type of job you are seeking. Your career services office should have current statistics.

You should consider a number of other factors in reviewing a salary offer:

- What fringe benefits are included in the offer?
- Specifically what kind of insurance program (life, disability, health) does the employer provide?
- Is there a starting bonus or an annual bonus?
- Pension or retirement plan?
- Vacation?
- Leave (illness, parental, sabbatical)?
- Does the employer provide a profit-sharing or other incentive program for the newer lawyer?
- What about "perks" such as club memberships, travel expenses, professional dues and journals, CLE, and parking?
- Will you have staff support, including paralegals and secretaries?
- What is the cost of living in the community?
- Will there be employment for a working spouse?
- When do you go on the payroll (after graduation, after the bar exam, after licensure)?
- When considered together, these many factors may give a very different picture of the compensation than the original salary quoted.

In some instances, salary is not negotiable, such as in government positions where the salary level is beyond the employer's immediate jurisdiction. Otherwise, you may have a minimum figure in mind that you believe is necessary to cover your expenses and financial obligations. If you have obtained information regarding ranges, you will know whether the offer falls in the acceptable pattern. Negotiation in such cases is acceptable. See Chapter 16 for more information on negotiating your job offer.

Here is where the problem may arise: if you give the interviewer an outrageous requirement, she is likely to think that you are unrealistic or simply pricing yourself out of the market. On the other hand, if you quote an unusually low figure, she may perceive you as underselling yourself and your abilities, and she may take that as a sign of little or no self-confidence. (Of course, she may also hire you on the spot because you are so cheap.)

The key to surviving this minefield successfully is to identify the employer's salary range, which is probably competitive within the geographic area and type of position for which you are interviewing. Large firms will offer the higher salaries and small firms will offer figures in the lower part of the competitive spectrum. Salaries for 2007 law school graduates are from under $30,000 to over $160,000, with a median of $70,000 according to NALP, so employers' offers may be anywhere in this range.

In recent years fringe benefits have become a major concern of law graduates, but often their importance is overrated. Most benefits are tied to long-range employment prospects, but today, increasing numbers of lawyers are moving laterally from position to position. The traditional pattern in which an entry position becomes a lifetime professional commitment is no longer necessarily the case.

Early in the game, therefore, your best evaluation of the fringe benefits probably will contemplate their immediate value to you. By the time their long-range value becomes important, you may have moved several times. One time when the benefit package may be a factor is when you are evaluating similar offers. The opportunity for professional growth should be your primary concern, but if that criterion appears to be equally met, consideration of fringe benefits in your comparative analysis may be helpful.

In addition to finding out about salary and benefits, ask how the firm is organized and whether cases are handled by teams, whether associates work with one partner only, how specialized the firm is, and how new clients are obtained.

There are certain areas where open discussion may not only be unnecessary, but may harm your chances of being hired. For example, many students are very interested in knowing the turn-over a firm has, or how many people come and go within a year. Rather than inquire directly and antagonize the interviewer, check *Martindale-Hubbell* and the law school placement office figures back on campus.

When you interview with a bank, public accounting firm, or other organization, you might be asked about the possibility of your leaving to enter private practice. It is not uncommon for the interviewer to raise such a question, and more often than not, she will be quite sensitive about this subject. The key to avoiding problems in this area is to appear enthusiastic about the work without really making a lifelong commitment.

Another rather sticky question involves the amount of time you will be expected to work. A direct line of interrogation about working hours is likely to create an impression of laziness and lack of ambition in the interviewer's mind. Instead, find out the answer indirectly by calling the office after hours or on Saturday. As a general rule everyone works hard and a sixty- or seventy-hour week is not unusual.

Another risky question is the potential for future earnings. While it is perfectly natural to wonder about your future, the question seems to disturb quite a few interviewers. It may be better to glean the answer to this question from several sources. Ask other young lawyers in the firm or check *Martindale-Hubbell* for a high turnover rate, which may indicate low growth potential.

You could also ask other related questions in the hope that the interviewer may mention growth potential as one of the firm's benefits. Try to get the interviewer to make a comparison among firms or between the firm and a corporation's legal department. Never ask something like, "How much will I be making in ten years?" or "How much do you make?" You not only come off sounding mercenary, you will antagonize the interviewer.

Similarly, avoid asking questions about the length of time until you reach partnership or how many associates make partner. Consult *Martindale-Hubbell* or use other indirect channels instead. Forget about asking questions about salary differences between new and senior partners. Ultimately, the answer is that, as a partner, you are getting a "piece of the pie," and your income is much more tied to your output.

There are, however, different ways of making partner. In some firms you spend the entire time you are an associate saving up to buy in or to purchase a share of the firm. In others, that is not a major consideration. It varies from firm to firm.

If you can get someone to talk about the organization, you can figure these things out very easily. Questions dealing with money or partnership should be raised with the person you believe to be the one with the most power in the hiring process—a managing partner, senior partner, or the chair of the hiring committee.

Another sensitive area involves conflicts of interest. Although Rules of Professional Conduct do not technically apply to law students, those who have worked for more than one legal organization before or during law school may discover that they possess confidential information or have an otherwise conflicting relationship with former firms or client. Do not be surprised to learn that a potential employer wants to scrutinize your prior employment relationships in the same way it would a lateral lawyer before hiring you.

The last area in the line of delicate questions is the skeleton in your closet. It might be your grades. It might be where you went to school. It might be something in your background. Everybody has some questions they would like to avoid, but it is best to be prepared for the worst. Here are some specific pieces of advice: First, do not apologize; second, do not be evasive; and third, prepare a response. Instead of praying that you will not be asked, make a list of the five questions you would least like to be asked in an interview and develop answers before the interview (see Chart 15).

In recent years, a number of students have learned the hard way that postings on social networking Web sites like Facebook and MySpace can come back to bite them. Spring break in Cancun sophomore year may have been great, but when you find your photos googled when you are a second-year law student, it may not seem quite as cool. What's done is done, but you may need to engage in some anticipatory damage control in some situations.

To summarize, do not hesitate to ask questions, even tough questions, but be sensitive to how the interviewer might react to your inquiries. Observe everything going on around you in the office. In this respect, the office interview is much easier than the on-campus session because new topics for discussion and conversation are constantly being raised. Prepare beforehand by researching the firm or organization and record your impressions and new information learned as soon as you leave.

Chart 15
Five Least-Desired Questions

Question	Proposed Answer
1.	
2.	
3.	
4.	
5.	

Making a Decision   **16**

How will you receive your job offer? Will it come by phone or letter or e-mail? How much time will you be given to make a decision? Will the offer be negotiable or not? These are questions that all law students eventually confront.

It is somewhat axiomatic to say that good news comes in person and bad news comes by mail. In the legal community, however, this is usually true. Sometimes offers are communicated by mail, and some firms may give you the courtesy of a call to tell you that you were not selected. Many times this information will be described in the employer's literature or in an interview, but if it is not, you should attempt to find out what to expect, so you will not have to worry with uncertainty.

What is probable is that that you will have to wait for news, good or bad. After completing the interview process, firms may not give you any direct indication of your status. While you may have some idea of how well you did, you may possess little or no indication of whether or not an offer is forthcoming. The official notification will be received several weeks later. Occasionally, offers are made during the interview process, but more commonly, you will have to wait.

Receiving an Offer

If you do receive an offer and are not prepared at that time to make a decision, it is vitally important to show a continuing interest in the employer. Explain that presently you are interested but are talking to other employers and you feel it would be unfair to accept this offer without reviewing all your options. You might stress also the importance of the decision by saying that you simply need time to think. Emphasize that you enjoyed your interviews and that you were very impressed with what you saw of the firm.

There is no need to succumb to pressure. The firm will want to know as soon as possible whether or not you plan to accept, but usually it will allow you a reasonable amount of time to make a decision. Firms interviewing on campus during the fall generally follow NALP guidelines requiring offers to be held open for 45 days, or until December 30, whichever comes first. (See Appendix B.) Check your own career services office for details and special policies at your school.

Some employers attempt to exert pressure on applicants to make a quick decision. Smaller firms, for example, may feel that they cannot play a numbers game, making ten offers for five spots on the assumption that they will have only five acceptances. They may make only one offer and will want to know if that candidate is going to turn them down right away.

Whereas the employer wants you to decide as soon as possible, you will want to keep your options open as long as possible. This is a matter for negotiation along with other issues such as salary, benefits, starting dates, etc. But remember that once you know an employer wants you, you are playing a much stronger hand than when the process started.

Negotiating an Offer

Many law students fail to think of themselves as negotiators when they get a job offer. They simply take the money and run. While negotiating varies according to issue and employer, many of the terms of employment are subject to negotiation.

Generally, employers that participate in fall on-campus interviews and other employers with highly structured personnel policies are more likely to have predetermined what they are willing to offer you. They are less likely to be willing to negotiate major terms like salary and benefits, but may be more flexible on issues such as practice area assignment or starting date. Smaller firms and other employers that do not hire associates on a regular basis are less likely to have a clear idea of what they will agree to give. These employers are more likely to negotiate a wider range of issues.

Many students have taken law school courses on negotiation and should recognize that the principles of negotiation are the same in a job offer situation. A few suggestions may help you negotiate the best possible terms for yourself:

- Figure out what you want out of the negotiation. What would you like to get ideally? What would you be willing to accept as a fallback position? Which issues are critical (non-negotiable) and which are you willing to concede in order to reach an accord?
- Try to find out what the employer wants out of the negotiation. What is the maximum you can expect? Which issues are critical to the employer?
- Construct an agenda for the negotiation.
- When you sit down to talk about terms have a plan for attaining your objectives. Keep in mind your bottom line. Both you and the employer have a bargaining range (See Chart 16). Do not expect the employer to go outside its bargaining range to accommodate you.
- Try to make this a win-win situation. Both you and the employer should walk away happy.

Employers hiring to fill a single position are more likely to negotiate terms than employers hiring two or more since it may be awkward (or illegal) to start different lawyers with comparable qualifications at different rates. Some of the specific areas that you may be able to negotiate include:

- Starting salary.
- Benefits. Health insurance may be fixed, but professional benefits (e.g., bar dues, CLE allowances, club memberships) may be subject to negotiation.
- Incentives/bonuses. Signing bonuses are uncommon except for genuine superstars, but many smaller firms are willing

Chart 16
Negotiating an Offer—The Bargaining Range

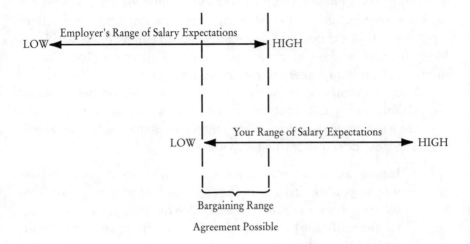

Bargaining Range

Agreement Possible

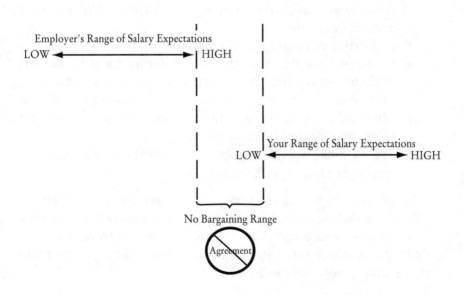

No Bargaining Range

to give associates an incentive to produce work or bring in clients (e.g., a percentage of the fees from all new clients brought to the firm by the associate).

◆ Practice areas. This is the most commonly negotiated term of employment.

◆ Working conditions. Support, office space, expectations.

◆ Special arrangements. Child care, part-time status, tuition for LLM program.

◆ Time off. Vacations, National Guard, parental leave.

◆ When you start and when you begin to be paid (before the bar, after the bar, when you are licensed).

Your own marketability can also be a factor. Does the employer want you because of your Ph.D. in genetic engineering? Are there other comparably qualified candidates in the wings who would take the job if you said no? How close is it until the time when you plan to go to work? How many other offers can you expect to receive in the near future? You should not hesitate to ask for specific terms once the employer has formally extended you an offer, or wait until after you start work to clarify terms and conditions of employment. Although you may feel somewhat uncomfortable initiating these discussions, you will be glad you did.

The Final Choice

Whether you receive a single offer or have several to choose from, take time to assess options in order to reach a sound decision. Develop a list of the advantages and disadvantages for you in any position. Then on a scale of one to five (1 = ideal; 5 = unbearable), rate the offer you have received according to the factors you have listed (See Chart 17). Use this rating system to help clarify your thinking about the offer.

As you go through the decisio-making process, ask yourself the following questions:

◆ Is this the type of practice I have been seeking?

◆ Will my family and I be happy in the community?

◆ Do I possess the requisite skills for the job?

Chart 17
Offer Rating Sheet

Offer	Pros	Weight 1 to 5	Cons	Weight -1 to -5
1.				
2.				
3.				
4.				

- Does the management style of the employer seem consistent with my working style?
- Will my peers be the types of lawyers I find interesting and congenial?
- Is the money offered satisfactory?

Although salary is important, especially for those with financial obligations, it should be weighed against a number of factors that receive your careful consideration. Only a relative handful of graduates can be expected to see the top dollar figures being quoted in newspapers and periodicals. For most applicants this is simply being unrealistic.

Because the first few years of practice represent an apprenticeship or internship and the beginning lawyer is learning how to practice law rather than generating a profit, starting salaries for new lawyers may not reach the impressive levels indicated by the legal press.

On the other hand, economic surveys show that you can expect your income level to grow year after year, reaching the top income figures after about twenty years of practice. Thus, initial salary and benefit packages are important, but these are only part of the overall picture.

Before you total up your ratings for the positions you are evaluating, take a second look at the list of disadvantages. In contrast to the pluses, the disadvantages are often thrust to the back of one's mind. On a day-to-day basis, however, they can tarnish even the advantages most eagerly sought.

What if you are not really comfortable with your office peers? Will you be excluded from the informal discussions at lunch or other moments of relaxation that contribute so much to your professional growth? Will you find a willing and able mentor at the firm? Some disadvantages are merely inconveniences, but others can have truly inhibiting effects upon your professional life.

One additional factor deserves special consideration: How will accepting the position influence your future? In their classic book, *The Making of a Public Profession*, Frances Zemans and Victor Rosenblum point out the importance of the selection of a first position on future potential. Reviewing their survey results, you cannot help but be impressed by the importance of your first position to your entire future career. Your potential for specialization is determined. Upward professional mobility is developed. Lateral mobility is defined.

Your question, therefore, is simply: What limitation will this first position impose if all does not go as well as you hope? If a chance for a partnership does not develop, how saleable in the legal marketplace will be the skills you acquire? Will your skills be easily transferable to another area of the country? How closely tied to your present community will you be by your clients, your business, and professional contacts, or the specialized practice experience you have acquired?

Should you have to choose from two or more offers, it may help to make lists of the pros and cons of each offer. But although a ranking may help you to review your own objectives, it may not answer the question of which offer is most likely to satisfy you. You might play out a worst-case scenario and imagine where you will be if the job does not work out.

In the end, it is frequently a subjective rather than objective decision. Carefully assessing an offer means considering personal feelings not just attempting to quantify advantages and disadvantages. Ultimately, you make a choice and go forward.

Finding Satisfaction

A number of different surveys of young lawyers report that for many their present work failed to meet their expectations for personal satisfaction. Those who are not happy frequently experience frustration either because of unrealistic expectations or because they chose the wrong type of position to meet their goals.

For many new lawyers, the biggest dissatisfaction is the amount of time spent on trivial matters. This is not surprising. Most clients have problems that loom large in their eyes but which to the trained professional are routine and simple.

Some offices are involved in large cases with millions of dollars at stake. A virtual army of attorneys may be involved for days or months in compiling data and citations and cataloging a myriad of documents. Many of the lawyers involved in such tremendous compilations will not be around to see their contribution to the final outcome. They may not know the overall objectives of the client representation for which they work so diligently. Although this situation is highly frustrating, young lawyers should be aware that this kind of data collection work is typical in firms where large issues are a way of life.

Dissatisfaction can also arrive after two or three years of practice when lawyers begin to feel they have mastered the skills of practice and that responsibilities are increasing more rapidly than compensation. Still another type of annoyance to many young lawyers is the administrative detail that the operation of any office requires but particularly larger firms. It is frustrating when there does not seem to be enough time to deal adequately with the challenging legal matters at hand.

New lawyers also may complain that they have insufficient time to do an adequate job on their assignments. The fact is, you cannot spend $5,000 worth of time on a case that will bring only $500. A new lawyer may also have several assignments from different partners or senior associates and feel they cannot all be completed within the time frame allotted. Or there simply may be too few lawyers to handle the total caseload.

Lack of feedback or evaluation from superiors represents another source of dissatisfaction. This is perhaps the most serious problem because it limits professional growth and development. It is also the most difficult to remedy because training must be initiated from the top to be truly successful. Forward-looking offices seek ways in which to improve the skills of both new lawyers and more experienced ones.

On an encouraging note, job dissatisfaction seems to dissipate after the third year in practice. As new lawyers gain experience, they develop a more realistic outlook on practice and better means of coping with its many irritants.

Although a certain amount of frustration is inevitable in the transition from law school to the real world, long term career dissatisfaction is often avoidable. If you match your skills and goals to the best position available, you are more likely to achieve satisfaction in your work. Seek out the possibilities, rather than accept whatever comes along, and take time to weigh the advantages and disadvantages of any offer. Negotiate to get the best employment package and choose the position that offers the best opportunities for personal and professional growth. If genuinely torn between career choices, use contacts in your network to help you decide what's best for you.

Renewing Your Options 17

$\mathbf{Y}$ou have spent the weeks following your office visit in a state of anxious anticipation. Then one day the mail brings a law firm envelope. Instead of seeing the words of welcome that you expected, it begins with the conciliatory "We certainly enjoyed having the opportunity to talk with you. Unfortunately . . ." Suddenly, you are aware that your job search is not over yet.

Not every letter and résumé you send out will get a response. Not every interview will come to a successful conclusion. These two facts of life tend to result in a discouraged frame of mind—the rejection syndrome.

Managing Setbacks

There are many reasons for such disappointments, many no fault of your own. If, after the first few weeks, your job search has not yet produced results, you may begin to wonder: Did I learn enough about the prospective employers? Were my cover letters as personalized as I could make them? Did I present myself effectively in the interview? Such self-analysis and criticism should not disintegrate into self-castigation. Your need is to overcome feelings of personal rejection because they produce an attitude that is virtually self-defeating.

One way of dealing with this attitude is through a program of rewards to yourself in an area that is specifically under your control: your job campaign. Establish benchmarks of achievement in your campaign: so many offices added to your files, so many personalized cover letters written, an interview obtained, and so many acknowledgments made. When you reach each benchmark, reward yourself. The reward need not be expensive. It may be the allocation of time to read a special book or article. It may be seeing a movie you have been longing to attend. It may even be a sinfully fattening sundae. When you do a good job, treat yourself well.

It has been said that a good trial lawyer is not unlike a good prizefighter. Both step into the ring knowing someone has to lose. After a loss, the best lawyers and prizefighters share the ability to rise confidently for the next fight. Rejection gives you an opportunity to hone an important professional skill.

The difficulty lies in learning to swallow this rejection and go on. For many law students, dealing with rejection can pose a major problem because they have not had much experience in being rejected, having succeeded at nearly everything they have tried.

So how does someone who has always been a walking success story cope with the "rejection blues"? The answer is simple—by preparing emotionally and mentally beforehand.

Perhaps the best way to deal with rejection is to build a list of specific options before the interview process even begins. As some options do not work out, others can be added to the list. It is important never to allow the list of alternatives to become exhausted (see Chapter 6).

It is also important to understand the meaning of rejection. First of all, everyone, even a walking success story, must understand that no one goes through life without facing rejection. So rejection is not necessarily synonymous with failure—it is merely a setback, and should be viewed as such. In baseball, a good batter gets a hit three out of ten times at bat. In business, a successful entrepreneur frequently experiences many business failures before finding a successful combination.

Secondly, remember that your response to rejection is influenced by several factors, such as the number of other rejections already received, the amount of energy and desire you invested in getting a particular position, and your basic orientation to the job-hunting process. The response may vary from situation to situation, and from person to person.

If this particular job was a big deal (i.e., you invested a lot of time and energy into getting it), then by all means, allow yourself to go through the "grief process." Grief for a lost job opportunity does not differ all that much from the grief following any significant loss in life, and you may experience the stages of loss:

◆ Denial
◆ Anger
◆ Bargaining
◆ Depression
◆ Acceptance (finally)

It sometimes helps to have someone with whom to share these feelings, and with whom you can work the problem through to the point of acceptance. The person might be your career counselor, a professional confidant, a mentor, a friend, or a family member. Despite the temptation to go hide in a cave, you will find it easier and more productive to talk to another person you can trust about your feelings.

This might be a good time for self-evaluation as well. Consider the following matters as you reflect on your situation:

◆ Determine whether there are areas over which you have control.
◆ Consider how much you can change.
◆ Get a handle on your basic abilities and goals.
◆ Try to generate some new alternatives for yourself.

Ironically, the rejection period can be a very creative time. The road to acceptance should be one of growth. You should learn about yourself and change. Ask yourself how the situation could have been different. Ask what you can do in the future to avoid a recurrence. The most important thing is to get in touch with the positive side of the experience.

Do not take too long "getting in touch" or you will lose possible advantages and opportunities that have come up in the meantime. Do not let your job search grind to a complete halt. Sometimes students who do not get job offers in their first attempts do nothing more until after graduation or even after the bar exam. In such cases, the passing of time forecloses many options, and the pressure to get a job only becomes more intense.

Revising Your Goals and Strategies

Sometimes not receiving the offer(s) you hoped for will lead you to reevaluate your position in the market. You may want to look at other alternatives. Or you may decide to press forward in the same direction and hope that fortune will smile on you soon. You may, however, conclude that in order to move forward or to change directions you need to strengthen your skills.

If you have evaluated your skills already, you may be able to identify problem areas. If not, you should look back to Chapter 4 for help on identifying career skills. Either way you should attempt to identify not only a picture of your shortcomings, but a plan for overcoming them.

In some situations you may be able to make adjustments, either academically or experientially, while you are in law school. In other cases you may need to consider post-graduate solutions.

Graduate Law Study

Many law schools offer master of laws (L.L.M.) programs. These vary from general studies to highly specialized curricula in fields such as tax, environmental law, intellectual property, and other specialty areas. For some fields such as law teaching, an L.L.M. at a prestigious law school can add luster to the résumé of a candidate from a regional institution.

As a rule, however, an L.L.M program is not the place to go to avoid the job market for another year. It should be utilized to enhance your skills and credentials when you have a good idea where you are going. The ABA Law Student Division magazine, *Student Lawyer,* lists graduate law programs, and many of these programs send application information to other law schools as a matter of course, and post information on their Web sites. See also *Barron's Guide to Law Schools* for more information.

Graduate School

Some students believe that by combining different degrees, they can qualify for jobs in which they would otherwise not be considered, including both specialized legal jobs and nonlegal jobs for which a J.D. would be an asset but not a qualification. Although many students do graduate work before law school, some choose to do it afterward. At some universities, it is possible to complete a law and graduate degree at the same time (e.g., J.D./M.B.A., J.D./M.P.A.). Check with your university to find out whether such programs exist and whether you can enter a joint degree program after starting law school.

Among the most common graduate programs for law grads are the M.B.A., M.P.A. (Public Administration), and Ph.D. As with the pursuit of an L.L.M., you should seek other advanced educational degrees only when it is consistent with your other career goals, not just to escape reality. You will find considerable literature on graduate programs in a variety of publications, just as you found information about law schools when you were applying to J.D. programs.

Fellowships

You may also want to explore a variety of post-graduate fellowships. Some of these are well known, and others less recognized. The competition for all is stiff but the benefits can be great. Details about available fellowships can be found in your career services office. For example, consider the White House Fellowship program. The purpose of the program is to give the fellows firsthand, high-level experience with the workings of the federal government and to increase their sense of participation in national affairs.

The fellows are younger men and women, ages twenty-three to thirty-five, chosen from business, law, journalism, the humanities, architecture, or other occupations. Fellows are assigned to the office of the vice-president, to cabinet officers, and to members of the White House staff. In addition to their daily work, the fellows take part in seminars and other activities especially planned to advance the purposes of the program.

There are a number of similar post-graduate fellowships and research grants each year. Because lawyers tend to be highly goal-oriented, most move directly into positions with law firms and other legal employers. Law school career services offices often do not publicize the availability of many fellowships because so few lawyers pursue this route. For some students, however, such a move might make sense to develop their skills and marketability.

Re-Structuring Your Plans

In short, you are not out of luck if your first options do not pan out. At the beginning of Chapter 6 (page 69), this book recommended developing a ranked list of options. As you proceed and find that one alternative does not work out, you should still have other choices in mind. And you can periodically cast your net wider and add alternatives. At some point, it might even be necessary to re-structure your search. But the most important thing to remember: It will work out, you will find a job. It might take longer than you thought, or require some compromise but, if you persevere, things will work out.

The Marketplace for Legal Services

Lawyers and the Practice of Law Today 18

Demographics

Surprisingly, there is very little empirical research on lawyers and the legal profession. Much of what we know about where and how lawyers practice law is anecdotal, or derives from non-scientific surveys. Nevertheless, it is possible to piece together a picture of the practice of law from a variety of sources. As you conduct your own research on career opportunities, you may want to drill deeper into the information pool to get an accurate picture of options you are considering.

Since the early 1950s, the American Bar Foundation has conducted surveys of the lawyer population, derived from *Martindale-Hubbell Law Directory* files. According to the foundation, there are over 1,100,000 lawyers in the United States today. Extrapolating from that figure, there were more than nine hundred thousand lawyers in the United States at the turn of the century. Because the number of new law school graduates exceeds the number of deaths, the total lawyer population will continue to grow, although *Martindale-Hubbell* and the ABF lose track of some living lawyers each year. Many of these "lost" lawyers have left the legal profession to pursue other careers or have retired from the world of work.

The ABF reports that the number of lawyers working in large law firms has increased dramatically in recent years. In fact, the concept of the large firm evolved as well, as the largest firms grew from tens to hundreds to thousands. Interestingly, the largest law firms are very small business organizations. Although the largest of the large firms come from the largest cities, many moderately large firms (which would have been behemoths fifty years ago) make their home in smaller cities.

One important trend in the practice of law today is the development of branch offices. As law firms expand their services beyond a narrow geographic locality to serve clients in a nationwide or global market, it often makes good business sense to open branch offices with resident lawyers, rather than operate a far-flung legal empire from a single home base. Some firms dispatch lawyers from their main offices to open branches; more often, however, they assimilate one or smaller law firms from the city into which they move.

Mergers, the second trend, also involve the combination of two or more law firms, and often from different cities, although mergers typically involve law firms of similar size. The integration of differing firm cultures can be a challenging and even insurmountable barrier to law firms hoping to merge. A variation of this phenomenon involves a practice group or a substantial part of a practice group defecting to another firm. All these activities suggest that the makeup of law firms is constantly changing and that many firms are growing larger to meet the needs of clients in the national and international arena.

The largest law firm in the world employs several thousand people, including lawyers and support staff, compared to hundreds of thousands employed by "Big Five" accounting firms, banks and other international professional-service organizations. Professional-service providers worldwide compete for the business of global companies, and even stateside firms compete with each other; the pressures to grow have fueled a shakeout and consolidation of high-end *Fortune 500* practices.

Of course, not all lawyers represent large corporations. Many law firms service small, start-up companies, individuals and other legal interests. These lawyers are disbursed throughout the United States in cities, towns, and rural areas. They work primarily in smaller firms and solo practices. The typical American lawyer still practices in a small firm or alone, despite the impression left by coverage in the legal press, suggesting that large firms make up a larger portion of the profession than they do.

The percentage of lawyers who are solo practitioners is less than 40 percent of those in private practice (one in four of all lawyers). On the other hand, the number of solo practitioners has remained fairly stable, pointing to an increase in the number of lawyers practicing in firms with other lawyers as a cause for the change in percentage.

Over the years, the percentage of lawyers engaged in the private practice of law has remained fairly stable. About 40 percent of all lawyers practice outside of law firms. This includes 12.5 percent in corporations, 12.2 percent in government service, 11.4 percent in the judiciary, and 5.2 percent in a variety of other positions, including military law offices, public-interest law offices, and related activities.

Because there is probably some underreporting in the ABF survey of those lawyers not engaged in private practice, especially those who work in jobs outside the legal profession, it is more difficult to get a clear sense of the career patterns for this segment of the lawyer population. Many of these lawyers work in nonlegal jobs and never practiced law, while others left the practice of law after some period of time, frequently to go to work for clients. Some lawyers move in and out of the legal profession periodically.

Work and Lifestyle

Given the complexity and diversity in the legal profession, is it possible to make any generalizations about the work and lifestyles of lawyers? It may not be easy, but several observations deserve mention:

- ◆ A high concentration of lawyers lives and work in urban areas. In rural areas, there may be fewer than one lawyer for every thousand people, but the ratio is one lawyer for every one hundred persons in many of the largest cities. Perhaps it was this ratio that prompted a cartoon showing one person saying to another at a cocktail party, "How did I know you're a lawyer? Everybody's a lawyer!" The odds are three out of four that you will live and work in a metropolitan area of one million people or more when you graduate, according to the *NALP Employment Report and Salary Survey* for 2000.

◆ A substantial number of lawyers are relatively young, due to the fact that over forty thousand students graduate from law school every year.

◆ The demands of practicing law have generated an undercurrent of dissatisfaction with the private practice of law, and calls for greater attention to quality of life issues by law firms.

◆ Lawyers enjoy relative affluence, compared to the general population. Surveys of lawyer income peg the average at $150,000 or more per year. NALP reports the median starting salary for law school graduates at close to $70,000. In 2006, the top law firm salaries exceeded $165,000 plus bonuses. Differences in sampling and collection methods of these surveys may produce seemingly inconsistent results. Surveys that focus on smaller towns are likely to indicate lower salaries. Surveys that include lawyers in government and public interest legal work produce lower figures than surveys of private practitioners alone.

◆ The advent of two-career families has resulted in a doubling of income for many couples. Two 2007 law school graduates could earn combined salaries of almost $400,000 per year. The pressures and the burdens on a relationship from such a commitment may be staggering. The lifestyle considerations facing two-career couples impose additional career planning problems for both the short and long term.

◆ The pressures of work for all lawyers, not just those in large firms, can be stifling on a personal life. The average number of hours per year billed to client matters by lawyers has increased every year since the 1970 to over 1,850 today. It is hard to say whether this trend will continue.

- Despite the fact that the percentage of women in the legal profession has increased dramatically, women, must make difficult decisions about career and family.
- The profession is becoming more diverse in terms of ethnicity, lifestyle, background, and age. As America becomes more diverse, so does the population of lawyers.
  - Lawyers having an alternative sexual orientation (i.e., anyone but traditional heterosexuals) have increased in numbers as acceptance of different lifestyles becomes more common. Obviously, some communities have a tradition of embracing lifestyle diversity, while others remain less open, but the situation has improved in recent years, particularly within the legal profession.
  - Similarly, religious and cultural diversity is on the rise, and lawyers whose religious faith is outside the Judeo-Christian mainstream as well as lawyers from minority ethnic cultures are becoming more visible among the lawyer population.

Practice Concentration

Another trend that is having a wide-ranging impact on the legal profession is specialization. Increasingly, lawyers are utilizing their legal skills in combination with the skills they have acquired in other disciplines. Specialization includes not only formal recognition as a specialist under a jurisdiction's rules of professional conduct, but also *de facto* specialization in the form of practice concentration or limitation.

As society has become increasingly complex, the number of areas where legal representation is needed has increased. In many cases, lawyers have developed expertise in a single area (e.g., tax, EEO). An increase in the willingness of clients to sue their lawyers if they are not satisfied with the outcome of a case has made many lawyers reluctant to take cases if they lack experience in the area.

The demise of the lawyer as generalist and the evolution of the lawyer as specialist have profound implications for those who are entering the practice of law today.

The concept of specialization has become a term of art within the professional responsibility context. The ABA's Model Rules of Professional Conduct define the circumstances under which a lawyer may hold himself or herself out as a specialist. Traditionally, only patent lawyers and admiralty lawyers, due to the uniqueness of those practice areas, were allowed to call themselves specialists. In recent years various state bars have promulgated rules governing the certification of specialists. Those jurisdictions now allow lawyers certified under procedures established in their jurisdictions to call have raised the bar for lawyers seeking to establish their credentials as experts through certification.

Why should a lawyer specialize? The simple answer is that specialists earn more money than generalists. The GP has to handle a variety of different cases, which might be interesting as an intellectual exercise, but it makes it impossible for the lawyer to develop systems that increase efficiency by leveraging knowledge and process. Just as you became proficient at various activities growing up through repetition or practice, specialists become efficient by doing the same kinds of cases over and over again. Moreover, specialists develop a reputation in their fields of expertise, and a defined client base, which tends to reduce the cost of marketing. Perhaps the greatest benefit of specializing is the reduced risk of professional error, leading to malpractice or other action against the lawyer. If you know what you are doing, you are less likely to make mistakes. This protects clients and the public, while enhancing the image of the legal profession. Some critics of specialization see it as simply an advertising tool, even as a way to get around regulations regarding lawyer advertising.

The original comments to Model Rule 7.4 suggested that it would be improper to use the terms "concentrated" or "limited to" when referring to uncertified specialization. In February 1988, however, the ABA House of Delegates amended Rule 7.4 by eliminating reference to the terms "concentrated" or "limited to," an action confirmed by the United States Supreme Court in *Peel v. Attorney Registration and Discipline Commission of Illinois*, 496 U.S., 91 (1990), invalidating an Illinois disciplinary rule restricting communication of specialty. Thus, presently, a lawyer may use such expressions without implying specialist status. This discussion will use the term "practice concentration" to denote expertise in a substantive area of law.

Although it may be clear that patterns of *de facto* specialization have emerged in the legal profession, such practice concentration should not be confused with officially sanctioned legal specialization. Many jurisdictions provide for the certification of specialists in certain areas of practice, but no state has taken the next step of restricting certain areas of practice to specialists in those areas. It is not clear at this time what the future holds for specialization in the legal profession. Will we move closer to a medical model where practice areas are carved up and reserved for particular subgroups within the profession and where the lack of advanced specialized training becomes a barrier to entrance into the specialty practice? Or will lawyers adopt a free market approach to the designation of specialization?

The potential for malpractice drives many lawyers to avoid cases outside their particular field of expertise. There is also some evidence that lawyers who hold themselves out as possessing greater expertise than the average lawyer can charge and collect higher fees for their services. The prospect of greater income may offset the risk of greater liability for malpractice resulting from a higher standard of care.

What does this trend toward practice concentration mean for you, the law student? Just as the generic lawyer is giving way to the specialist, the generic law student is finding it increasingly difficult to compete with classmates who possess special skills and abilities.

There are increased pressures to make longer-term career decisions at an earlier stage in your legal career. The consequences of poor career decisions can have more impact on the direction of a legal career than in simpler times. The trend toward specialization means students must recognize that they cannot keep all of their options open forever. When you cross a particular bridge, you frequently burn other bridges behind you.

When there were generic law graduates, factors such as class rank, law-review status, and law school attended were often the only distinguishing characteristics among candidates for jobs. The trend toward practice concentration tends to impel employers to consider more diverse criteria than in the past. Thus, there is greater emphasis on credentials related to many areas of practice concentration, including not only practical experience in the field during law school, but also educational and pre-law work experience. Law graduates today are simply not fungible.

The corollary of the specialization movement has been the development of a cottage industry in legal consulting and support services. An increasing number of organizations provide expertise, specialized technical services, and other assistance to law firms.

Usually, these services have grown up in areas where the firm either lacks expertise (e.g., computers) or cannot provide the service in-house as cheaply as it can buy it outside (e.g., legal-research services). The service companies tend to be small entrepreneurial ventures doing highly specialized work. Many of the practitioners in these support services are lawyers, and frequently have training both in law and some other discipline.

Competition

A final trend that affects everyone getting out of law school and entering the profession today is competition. The fifty thousand law students who graduate annually have increased competition for jobs. The large number of lawyers has increased competition for legal work. The large number of large law firms has increased the competition for institutional clients that hire such firms. This competition is all within the legal profession.

♦ Outside the profession, many other organizations—from banks to title companies to psychologists—provide the same services as lawyers, and frequently they do it better or more cheaply. There are fewer and fewer activities from which lawyers can exclude individuals who are not licensed to practice law.

♦ This, in turn, has blurred the lines between what is the practice of law and what is not. Lawyers have reacted by expanding the scope of their professional services into areas that would have been taboo even a decade ago. In addition, as formerly nonlegal work becomes "legalized," more lawyers go to work for organizations in direct competition with law firms.

- The line between services that fall within the domain of the legal profession and those that do not is not at all clear. As the number of institutions and individuals providing services in competition with legal services increases, the gray area between law practice and nonlegal work expands.
- In many states, title companies have taken most of the real-estate closings from private practitioners. These companies are nonlegal business entities, yet many lawyers work for title companies or own them. Are these lawyers practicing law or engaging in extra-legal business? Should work that is considered "legal" when performed by a lawyer become "nonlegal" just because a nonlawyer does the very same thing?
- Representing sports or entertainment figures as an agent is another good example. Both lawyers and nonlawyers may be involved in negotiating contracts representing clients' interests and in making financial decisions. Is a lawyer-agent practicing law or doing something else?
- American lawyers may compete for positions with lawyers from other countries, as more legal work is outsourced, or they may compete with nonpayer professionals, such as CPAs and MBAs for jobs that have legal components but do not involve practicing law in the strictest sense.

Lawyers provide advice and representation to clients concerning legal problems. Significantly, almost no problem is exclusively legal in nature; and almost every problem has a legal component. Lawyers who are licensed to practice in one or more jurisdictions may represent clients in court. Many lawyers, including a large number of private practitioners, never see the inside of a courtroom. For these transactional lawyers, there is no envelope of professional monopoly, as there is for litigation, and the marketplace for transactional services is essentially unregulated. Even in the litigation world, many clients (and service providers) seek to pull cases out of the court docket for alternative dispute resolution.

Lawyers represent both individuals and institutions (e.g., corporations, government agencies, etc.). Lawyers who work for institutions have a single client—the organization that employs them. Lawyers in private practice, on the other hand, sell their services on the open market to people and organizations who hire them. Whether or not you accept a position in private practice, you will probably be giving legal advice to clients. In either case, you may or may not be involved in litigation as an advocate for your clients' interests.

A Service Business

Law firms deliver professional services to clients for profit in order to function efficiently, firms need to operate in a businesslike way, and the law student needs to understand how his or her future employer functions economically.

In a service business like law, income is limited by time. If there are 8,760 hours in a year, and a lawyer spends 3,650 of them eating, sleeping, and commuting, only 4,060 hours are left to spend in the office, assuming that the lawyer does absolutely nothing else! And if that lawyer could manage to spend two-thirds of his or her time on client matters, it would be possible to charge 2,707 hours to clients for work.

In reality, most lawyers do not attain this level of productivity. A number of surveys have confirmed that the average number of billable hours for lawyers in the United States is around 1,850. The surveys show that associates bill over 1,900 hours annually, slightly more than partners. A law firm that expects its associates to bill over 2,000 hours per year is actually expecting 3,000 to 3,500 hours of work annually, which translates into 60 to 70 hours per week.

Since there is a natural limit to the amount of time available to provide legal services, there is a cap on the equity a lawyer can generate as well. There are basically three ways that, the owners of the legal business (the partners), can make more money:

- ◆ They can charge more (e.g., $200 per hour instead of $150 per hour) or they can repackage the fee so that it does not look like an hourly bill (e.g., $2,000 for a contract that took two hours of work, thanks to automated document processing; or a one-third contingency fee that produces a $600,000 settlement for twenty hours of work).

◆ They can unbundle their charges, that is, bill the client for the secretary, the paralegal, the photocopying, and other charges as well as the time of the lawyer. In other words the law firm can pass more of its costs on to the consumers of legal services.

◆ They can practice law more efficiently. With computer and management systems, lawyers can increase the bottom line by reducing the cost of the production of the legal service while keeping the cost of the service to the consumer the same. One way to accomplish this is to practice in larger organizations. Economies of scale disadvantage the small law firm just as they do the mom-and-pop grocery store, the tailor, or the home builder.

◆ Finally, lawyers can make money off the work of other lawyers. The idea is simple. If lawyer A has enough clients to keep two lawyers busy, lawyer A could hire lawyer B at a salary low enough to allow A to make a profit from B's work. The alternative would be for A to refer excess business to B and let B profit directly, or to share the profit with B, in which case A and B would be partners. The concept by which the As of the world hire and make a profit from the Bs is called leveraging.

To make the game more interesting, the As usually hold out a carrot for the Bs ("We'll make you one of us in seven years, if you'll let us make a profit on your work in the interim. And when you're one of us, we'll get more like you. There are plenty more where you came from.") Many law firms even skip the carrot step, and go directly from making a profit to "there's more where you came from."

These economic realities are changing the makeup of law firms and law practices. More importantly, these changes are altering the career opportunities available to law school graduates. In this environment, some of the assumptions of yesterday must be reexamined in light of new evidence. And old answers will not necessarily be the best ones to the questions raised in tomorrow's job market. Some law firms are experimenting with how to pay new lawyers, how to structure their jobs, and how to accommodate alternative work and life choices. Some of these changes appear to benefit the employers by reducing costs, but others reflect employers' genuine desire to respond to the expectations and aspirations of newer members of the profession.

Interestingly, the rapid increase in legal salaries among large New York law firms was fueled by competition for legal talent from investment-banking houses during the heyday of mergers and acquisitions practice. In the early twenty-first century legal market, law firms must also compete with multidisciplinary professional service firms, online service providers, and other competitors for legal talent.

Because the job market has fractionalized over the years, there is not one job market for lawyers today but many. The job market for lawyers entering private practice may be the predominant market, but it is not the only one. All this makes job hunting significantly more complicated, although ultimately it means more opportunities for more people.

Is the job market infinitely elastic? There is evidence that certain segments of the market already may have become saturated in some geographical areas and some areas of practice. There is also evidence that the increased size of the profession has increased competition and reduced law firm profitability.

Competition with Internet services that provide legal information, online law firm services, unbundled legal services, and an increase in *pro se* representation have all had an impact on delivery of commodity legal services. When services are relatively simple and routine, more lawyers (and many nonlegal providers) are capable of delivering the services, increasing competition, and driving down prices. Consumers in such a commodity marketplace shop for price rather than quality on the assumption that if all services are comparable in quality, the less expensive service is the better choice.

This means that less successful practitioners may be driven from the market because they cannot make a living practicing law. In addition, the market may contain an underbelly of marginal practitioners and underemployed young lawyers. Again, evidence exists that such an underbelly will persist in the foreseeable future, and that underutilization of some lawyers will create special image, professionalism, and ethics problems for the legal profession.

Aside from the question of how the legal profession should deal with these developments, there is a more personal question of how you should cope. Some students may have difficulty finding a job. The reality is, however, that despite the challenges, you can find a job. The simple answer is to plan carefully and remain flexible. This theme is repeated throughout this book. Beyond doing homework, however, you must have confidence that hard work and competence will pay off in the end.

Note that there is a difference between naïve doggedness and savvy dedication. More than a few lawyers have learned the hard way that long hours and blind loyalty do not assure success. In these volatile times, a constant self-awareness and sensitivity to the external environment are prerequisites to long-term success. The following chapters briefly describe some of the more important job markets for lawyers. They represent jumping-off points rather than final words on the topics covered.

Employment Patterns

The *NALP Employment Report and Salary Survey* for each year is based on data from ABA-approved schools. The summary of the 2006 NALP Employment Report in Appendix C gives an accurate picture of where graduates go and what they do. There will undoubtedly be some differences from school to school, so students should check with their individual law schools for a more detailed report or more current data.

Employment statistics do not provide any information about long-term career patterns such as job mobility, or intangibles such as job or career satisfaction. There are over nine hundred thousand licensed lawyers in the United States with some forty thousand new members admitted to the bar annually. There are many different career patterns open to all these lawyers. While some are more common than others, the diversity of legal and legally related jobs is amazing.

Salary Patterns

It may come as no surprise to law students that starting legal salaries have risen along with the cost of everything else. It takes more money to live these days, and recent law graduates feel this as acutely as anyone, especially if they have education loans to repay.

For potential employers, the question of how much to pay is difficult. Career services directors frequently hear phrases like "the going rate," "competitive," or "comparable" that describe a salary by comparison with other employers, but there is also an easy formula. Generally, summer and part-time law clerks can expect to make two-thirds to three-fourths of what an employer would pay a newly licensed attorney to go to work. The actual range of these salaries is more like one-half to nine-tenths, but the two-thirds to three-fourths figure is a good rule of thumb, using two-thirds for first-year students, and three-fourths for second-year students. Clerk salaries may be described in terms of hourly, weekly, or monthly rates. The highest summer salaries in 2008 were over $2,100 per week, and the bottom seems to be very close to minimum wage.

There is no way to escape the escalating cost of hiring legal talent these days. On the other hand, employers must continue to grow to meet the needs of their clients, and many will be willing to compete fiercely to attract the best possible legal talent. It is worth noting, however, that a law graduate today receives very little more real income than a graduate did in 1970.

Diversity in the Profession

Women and minority law students in the job market deserve mention. Much of the advice in this book applies equally to men and women, and to majority and minority law students. That does not mean that all law students will always be treated equally. Nor does it mean that the concerns of all law students are identical.

Although the blatant exclusionary practices that characterized legal hiring in the past have diminished, subtle forms of racism and sexism remain. In fact, many women and minority law students profess concern that discrimination simply has gone underground. Many law students are reluctant to challenge employment practices they consider improper, or at least they are uneasy about their situation *vis-a-vis* employers. It is true that women and minority students have special concerns, and they may face career issues that do not impede their male or majority counterparts.

If you have particular questions about the career planning or job search process related to your status as a woman or minority law student, you should discuss these questions with a career counselor at your school. You may also find it useful to share your concerns with fellow students, or to speak with graduates who have completed the job search successfully.

Private Practice 19

The broad heading of "private practice" encompasses work in organizations that provide legal services to clients, from sole practitioners to firms of over a thousand lawyers. The most recent NALP Employment Report indicates that 55.8 percent of law school graduates who responded to the survey chose to enter private practice in 2006.

The category of law firm employment includes small, medium, and large law firms, as well as sole practitioners. Differently sized organizations will obviously be different in many ways. Smaller firms are more likely to be like a family where everyone knows everyone else, whereas larger firms are typically more institutional. The common element, however, for all private practices is that they must be profitable to be viable. On some level law firms and the lawyers who run them are entrepreneurial.

Small Firms

Smaller firms often attract graduates who hope to avoid the pressures and impersonal demeanor of large firms.

The NALP survey shows that 31.9 percent of law school graduates who enter private practice choose a firm of between two and ten lawyers. Graduates who choose to practice in small firms often are attracted by the chance to be their own bosses, set their own hours, and handle their practice in the way that they deem most satisfactory personally.

Smaller firms can be found in every size city and metropolitan area throughout the United States. Although such firms almost certainly promise lower initial income than the larger firms, they may present earlier opportunities for client contact, independent work, and partnership.

For those who prefer living in small towns or rural areas, solo and small firm practice may be the only private practice option. Some individuals might consider small-town life stifling due to the lack of cultural opportunity or professional recognition. The type of legal work that you would handle in a small town is likely to differ markedly from the work you could expect in an urban setting. At the same time, small-town life is changing. Walmart, satellite television, the Internet, and modern transportation have given rural Americans unprecedented access to the advantages that only city dwellers enjoyed in other eras.

Many small firms choose to specialize because they can more easily maintain competence, charge higher rates, and market to a targeted audience. These boutique firms represent a growing trend in law practice, as it becomes harder and harder for law firms to be all things to all people. The last bastion of true general practice is in small communities, but even in the smallest towns, lawyers who limit their practices are often more prosperous than the "jacks-and-jills-of-all-trades."

Small law firms may be organized as partnerships, either informally (a handshake partnership) or formally (with a written agreement). In many jurisdictions today, it is possible to elect to become a limited liability partnership or company, a professional association, or a subchapter "S" corporation. In many cases a group of sole practitioners may share office space and expenses such as secretarial assistance, technology, and legal assistants, with each practitioner keeping his or her own clients and retaining fees on an individual basis. Such office-sharing arrangements risk being treated as implied partnerships for purposes of professional liability if the practitioners are not careful.

Generally, small law offices do not recruit on a regular or even on an annual basis. Small firms are most likely to recruit new lawyers only when a specific need for additional help arises. As a result, recruiting efforts are likely to be more informal, and openings are likely to arise at times other than traditional recruiting periods (the on-campus interviewing season). It is not unusual for small offices to contact the career services officer of a law school three or four months after graduation and ask for assistance in locating a graduate for a position that has suddenly developed.

Students often fail to address two special aspects of small-firm recruiting. First, it may be critical for the candidate to be admitted to the bar. The potential for full utilization of the lawyer from the first day of employment is often a vital consideration, so do not be surprised if you are not a viable candidate until you have passed the bar exam. That is an economic dictate, not a rejection of you personally.

The second consideration is that both you and the employer share a high degree of mutual visibility in a small firm. If you and your colleagues are not compatible, there is no back room in which you can hide. Small firms are aware of this fact, and are extremely careful in their selection of new lawyers. You owe yourself the same carefulness.

The very closeness of small-firm lawyers and staff, however, also provides distinct advantages for a graduate. Because of your high degree of visibility, you will meet clients earlier than you would in a larger office. As you prove to be capable, you will receive additional responsibilities.

It would be a mistake to make generalizations about small firms without knowing specifics. Young lawyers sometimes assume that intellectual stimulation can be found only in very large firms. They eventually may realize they have misjudged the situation when they spend time in the real world.

Solo Practitioners

Solo practitioners work alone with only secretarial or legal assistants in the office. As soon as an associate lawyer is added to the office, the lawyer cannot be said to be practicing alone. This situation becomes confusing because of office-sharing arrangements, and work-for-space agreements. As a percentage of all lawyers in private practice, sole practitioners have decreased steadily from 70 percent in 1950 to less than 40 percent today.

Some brave souls would argue that the most effective way to achieve valuable experience in actually practicing law is to plunge into private practice immediately upon graduation from law school, and hope that experience will indeed be the best teacher. This has rewards and inherent problems, both of which should be given careful consideration.

Hanging out a shingle, as the practice is sometimes called, is certainly not the path for the fainthearted or for those who must rely on a steady income to provide for their family or to repay law school debts. Less than one percent of all law school graduates start their own practices immediately after law school, although large numbers of lawyers leave other practices, as both associates and partners, to open their own offices, either individually or as a group.

Some law school graduates are more likely to succeed at opening a practice than others. Desire and determination are not the controlling factors. Probably the most apparent factor in succeeding as a solo is competence. Although competence is difficult to define, it is clearly more than legal knowledge. The Model Rules of Professional Conduct define competence as "sufficient knowledge, skill, preparation, and thoroughness to adequately represent the client." It is often said that when you pass the bar exam, you know more law than at any other time in your professional life.

Many of those contemplating solo practice express fear about their competence. This fear may be rooted more in the absence of necessary skills to practice competently than the lack of substantive legal knowledge. When you practice alone, you can look up the law if you are unsure of something, or associate with another lawyer if you lack expertise. But knowing how to handle a case, run an office, and collect your fee are much more elusive skills, and these are generally not taught in law school.

The prospective solo practitioner should have experiences in two distinct areas: running a small business and working in a small law firm. The principles of running any business are similar, and the skills are transferable from one experience to another. If you lack business acumen built upon practical experience, you should be wary of opening a law office. You also should have experience working in a law firm that handles cases like those you will encounter as a practitioner so you can develop a working knowledge of how to handle legal matters from start to finish.

For the first few years, it is almost essential that the self-employed lawyer have a professional mentor to turn to for advice and counsel. Those who choose this path have no more knowledge of how to practice law than any other graduate, and the guidance and instruction provided by a mentor may substitute in part for that provided by the more senior members of a law firm. The problem is that the majority of lawyers today may not have experience at practicing alone themselves, and, therefore, cannot serve as role models for younger lawyers who choose solo practice.

Financing a start-up law practice can be a major hurdle as well. Law firms tend to be under-capitalized, because law has not tended to be a capital-intensive business in the past, and the Model Rules of Professional Conduct prohibit nonlawyer investment in law firms. Inadequate financing is probably responsible for more new practices failing than any other cause. If you open your own law office, you should not plan to take anything out of the practice for the first year, and you should have sufficient reserve to cover inevitable cash-flow problems in the early months of the practice.

Even if a client walks into your office the first day you open your doors, you may not see the fee for several months. During this time you still have bills to pay. Jay Foonberg, author of the classic *How to Start and Build a Law Practice* (Fourth Edition, ABA Law Practice Management Section, 2006) suggests that you set aside living expenses for one year before attempting to start your practice. For some people this may not be a problem. They have a working spouse, or they will retire from another job with a good pension when they graduate from law school, or they are independently wealthy.

For many entrepreneurial lawyers, the process of opening a law practice includes obtaining loans to finance the business. Whether you go to family or to a lending institution, the lender will want to be convinced that you will repay the loan, that is, that your practice will be successful. You will need to show more than good intentions. To convince a lender that you are a good risk, you will need a good credit history and a well-thought-out business plan.

You can take steps to solidify your credit rating long before you go to ask for a loan. Aside from paying your bills, you should attempt to develop a relationship with a banker in the area where you hope to practice and take out smaller loans, which you will then pay back promptly.

Planning is the third factor related to successfully opening up practice. A document called a business plan is a key part of the planning process. Not only do you need a business plan for the lender, you need it for yourself. A business plan should be organized as follows:

- First, you should conduct a market analysis. Look carefully at the area where you plan to open your office. What are the demographics? Where do people live and work? Who are your potential clients? What drives the economy of the area? Where are the banks? What are the opportunities for business growth?
- Second, who is your competition? How many lawyers practice in the area and what do they do? Do nonlegal institutions provide any law-related services?
- Third, you must figure out where you fit in. What is your market niche? What clients do you hope to attract and how? What services will you provide? Where will you locate in order to assure that potential clients reach you?
- Fourth, the business plan should contain an organization and resources plan. Even if the office will just include you and a secretary, that structure should be described. You should also cover office space and equipment, furniture, and information resources.
- Fifth, the business plan should include financial projections, including anticipated profits and losses and cash flow. The more realistic your budget, the more likely that it will impress a lender as well as serve you in your practice.

Opening a law practice may be a legitimate career option for some people, but a disaster for others. Entering a solo practice right out of law school should be an affirmative choice and not a selection of last resort. For the right kind of person, however, hanging out a shingle remains a viable option.

Large Firms

The decline in the percentage of lawyers practicing alone has paralleled an increase in the percentage of lawyers who practice in large institutional law firms. Why have more and more lawyers chosen to practice in larger and larger firms? And what lawyers are more likely to be happy as employees or owners of a larger law firm?

First, large law firms have emerged to meet the needs of clients. Individual practices serve individual clients. Larger business organizations frequently have a large volume of complex legal problems that cannot be dealt with by a single lawyer. A very large firm essentially serves the legal needs of very large corporations. Smaller firms serve smaller business entities. It is no accident that more of the lawyers whose work involves representing individuals choose to practice by themselves.

A second factor that has promoted law firm development has been economics. Economies of scale work in the legal services industry the same way they do in other businesses. The practice of law requires the use of sophisticated equipment, which represents a substantial capital investment for a sole practitioner. Overhead has taken an increasingly large percentage of firm profits in recent years for all firms, but the bite is particularly painful for individual practitioners.

A third factor is specialization. Lawyers increasingly must become experts at one, or at most a few, areas of law. In order to offer potential clients a full range of legal services, it is increasingly necessary to bring together a group of lawyers with different specialties in order to have a full-service law firm.

About 36.7 percent of the law graduates surveyed by NALP who entered private practice in 2006 joined firms of more than fifty lawyers. Approximately 6.4 percent accepted positions in law firms of more than fifty.

The patterns of practice at larger firms have been well-documented in a number of books, both fiction and nonfiction. Some discussion concerning the recruitment practices of very large firms, however, may be helpful.

These firms recognize that their continued growth and vitality depend upon the recruitment of highly capable people.

Consequently they undertake sophisticated recruitment programs that include on-campus recruiting, deadlines for offers, and careful selection of schools for maximum potential results and the use of professional staff.

Large firms are aware that they must hire far more associates than can possibly be expected to become partners. Such firms, however, are also aware that the training they provide and the standards they require are such that those who do not remain at the firm, for a variety of reasons, are sought-after candidates. Some of the career paths of those who leave large law firms include: other law firms as well as in-house counsel offices of clients, government regulatory agencies, business consulting firms, investment banks, and lobbyists.

Larger firms tend to provide greater opportunities for specialization, the highest initial starting salaries, and the most comprehensive training and professional development. These firms also offer a chance to practice law with other lawyers who are generally quite competent, and therefore able to provide the benefit of valuable experience.

The problems of being an associate with a big firm cannot be overlooked either, and in recent years these problems have been a source of increasing concern to law school graduates, who want freedom in the hours they work, the kind of legal work they handle and level of responsibility they are given.

Not Large, Not Small

Some firms are neither large nor small; in a sense these are transitional organizations. When a firm reaches a size of about ten lawyers, it becomes institutionalized: it hires more regularly; it departmentalizes; it becomes more structured administratively. Such a firm will become more and more like other large firms as it grows, even though it may try (usually unsuccessfully) to retain its small-firm attributes. These medium-sized firms that do not make the transition to large firms often splinter into smaller firms again or find themselves taken over by larger organizations.

In fact, there have always been small firms, but today more and more of them represent the fallout from the breakups of larger organizations, or boutiques of lawyers choosing to practice in small groups within narrow specialties. Even in small towns, many lawyers are deciding to narrow their practice areas, as discussed earlier, page 228.

Some small-town boutiques are joining other lawyers similarly situated to create regional specialty firms or alliances. Other small-town practices are creating referral networks with lawyers in areas outside their practice concentrations to cross-refer clients to assure competent representation. What all this means and where it will lead is uncertain, but it does demonstrate a willingness for lawyers to experiment with nontraditional organizational structures in order to improve their position in the marketplace and the quality of services delivered to clients.

Organizational Practice 20

In the first decade of the new millennium, over 40 percent of all lawyers do not engage in the private practice of law, an increase from less than 20 percent in 1950. Think of it: Almost half of all lawyers ply their trade in organizations that do not deliver legal services directly to private clients, but rather serve organizational clients. These institutional lawyers sometimes struggle with their identities in a profession that still sees itself as primarily composed of private practitioners.

This chapter divides lawyers for organizations into several groups: corporations and other business associations (house counsel), government lawyers, and nonlegal organizations. Where legal duties extend beyond the organization to its customers, the ethical challenges for lawyers, including independent judgment, confidences, and loyalty, can prove significant. Yet there are no signs of this trend retreating.

Some multidisciplinary professional practices represent a hybrid between traditional practice involving service delivery to clients and organizational practice.

The organized bar has resisted MDPs, as they are often called, but outside the United States, law firms, accounting firms, and other professional services offer clients one-stop shopping for their professional services needs.

House Counsel

The number of lawyers employed by a corporation will vary widely with the size and type of the corporation. Many smaller and some larger corporations farm out all their legal problems to private law firms. Many others have in-house counsel for only certain matters. Other corporations have a legal staff large enough to handle most legal problems in house. The responsibilities:

- Corporate secretary functions
- Advising senior management
- Corporate compliance
- White-collar crime
- Managing outside counsel
- Government relations
- Contracting
- Handling other legal work of the corporation

In a small corporation, a lawyer may have responsibilities other than the legal business affairs. An increasing number of corporations are seeking young lawyers to handle legal problems and assume management duties as well. If there is a legal department or a full-time lawyer employed by the corporation, the individual is often referred to as the general counsel.

Some corporations hire lawyers outside their regular legal departments. Oil companies typically have exploration or land departments totally distinct from their legal departments. Some companies hire lawyers in tax departments, in intellectual property, in research and development, and in other capacities that require an ability to deal with the law.

Starting salaries in corporations tend to be higher than for small firms, but less than the highest paying large firms. On the other hand, law firm associates, especially in large firms, may work more than sixty hours per week, while a corporate staff lawyer may follow a typical 8 a.m. to 5 p.m. schedule. In addition, the fringe benefits, amenities, and working conditions are often more palatable in a corporation than in a firm.

In business, as in government, many management decisions, such as those involving the number of lawyers and salary ranges, are made outside the legal department. Top leadership has relatively little turnover, so variations in form and procedure remain relatively stable.

Law graduates can expect a wide range of opportunities in corporate practice depending upon the nature of the legal work of the individual organizations. Although form and structure may be dictated by outside forces in both government and business, each legal department has a unique personality formed by the individual viewpoint of the general counsel and senior staff of the department. See Chapter 23 for a summary of nonlegal positions in corporations.

Government

The rise of the regulatory state has coincided with the emergence of administrative agencies to carry out legislative mandates at all levels of government. Many of the rules and budgets for these agencies are established by legislative bodies rather than by the agencies themselves, although agencies often exercise considerable discretion and great power in carrying out their mandates.

Differences among government agencies depend upon the scope and jurisdiction of each agency. For example, work in a district attorney's office will provide early exposure to criminal litigation, while work in the Office of the General Counsel of the Environmental Protection Agency offers exposure to environmental litigation.

Opportunities with the federal government are as varied as the departments themselves, and the departments are as varied as the problems facing the country today. There is a government agency designated to deal with almost every facet of American life. Within this framework, the opportunities for employment are virtually endless.

The diversity of activities within the broad scope of "government service" necessitates careful investigation of each individual department, because each is a unique entity with its own particular advantages and disadvantages. A person who would not be at all interested in consumer-protection and anti-trust law with the Federal Trade Commission or with the Tax Division of the Justice Department might enjoy dealing with the problems of rural America in the Department of Agriculture.

Many would criticize the federal government for its bigness; however, in terms of employment, this is not always an accurate perception. Each department retains a certain degree of autonomy and self-sufficiency with a group of people all working in the same general direction within the department.

For graduates seeking jobs with state agencies, the road to employment may seem strewn with obstacles and at times impassable. A plethora of agencies exists in each of the fifty states and in the territories. Many states provide no centralized organization or bureau, such as the U.S. Civil Service Commission, that coordinates the hiring of personnel. Yet, despite this, it is possible to traverse the course and find the way to gainful employment.

The key to success may well lie in the right combination of luck and perseverance. Many state agencies hire someone when a position becomes open, unlike large law firms that know how many new lawyers they will need in any given year. Thus, retracing ground may well be necessary. You should not become discouraged if your initial efforts are unsuccessful.

At the local level, jobs with governmental entities are often harder to find because there are so many potential places to look. District, county, and city attorneys' offices often hire recent graduates. In larger cities, these offices have regular openings as well as more coordinated hiring policies; in small cities and towns, getting hired is likely to be much more difficult.

Local government may present opportunities in fields such as land-use planning, zoning, utilities law, and other substantive areas that correspond to local political issues. Jobs may be funded in departments within city government and in special districts (e.g., water, school, regional planning). Local government agencies are more likely to recruit from the local bar than to solicit applicants from law schools. There is no comprehensive list of such local government jobs, so you should discuss your plans with a member of your career services staff for personal guidance.

Each branch of the military service has its Judge Advocate General's Corps or equivalent. The salary, benefits, and relative security of military life may be attractive to many graduates. Significantly, the military services represent one of the largest employers of law graduates in the country and. despite the fact that the military legal system is different from the civilian one, military legal alumni testify to the excellent preparation for law practice that they receive.

NGOs, Foundations, and Private Associations

Nongovernment organizations and private associations have proliferated in recent decades. Government-business partnerships are not new, but they have become increasingly popular as devices for accomplishing social, political, religious, or economic objectives where traditional funding or organizational models have proven ineffectual. On the international stage, sometimes only an entity that is not officially connected to any government can undertake certain jobs. In 2008, the government of Myanmar (formerly Burma) refused to permit relief from other countries to assist victims of a devastating typhoon and strictly monitored private organizations like the International Red Cross.

It is beyond the scope of this *Guide* to describe all the different variations on the theme of organizations that are neither governmental nor corporate in nature. It is worth noting, however, that many of these entities perform legal or law-related functions and many lawyers work in these settings. For these reasons, law students looking for nontraditional opportunities owe it to themselves to investigate these options, See also Munneke, Henslee, and Wayne, *Nonlegal Careers for Lawyers,* ABA (2006).

Judicial Clerkships 21

Judicial clerkships are a sought-after opportunity. These positions are unique for many reasons that relate to the nature of the experience and the opportunity to work directly in the justice system. Perhaps more than any other type of legal position, a clerkship, in terms of the quality of the experience, is strongly related to the personality and values of the judge with whom one serves. Due to their close working relationship, judges and clerks often develop a special, long-lasting professional bond. Because clerkships are of limited duration, they are not generally considered as career paths in and of themselves, but as gateways leading to future career options.

Deciding whether to apply for a clerkship requires an understanding of the different functions and range of responsibilities of each court. Judges in different courts provide different experiences depending upon their jurisdiction, types of issues brought before their court, and individual use of their clerk's time. Some judges use their clerks as sounding boards for working through the thought process for making a decision; some require their clerks to be in the courtroom at all times, and others not at all; and some judges allow clerks to create a first draft of an opinion while others request initial research as they prefer to work through the legal aspects of the case alone. Finding a judge who will enhance your research and writing skills, as well as one who will become a mentor throughout your professional life, is one of the most treasured aspects of serving as a judicial clerk.

To decide whether a clerkship is the right choice for you and to determine the court level that will be the best fit for your skills and interests, it is important that you invest some time in researching the courts, speak to others who have clerked for the court or judge and, especially with the federal courts, be geographically flexible. One important aspect of that research should include determining the jurisdiction and focus of the specific courts that you are considering. These differences can make an impact upon the experience that you will have during your clerkship year(s).

Federal Courts

Because federal courts hear issues of federal jurisdiction, judges do not expect a clerk to have a geographic connection to the area where the court is located, nor do the judges expect a clerk to reside in the local area after the clerkship has ended. Clerks are also not expected to take the bar examination in the local jurisdiction. The duration of the clerkship can range from one to two years, depending upon the judge's preference.

The Supreme Court

This section starts out by mentioning the U.S. Supreme Court but, in a sense, it should be listed last. Few students will have the opportunity to serve in one of the thirty-seven positions, four for each associate justice and five for the chief justice. Given the prestige and competition associated with these positions, it should be obvious that only the most stellar candidates need apply. As a rule, Supreme Court clerks come from the ranks of the best students at the most elite law schools. Additionally, in recent years, the justices have selected most, if not all, of their clerks from individuals who have served as clerks for the U.S. Court of Appeals (see below). If you think you might have a chance to attain one of these positions, you should work closely with a faculty advisor, typically someone who has ties to the Court and who can work with you to maximize your chances.

Courts of Appeals

A clerkship for the court of appeals tends to involve less courtroom action and more scholarship than a clerkship for a federal district court judge. A major portion of an appellate clerk's time is consumed by research and writing. When a case comes to the court of appeals, most of the routine questions have already been resolved at the district court level, while the complex, more difficult questions, are left for the appellate court to consider. Thus, the appellate clerk is afforded an opportunity to study fewer questions, but in more depth.

The range of legal problems encountered in the federal court of appeals is quite wide. A sampling would include *habeas corpus,* criminal law and procedure, labor, administrative procedure, tax, admiralty, antitrust, securities, bankruptcy, civil rights, poverty, social security and welfare.

In addition, because of the federal courts' diversity of jurisdiction, an appellate court also encounters the standard range of common-law matters, including contracts, torts, and real property matters. The clerk always attends oral argument and, therefore, learns a great deal about the best practices for presenting an oral argument before a judge.

Although an appellate clerkship does not offer much direct contact with trial practice, it does provide an opportunity to learn a great deal of information about trial practice and procedures from the study of trial records that are always included in an appeal. By reading all of the motions and pleadings filed in the trial court and studying the trial transcript, the clerk learns how to prepare a record for appeal.

District Courts

The duties of a clerk for a federal district court are somewhat different than those of a court of appeals clerk. Individual judges utilize their law clerks as valuable adjuncts to the judicial decision-making process.

There is much activity outside the courtroom in connection with pre-trial motions and memorandum opinions. The law clerk examines all of the pleadings and briefs and prepares memoranda for the court. Active discussion may ensue between the judge and the law clerk concerning the positions taken by the respective parties and their merits.

A law clerk is a valuable sounding board against whom the judge can, in confidence, "bounce" legal theories offered by the litigating parties, legal concepts overlooked by the parties, and the consequences of a decision to be rendered.

State Courts

Although much of the attention at law school is focused on federal judicial clerkships, at least in part because the faculty considers such appointments prestigious, every jurisdiction has a system of state courts that utilize judicial clerks to some degree. Some states only provide funding for clerkships at the appellate level. Others offer trial court clerkships just like the federal system. In either case, state courts offer an excellent opportunity for students and graduates interested in judicial clerkships in their home community or with courts having a more limited jurisdiction. State court judges tend to seek clerks with a connection to their state and may expect clerks to become licensed in the state and to be interested in practicing locally after their clerkship.

The procedures for applying to judges at the state court level are similar to those in the federal courts, although the specifics will vary from jurisdiction to jurisdiction. The timing for applying to state courts is generally, but not always, at the same time as the federal courts—especially for the appellate courts. If you are interested in a state court clerkship, consult with your career counselor, court administrator, or an alum who has clerked in the state, for information on the timing of the application process.

Administrative Courts

Another opportunity for a clerkship experience exists in applying to the administrative courts, including the Tax Court, Court of Claims, Court of Patent Appeals and Magistrates, among others. The number of applications for these positions is often less than for the other more general courts because many potential applicants are not as familiar with their focus.

Many of these courts seek applicants who not only have an interest in the specialty jurisdiction of some of these courts but also have some experience in the practice area (e.g., Tax Court). These courts accept clerkship applications within the same time-table as the federal court process.

The Application Process

The application process for judicial clerkships at both the state and federal levels is different from any other career path. Understanding this process is critical to securing a clerkship, but it is not an impossible task.

Getting Started

To learn something about the specifics of a law clerk's responsibilities, it will be useful to do some research. The Administrative Office of the Federal Courts has a link to a description of the responsibilities of a federal court law clerk on its clerkship hiring plan Web site at *http://oscar.uscourts/gov*. This home page will allow you to enter a site that provides information about what a clerk does in different federal court contexts. It is also the link to the application information (see the Application Process below) and a database of judges participating in the clerkship hiring process.

Another resource is the clerkship handbook or other information that is available from the administrative office that is charged with counseling clerkship applicants at your law school. Many schools have lists of faculty who have clerked, alumni/ae who are either judges or who have served as clerks at many clerkship levels, and information from law students who have interviewed with judges and are willing to share their information with other students. There are also blogs and Web sites that provide information and allow students to share information about the clerkship application and interview process.

Students

If you are interested in serving as a judicial clerk, you should begin to prepare your application package during the spring of your second year of law school. The standard application for most judges consists of a résumé, cover letter, transcript, writing sample, and at least two faculty recommendation letters. It is best to identify the writing sample that you will use and to request recommendations from faculty before you leave law school in the spring.

For federal clerkships, almost all judges elect to participate in a national hiring plan that provides a standardized process for application and interview timing. Information concerning the details of the applicable hiring guidelines and a searchable database can be found at: *http://oscar.uscourts/gov.*

Application Timetable

- *Check the U.S. Courts Web site* for accurate information as each year the judges meet to decide the timetable and process for the next clerkship season.
- *The day after Labor Day:* Applications and recommendations are mailed by law schools or individual students (depending upon the system in place at each law school). These applications are sent nationwide to a list of mostly federal judges identified by students interested in a clerkship in the judge's chambers. Some law schools collect and bundle these applications and mail them for their student applicants; others prefer that students mail their applications independently.
- *One week later:* This is the first date that judges who are involved in the hiring plan may contact applicants to schedule interviews.
- *Two weeks later:* This is the first date that judges in the hiring plan will begin to interview applicants. The clerkship process begins in the late summer of the second year of law school. The application process was changed a few years ago in order to enrich recommendation letters from faculty. The faculty requested additional time and experience working with students before they were asked to write a recommendation letter to the judge to whom the student was applying.

How to Apply

Judges either elect to participate in the Online System for Clerkship Application and Review (OSCAR) found at *http://www.oscar*

.uscourts.gov or they ask that students apply by mail. (Many students overnight these applications so that the judge receives them at the same time as the online applications.) The smaller number of individual judges who elect to accept application materials directly by mail from students expect students to send their materials at the same time as the timing guidelines specify. (Check with your law school to determine if the school has administrative support or a collection process.) At present, almost nine hundred federal judges elect to participate in the online application process.

For state court clerkships: The state courts are not specifically bound by or involved with the federal timing guidelines for the clerkship application process. However, many state supreme or courts of appeals utilize the same guidelines and timing as the Federal courts. The best resource for determining the application processes of the various state courts/judges is either by checking the Web sites of the various courts of interest or consulting *http://www.vermontlaw.edu/career* and requesting login information from your law school. Most law schools subscribe to this resource.

Graduates

In past years, it was rare for experienced law school graduates to clerk. It has now become not only common but also preferred by many judges. Clerkship positions are now commonly held open for at least one experienced clerk, in addition to the recent graduates who traditionally have clerked in the judge's chambers. The application timing guidelines for student applicants do not apply to graduates applying for experienced clerk positions.

Graduates may apply whenever they are ready or interested in applying. For graduates who are able to plan at least one year ahead, it is preferable to apply at the same time that students apply so that they may take advantage of all of the clerkship openings available for the following year (Labor Day of one year for a clerkship that begins the following year). Graduates who decide to apply "off cycle" often fill positions with new judges, open positions with judges who have unexpected openings or to complete a clerkship year for a current clerk who leaves early. Although the basic application is the same as that requested of law students and includes a résumé, cover letter, writing sample, transcript, and two recommendation letters, the longer that a graduate is out of law school, the more difficult it may be to obtain recommendation letters from faculty.

If you think that you may apply to clerk some time in the future, it is advisable to approach faculty while you are still a student or a recent graduate. Many schools or individual faculty will create a file with reference letters that can be utilized when the graduate decides to apply for a future clerkship. If you decide to clerk after two or more years of employment, judges still prefer at least two faculty recommendations but they will also accept at least one recommendation letter from a work-related supervisor. It is advisable that the work-related reference concentrate on writing, research, and legal analysis skills in the letter. One difference in applying as a graduate involves salary levels. The salary scale for the federal courts will take into account prior legal experience. The judge can recommend an advanced salary level for an experienced clerk.

Many law school clerkship advisors will assist graduates with their clerkship applications. Some will collect and "bundle" graduate applications and send them to the judges a few months before student applications are sent, others will "compile" application materials individually, and still others request that graduates send their applications independently. Check with your clerkship office to determine the resources and support available to you.

Graduates should consult the Online System for Clerkship Application and Review, http://oscar.uscourts.gov, for a listing of judges with clerkship availability outside of the annual clerkship timing guidelines (see also Appendix A for additional resources).

Yearly Updates

The clerkship timing guidelines are reviewed each year and may be adjusted. For the most up-to-date information, view the Web site of the Administrative Office of the Federal Courts (http://oscar.uscourts.gov) and contact your law school clerkship office.

Interviewing Judges

Interviewing with a judge takes an understanding of the process and an appreciation of the differences between judicial interviews and those of a law firm or other legal position.

Federal court judges will most often schedule an interview within days of the allowed interview dates (in accordance with the guidelines). They may contact you by telephone or by e-mail to arrange for the visit. Be prepared to take the first appointment available—even if it means taking time off from school or your employment. Keep in mind that judges do not wait to interview all candidates before making offers. They will be hiring only two, or at most three, people. Many judges involve their clerks in the screening process and the office secretary/administrator also has an important role.

State judges either interview individually or participate in the rotation of a pool of clerks assigned to them by the court administrator. If the court uses a pool of clerks, the candidates will most likely be interviewed by a group of judges who evaluate candidates for the entire court. Appellate court judges will most often follow the federal court model. District court judges tend to interview at a later date and will usually contact candidates by mail or a call from their court administrator. It is important to understand the process being utilized by the judge. Interviewing as part of a pool is different than interviewing with one judge's chambers.

Based upon the timing of the interviews, once a judge has called to offer you an appointment, you may have very little time to prepare. It might appear that the judges are in a "race" to find the best clerk for their chambers. Its best to begin to prepare as soon as you send out the application so you are ready to accept an interview invitation.

Resources

In preparing for the interview, some of the following resources will prove to be useful:

◆ A judge's or courts most recent opinions. A judge may ask an applicant about an issue that has come before the court because it is the most current topic in chambers.

◆ Any and all biographical information about the judge. *The Almanac of the Judiciary* can supply basic information and do not assume a judge's political leanings based upon the U.S. president who appointed her/him. Judges on the federal bench are recommended by senators who often cooperate on selections even if they are of a different party.

- Legal press coverage of the judge or her/his court opinions.
- Judicial blogs and commentary about the court.
- Any faculty member or graduate who clerked for the judge and can provide information about the selection process.

The Interview

Most interviews will include a meeting with both the current clerks and the judge. The clerks will explain how the chambers operate (e.g., some judges ask clerks to draft opinions; others utilize their clerks as sounding boards as they formulate their opinion; and others use their clerks to conduct research). As you are asking questions of clerks, keep in mind that they are part of the interview process. The judge's secretary/assistant is also an important part of the interview. Although he or she may not ask you questions, he or she is the permanent employee who works closely with the judge as the clerks come and go. No one is going to be hired who has not been cooperative and respectful of the judge's closest employee.

After meeting with the clerks, the judge will meet with you. In most cases, the interview will be different than that in other legal organizations. You are joining a "team" of individuals who work with the judge closely and all of the personnel must work together smoothly. In addition, the judge will evaluate how you analyze information and how you will fit with the judge's personal work style. In addition to standard interview questions, don't be surprised at the more unique questions you might be asked. Judges have been known to ask: What is your favorite movie? What was the last fiction book you read? Can you can fly fish? (This a standard question for some judges in fly fishing territory.) One judge asked applicant to name their favorite U.S. Supreme Court Justice and why. These are questions that you cannot easily prepare for. The best way to handle these questions is to answer truthfully and be comfortable, but not informal, with the judge.

Selection

As you would expect from the process, each interview is unique to the judge. You will be joining the "judge's family" for the rest of your career. Once you are selected for the interview, everyone interviewing you is seeking the illusive concept of "fit" with the others in the chambers. The bond among former clerks with their judges is usually so close that many judges hold reunions with their clerks every year. Judges are the most sought-after reference by future employers.

Once a judge interviews a candidate, a decision usually is made very quickly. You may receive a telephone call from the judge the next day or within a few days. It is expected that you will be able to respond to the offer quickly—within a day or at most two. Some judges are known to make offers at the interview and will expect an immediate answer. This is a very personal process as the judge is offering an opportunity to work individually with the selected applicant for a year or two (depending upon the length of the clerkship term).

It is advisable to prepare carefully for the interview so that you are ready to make a decision very quickly based upon your research, the information provided by former clerks, and your evaluation of the interview.

Clerking provides a unique experience. It is an opportunity to see the inside workings of the legal system guided by a judge who will be a mentor and reference for you for the rest of your career. It is rare to speak to someone who has clerked who did not feel that it was the most educational and best year of his or her career.

Judicial Administration

Although most law students and graduates only think about judicial positions in terms of clerkships, the broader field of judicial administration is worth considering for the longer term. Many practitioners transition to the bench, either for limited terms or lifetime appointments. Because most (although not all) judges are lawyers, appointment or election to a judgeship provides an interesting alternative to practice.

Contrary to stereotypes of judges being more senior attorneys, many judges are surprisingly recent graduates from law school, mid-level associates, law firm partners, and public interest/

service attorneys or law professors. As with anyone who hopes to pursue a life in politics, it is never too early to start developing contacts that will lead to a judicial position.

If you are interested in working for the courts in an administrative position, as a staff attorney, a full-time law clerk (a more permanent position), or in human resources, check the specific court's Web site for position openings.

Pro Bono *and Public* 22
Service

The term *public interest* means many things to many people, because different people have different ideas about what constitutes the public interest. For many, public interest work includes employment with programs that provide legal services for the indigent, and the law reform activities related to civil rights organizations. In recent years, the definition of public interest law has broadened to include private associations with broad social or political agendas, such as environmental protection, as well as groups advocating the interests of a variety of causes. In this broader context, activists from all corners of the political landscape claim to act in the public interest.

Legal Services for the Poor

Legal services programs have existed for decades in every jurisdiction throughout the United States. Many programs are a part of the Legal Services Corporation funded by Congress. These programs provide legal assistance for a variety of civil problems, including landlord-tenant disputes, domestic relations, employment discrimination, social services, and other legal issues.

Other notable programs include federal and state public defenders which provide constitutionally guaranteed legal assistance to defendants in criminal cases who cannot afford a private lawyer. A variety of other private legal-services organizations assist individuals with specialized problems and provide access to the justice system for those who would not otherwise receive it.

If you decide to pursue a career in public interest law, you should not expect wealth or fame. Your primary rewards are more likely to be personal ones, such as knowing that you have done something useful for society or helped someone to resolve a problem that day. There is a great need, however, for legal services lawyers, because those who enter this type of practice are in short supply.

Although opportunities in the poverty law area have diminished since the mid-1960s, legal services programs continue to seek and attract motivated, competent individuals to practice law on behalf of the poor. Because ethnic and racial minorities constitute an inordinate percentage of the poor, lawyers from ethnically diverse backgrounds who communicate effectively with minority clients are in great demand. The influx of Spanish-speaking immigrants over the past two decades has produced particular demand for bilingual lawyers in this field.

As a legal services lawyer, you have the ability and training to contribute significantly to the public interest, but such dedication involves some sacrifice in terms of your own personal comforts. The degree to which you dedicate yourself to solving these problems could range from an entire career devoted to legal aid, to limited terms of service during your career, and *pro bono publico* work while you are in private practice.

Public defenders should also be included in this category, although they represent indigent and low-income individuals in criminal, as opposed to civil, matters. Public defenders may work in separate organizations, but they face many of the same challenges of heavy caseloads, low pay, and high stress as their legal services counterparts.

Work in a legal services program can be frustrating but it is ultimately rewarding professionally (if not financially), and is always excellent training for young lawyers. Are you willing to sacrifice a lucrative position in private practice for the satisfaction of doing something that must be done? It is eventually a question of ordering priorities to determine what you want from your career. Your profession has prepared you for a vast range of other alternatives, so the decision to pursue a career in legal services is an extremely difficult one.

Public Service Organizations

Americans view the law as a vehicle for promoting their interests, which they perceive as the public interest. Conversely, they often refer to the interest of those with whom they disagree as special interests. Over time, new interest groups emerge to represent interests and causes that evolve in society. This multiplicity of interest groups represents a means for broad social and political questions to be resolved through the judicial system, and the fact remains that more people than ever before are getting involved in the legal process.

Some of the areas that have aroused considerable interest are consumer protection, environmental law, land-use planning, communications, governmental responsiveness, and ethics. Whenever a group of concerned citizens attempts to assert or defend its rights, lawyers are likely to be involved.

Funding for public interest representation derives from both the government and charitable sources; citizens who are actively involved in the cause have shouldered a large part of the burden. If these individuals are not indigent, they can contribute to the funding. If they do not have money, resources must come from somewhere else. In some cases, statutory and contingent fees may provide access to the courts, but in others independent funding is needed.

Just as in legal services for the poor, other branches of public interest law may involve either legal advice and representation or law-reform activities. Groups may secure someone in a law firm to represent them, hire staff counsel, or rely on volunteers to handle their legal work.

Lack of government support and tight foundation budgets make good-paying jobs in the public interest field scarce and competition fierce. But for persons willing to make the commitment, the need is there. It is exciting to view the significant numbers of good law students who find the problems impossible to ignore.

In recent years, the term NGO, standing for Non-Government Organization, has come to be used for almost any association or government organization that performs a quasi-governmental function outside the formal government structure. Funding may come from the government, private sources, or from combined contributions. The category might include an international agency that is not a part of any government, or a small private association with a narrow public service agenda. Although it is not always clear what an NGO is and what it is not, it is clear that these organizations are on the rise and many of them are hiring lawyers.

Pro Bono Publico

Rule 6.1 of the ABA Model Rules of Professional Conduct says that all lawyers should engage in fifty hours per year of *pro bono* legal work. The comments to the rule state that, although this requirement is typically met by providing legal services without charge, it can be met in other ways. Although there is no provision for disciplinary enforcement against lawyers who do not abide by the rule, its inclusion in the ethics code is a strong statement on behalf of public interest representation.

In practice, many lawyers reduce or do not charge fees to clients who are unable to pay. Although not often reported by the press, many lawyers take on cases that do not provide remuneration simply because they believe that a client deserves representation. Many larger firms engage in *pro bono* work on an institutional basis, and give associates and partners who wish to provide public service leave to do so.

In a larger sense, however, lawyers should remember that a license to practice law is a privilege, and that in return for the benefits associated with serving as officers of the courts, they should give something back to the community. For some, this may mean taking on *pro bono* cases; for others, it may involve community service, participation in local government, writing and speaking about the law, or providing contributions to public interest causes, however they define them. When lawyers participate visibly in their communities as public citizens, one positive by-product is that the image of the legal profession undoubtedly is enhanced. For those entering the profession, meeting the letter and spirit of Rule 6.1 should be a part of their career planning, whether they intend to practice public-interest law full- or part-time.

Student Loan Forgiveness

In 2008, Congress adopted legislation allowing law school and other graduates to work in government and other public service jobs in return for partial forgiveness of student loan obligations. Thus, many graduates who felt compelled to accept higher paying law firm jobs over government and public service jobs to repay student loans will now be able to make career choices based on their public service ideals rather than economic necessity.

Law-Related and Nonlegal Professional Services

23

$\mathbf{A}$n increasing number of organizations outside the traditional types of practice are choosing to employ lawyers. Among these new employers are organizations such as foundations, labor unions, trade associations, bar associations, universities, consulting firms, and other groups that have found that having a lawyer on staff is sound business.

For the most part, these staff lawyers perform the same kind of role as corporate or government counsel—advising their employers. At the same time, many non-lawfirm entities are hiring lawyers to provide services directly to clients and customers. Although such services are generally not called legal services, there is often a legal element to the lawyers' role.

Some organizations, such as the large accounting firms, have been more aggressive in melding legal services with other professional services in so-called multidisciplinary firms. Although lawyers in the United States are prohibited by Model Rule 5.4

from participating in such organizations, a proliferation of multi-disciplinary service providers offering one-stop shopping to professional service customers has changed the international legal-services market in significant ways.

Within the United States, accounting firms, banks, and other nonlegal organizations are broadening the scope of services they provide, defining law-related work as "consulting" to avoid prosecution for the unauthorized practice of law. These organizations have recruited law school graduates, associates, and partner-level senior lawyers to work for them. They have formed a variety of business alliances with law firms that fall short of prohibited partnership status. They have established creative referral arrangements that fall short of formal fee-sharing.

In addition, significant numbers of lawyers work in nonlegal positions throughout business and industry. The growth of these nonlegal positions can be attributed to two factors.

First, individuals with a legal education possess a set of skills and a base of knowledge that is useful in a wide variety of settings. The process of legal analysis can be applied to a multitude of problems to achieve favorable resolution. Many employers, therefore, find that it is strategically advantageous to have people with legal training in key positions. For example, an advertising account executive with legal training can alert management and the agency's counsel that certain ads under preparation may pose legal problems long before they reach media distribution. A contract administrator with legal training can more easily spot the failure of a supplier to meet contract specifications long before expensive problems and delays develop.

Second, many lawyers become disenchanted with the practice of law, either after practicing for a short time or as a result of burnout after years in the trenches. Whether some of these lawyers could have found satisfaction in other careers within the profession is a separate question. The fact remains that every year an uncertain but significant number of lawyers defect from the practice of law to nonlegal work. Even allowing for death and retirement, a large cohort of lawyers has disappeared from the roles of the profession.

Many law students either do not want to practice law upon graduation or have serious questions as to whether they would really enjoy doing so. Unfortunately, many career services offices are not geared to handle their needs because the great majority of law students seek law-related jobs. The law school, friends, and family may put tremendous pressure on students to pursue a traditional career in practice.

Students, however, should consider nonlegal career options if they have completed a careful self-analysis and really want to go that route. They should not refrain from considering nonlegal employment just because a majority of their classmates choose legal alternatives.

The Bureau of Labor Statistics recognizes literally thousands of job titles. If you focus on positions where legal training is a special asset, you will identify a plethora of opportunities while pursuing almost any job listing service or reviewing the Bureau's *Dictionary of Job Titles*. Although they may not be practicing law *per se*, law graduates, by virtue of their legal training, often have a distinct advantage over other applicants in nonlegal positions, and find their knowledge of the law to be a valuable asset on the job.

Pre-legal training combined with a legal education may provide special qualifications for young lawyers. If additional training or experience would be necessary to be considered for such positions, students should not hesitate to obtain these qualifications. It is worth noting that opportunities abound in the world of law firms besides working as a lawyer:

- ◆ Legal technology support
- ◆ Electronic data discovery
- ◆ Economic market research
- ◆ Jury selection
- ◆ Law firm administration
- ◆ Legal research
- ◆ Human resources
- ◆ Diversity

In today's world, unique skill sets combining more than one professional field are likely to open doors that would not be possible for a generalist. This chapter lists a variety of career opportunities outside the traditional practice of law. For more information on this topic, see the ABA Career Series book *Nonlegal Careers for Lawyers,* by Gary A. Munneke, William D. Henslee, and Ellen Wayne (ABA, 2006).

Business and Industry

The first group of nonlegal jobs includes that broad category of things we generally term as business. The most logical place to go to get information would seem to be the business-school career services office at your university, if your university has a business school. Check out your law school career services office first, but then go to the business school career services office. Your law school career services professional may even be able to set up an appointment or provide a letter of introduction. Some business schools may be unwilling or unable to assist law students, but it is worth a try.

As in the case of legal jobs, the business school may have an over-representation of corporate giants, conglomerates, and so on, forcing those who would choose a small business enterprise to look on their own. Still, you have to start somewhere. Some of the areas in which law students have expressed an interest include the following:

- ◆ Accounting
- ◆ Commercial and investment banking
- ◆ Entrepreneurship
- ◆ Information technology and knowledge management
- ◆ Insurance and financial planning
- ◆ Business planning
- ◆ Management
- ◆ Real estate
- ◆ Securities
- ◆ Systems analysis
- ◆ Title companies and land development

Government

Many nonlegal government positions involve work for which legal training is an asset. These opportunities may be found at the federal, state, and local levels. Federal jobs can be investigated through the U.S. Civil Service Commission, the U.S. Government Organization Manual, and a variety of listing services and Web sites.

For state employment, the search may be more problematic, as states may vary in the quality of access to information. If you are looking for jobs out-of-state, the geographic barriers may be greater, and you may have to search for information online if you cannot visit the area. Due to myriad local governments and special districts, local jobs must be researched separately. Some of the general categories of law-related work in the government are the following:

- ◆ Research
- ◆ Land-use planning
- ◆ Police work
- ◆ Administration and management
- ◆ Systems analysis
- ◆ Information technology and knowledge management
- ◆ Lobbying and political action
- ◆ Campaigning and running for office
- ◆ Law enforcement

Many law graduates who start out in an agency as lawyers find that as they move up the ladder in the organization, they assume an increasing number of nonlegal administrative responsibilities. Those at the top echelons of responsibility may do little legal work at all and, at some point, promotion at the agency may mean choosing a nonlegal job over a legal one. In this sense, long-term promotion in the government may involve moving from a legal position to one that is essentially nonlegal.

Education

One of the real growth areas for legal employment is in the field of education. Not only are lawyers going into teaching, but also into a variety of administrative positions in law schools, universities, and other educational institutions. In addition to law school teachers, where aging baby boomers who dominate faculties are reaching retirement age, business schools, medical schools, and other disciplines with a legal interface are hiring lawyers to teach law-related courses. At the same time, many students today come to law school with credentials in other graduate fields and some of these are going back into those fields. Although hardly complete, here is a list of positions in education:

- ◆ Teaching
- ◆ Educational administration
  - • Career services
  - • Student services
  - • Financial services
  - • Admissions
  - • Development
- ◆ Information technology (IT)
- ◆ Public relations

Communications

The field of communications attracts lawyers not only for their legal knowledge, but also for their verbal and cognitive skills. In fact, a perusal of the biographies of famous authors will show that a significant number were or are lawyers (e.g., Leo Tolstoy and John Grisham). Many investigative reporters, news anchors and commentators are lawyers (e.g., Geraldo Rivera, Catherine Crier). The viewing public finds high-profile legal cases fascinating, and coverage through the medium of television transfixing (from Lindbergh to Simpson). Although specialized training or education may be an important credential, many lawyers get into public media positions with little or no experience. The communications field includes:

- ◆ Advertising
- ◆ Creative writing

- Journalism
- Law-related publishing
- Radio
- Television
- Film
- Web-casting and publishing
- Sports and entertainment agents
- Painting and commercial art

Other Areas

Lawyers can be found in a variety of fields, from farming to architecture. An informal anecdotal survey suggests that most of these individuals use their legal training in some way. Graduates who pursue a nonlegal path, however, must realize that there may be no return. As nonlegal skills are acquired, and as the distance from day-to-day legal practice increases, it becomes less likely or possible to match current earnings with salary levels of law graduates in their first positions. Professionally speaking, going back to law may mean going back to square one professionally. There are exceptions, but the general pattern for nonlegal careers is that the defectors from law do not return.

Substantive Practice Areas

24

No book on career planning and the law would be complete without a discussion of substantive fields of practice. As law becomes an increasingly specialized profession (as discussed previously, pages 215–218), the need to make choices about practice areas will increase. This trend also places pressure on students to make career choices at an earlier stage in their professional lives, to make academic choices that reflect their professional interests, and to eliminate other options from consideration.

Law students fall into two major groups when it comes to choosing substantive areas of practice: those who have very definite ideas about their substantive preferences and those who do not. Those who do have strong preferences often come to law school with such attitudes already formed. They want to practice environmental law, labor law, patent law, criminal law, or some other specific field. Those who are not so sure about their interests frequently rank selection of a substantive area of practice below other considerations when they make career choices. These students are often quite flexible about the areas of practice they are willing to consider. Many assume that they can make choices about substantive fields after they leave law school and enter the real world.

Most law firms do not practice in just one field and most lawyers do not limit their practice to just one area. Even lawyers who practice in a discrete specialty often are called upon to deal with other areas of law that intersect their specialty. Unlike those who choose medicine, where a podiatrist may work only with feet or a cardiologist only with hearts, lawyers do not have the luxury of such narrow definition because legal problems seldom arrive in tidy substantive boxes. A client who comes to a lawyer for a will may also bring tax problems, property questions, family law issues, and a variety of other considerations.

Even the names given to substantive practice areas can be deceiving. International law may not mean that you look out of your office window onto the Champs Elysee as much as it means practicing corporate law for multinational clients rather than domestic clients. Entertainment law may not mean hobnobbing with famous actors and actresses, but rather drafting contracts, leases, and other mundane documents.

A useful discussion of many substantive areas of law would require an entire book. The 1999 ABA book for practicing lawyers, *Changing Jobs: A Handbook for Lawyers in the New Millennium,* edited by Heidi McNeil Staudenmaier, offers detailed descriptions of a variety of substantive practice areas. Other titles in the ABA Career Series focus on many of the more popular substantive areas of practice. See also Gary A. Munneke, *Careers in Law* (VGM Professional Careers Series, 2002). Appendix C also includes a fairly extensive listing of substantive practice areas from a study by Major, Lindsey & Africa, a leading legal search firm.

The selection of substantive fields of practice is an important consideration in terms of your initial career planning and your long-term career development. Various economic surveys conducted by bar associations have demonstrated that not all practice areas are equally prestigious, lucrative, or competitive. Neither are all areas equally demanding or stressful. Your earlier work in the area of skills analysis should help you to make decisions about substantive practice areas.

Unfortunately, many students make substantive choices for the wrong reasons. Sometimes students develop an interest in an area of practice because they like the professor who taught the course in law school. Their interest is triggered by the professor's enthusiasm, knowledge, and charisma rather than the actual work involved.

Some students simply fall into an area of practice. They clerk for a lawyer after the first year of law school and work on a few bankruptcy cases over the summer. Armed with this "expertise," they sell themselves to a subsequent employer on the basis of their experience in the bankruptcy field. When they accept a permanent job, they are (surprise!) assigned bankruptcy cases. Pretty soon they are the firm's bankruptcy lawyer. The only problem is that they absolutely hate bankruptcy law.

How do you make choices about substantive practice areas without pinning yourself down? How do you establish priorities about practice areas when you have no earthly idea what lawyers actually do in those areas?

Part of the answer to these questions is that you must simply explore different possibilities. Although you may not make a decision to specialize until you have practiced for several years, or you may decide not to specialize at all, you can begin to educate yourself early in law school about various substantive options. While you are still in school, you can begin to narrow the alternatives you are willing to consider.

Substantive practice areas are often defined by other factors such as geographic location, client needs, and organization type. As you explore these other questions, you will develop insights about a variety of substantive practice areas. For instance, the course listings in your law school catalog may provide insights into substantive practice areas.

Read as much as you can about what lawyers in different substantive fields do. Talk to as many people as you can: lawyers, professors, classmates, and career service professionals. Explore different possibilities: Take the clinical courses in law school, write papers, and look for law-related jobs in areas that interest you.

The technique of conducting information interviews can be particularly helpful in aiding you to form conclusions about what sort of practice interests you. Take notes on your impressions after reading or talking with someone. Try to identify specific skills of lawyers who practice in various specialties and compare these skills to your own. Try to narrow the field of possibilities as your base of knowledge increases. Chart 18 contains a list of substantive practice areas. Go through the list, checking areas that interest you and crossing off areas that absolutely turn you off.

Continuing legal education programs and bar associations provide access to lawyers who specialize. If you attend programs and

Chart 18
Substantive Practice Areas

Key Words to Describe Practice Areas

Administrative	ERISA	Mental Health
Admiralty	Employee Benefits	Military
Antitrust	Employment	Municipal
Appellate	Energy	Oil and Gas
Arbitration	Entertainment	Patent
Aviation	Environmental	Personal Injury
Banking	Estate	Probate
Bankruptcy	Family	Product Liability
Bond	Finance	Property
Business	Food and Drug	Prosecution
Children	Fraud	Public
Civil	Gender	Public Finance
Civil Rights	Government	Real Estate
Commercial	Health	Regulated Industries
Communications	Housing	Securities
Computer	Human Rights	Tax
Constitutional	Immigration	Telecommunications
Construction	Indian	Tort
Consumer	Insurance	Toxic Tort
Contract	Intellectual Property	Trade
Corporate	International	Trademark
Creditors Rights	Juvenile	Transactional
Criminal	Labor	Trusts
Defense	Land Use	Utilities
Disability	Legal Services	Welfare
Discrimination	Legislation	White Collar Crime
Domestic	Litigation	Wills
Education	Malpractice	Women
Elderly	Medical	Zoning

Source: National Association for Law Placement

meetings, you will have ample opportunity to meet some of these practitioners, many of whom will be willing to regale you about what they do. Conducting online searches of the *Martindale-Hubbell Law Directory* (see http://www.martindale.com), or keyword searches using other search engines can unearth a wealth of useful information.

As you proceed through the career assesment and job search processes, add new fields and delete others. If possible, try to prioritize your list. This activity, over time, will help you to focus your attention without unduly restricting you.

For those of you who have already made substantive choices, here are a few suggestions:

◆ First, give some thought to your reasons for making this particular choice. As mentioned above, many students make choices of specialty for the wrong reasons. Even if you know you want to practice criminal law, it may make sense to ask yourself if this is the best choice based on what you now know about skills analysis and career planning.

◆ Second, if you do know what substantive area you want, do everything you can to develop credentials in that area. Take all the courses your law school has to offer. Write papers, gain experience, work for pay or as a volunteer, and find ways to demonstrate your commitment.

◆ Third, start now to develop a network (see Chapter 13). In one sense, making contacts along substantive lines is relatively easy. Bar associations are often divided according to substantive sections; continuing legal education (CLE) programs generally have a substantive orientation; and directories and law school courses are defined along substantive lines. Even those who choose to be general practitioners have their own section in most bar organizations.

In short, if you are looking for lawyers who practice criminal law, finding them should not be a problem. A Lexis (http://lexis-nexis.com) or Westlaw (http://www.westlaw.com) search of cases in a substantive area will allow you to identify the attorneys of record, who you can then track down.

Although chances are you will probably end up as a specialist in one or two areas of law rather than as a generalist, use the time in law school to explore various substantive areas. Keep your options open, but begin to match your particular interests and skills with the types of practice that can best use them.

It might be difficult to make decisions about substantive practice areas early in law school, particularly if you do not come to law school with a specific interest. For many people, it is simply impossible to know what they like until they try it. This suggests that experimentation may be useful during law school and the early years of practice. This is really a part of the career assessment discussed earlier in this book, but for many people this is the most problematic choice. Many lawyers just fall into their substantive practice areas, by chance or serendipity. Here are a few ways you can become more actively involved in this decision:

- Take courses that interest you in a substantive sense.
- Tell employers what areas you are thinking about—don't just wait to be assigned to work.
- Read as much as you can about different practice areas.
- Find and talk to a mentor who can give you feedback based on experience.
- Network with lawyers in substantive practice areas at bar meetings, CLE programs, and law school events.
- Turn to your past experiences and interests to gain insights into areas you might want to pursue in the future.
- Work with your career services professional or other counselor to work through ideas.
- Do not be afraid to change your mind—if one path does not seem right for you or you start something and hate it, try something else.

If you are proactive in your approach and determined to make choices that are right for you, you will not have to tell your future mentees that you went into this field of practice because it was the first case the senior partner assigned to you when you went to work at the firm.

The Future of Law Practice 25

The world of work, often referred to in law school as "the real world" (as if law school were some kind of fantasy world), is complex, varied, and frequently confusing to the job hunter. Careful preparation beforehand can do much to make the trek through the job search minefield less treacherous. The task is made more difficult by the fact that the legal landscape is always changing

The practice of law today is not like it was in 1900, or 1950, or even 1980. Think of the monumental changes that have occurred in society during your lifetime. The future of the practice of law is influenced by these changes just as other institutions are. You need to prepare yourself for the practice of law the way it will be, not the way it was when your parents' or grandparents' generations got out of school. If you are a typical twenty-seven-year-old law school graduate in 2008, and you practice law until you are seventy (not unusual for lawyers), it will be 2051 when you retire. What do you think the world and the practice of law will be like by then?

Predicting the future is hampered by the fact that we can never know for certain what the future holds. We can make educated guesses based on trends and statistical tendencies. We can formulate alternative scenarios that rest on differing assumptions about what the future holds. Anyone who has played the video game *Sim City* recalls that you can project the growth of hypothetical cities by changing assumptions about their development.

For an interesting look at the future of the legal profession, see Gary A. Munneke, *Seize the Future: Forecasting and Influencing the Future of the Legal Profession,* (ABA, 2000). A number of other futurists have written on this subject and, in a period of rapid change, speculation about the implications of change is always rampant. The remainder of this chapter looks at several trends in society that will affect the practice of law in the twenty-first century.

Demographic Change

What is true is that populations change over time. The United States, over the last quarter of the twentieth century, has undergone a number of demographic shifts. Immigrants, particularly Spanish speakers from Mexico, Central America and South America, represent a growing population. Some demographers project that Americans of European descent will represent less than half the population by the middle of the twenty-first century. The population is growing older as baby boomers move toward retirement, and resort areas of the country have experienced an influx of older citizens. Two-career and single-parent households are on the rise. Diversity in religious belief, culture, and sexual orientation, as well as ethnicity contribute to what has been called a mosaic society.

The study of population movement is an inexact science because people (unlike atomic particles) do not always act in predictable ways. We can talk about trends, but trends change. War, famine, earthquakes, storms, new inventions, and serendipity can alter the course of events and reverse population and economic trends. Although exact prediction of the future may be impossible, we can seek out the best information and make our best guesses. We can identify favorable alternative futures and work to bring them about. What we cannot do is ignore the future if we plan to be living in it.

Changes in Society

Several significant trends in society deserve special attention because they represent forces that are remaking the world we live in at a dizzying rate. Some futurists describe these events as sea changes in the basic fabric of society. They include:

- ◆ Globalization and interdependence of nations, cultures and economies
- ◆ Telecommunications and access to information
- ◆ Technology and the Internet
- ◆ Attitudes about such matters as autonomy, self-determination, freedom of expression, and privacy
- ◆ A deregulated and competitive marketplace for goods and services
- ◆ The demise of legacy, from traditional monopolies to government institutions
- ◆ Dissatisfaction with the adversarial justice system, and by extension, lawyers

The Demand for Legal Services

All these changes affect the nature of legal problems that people have, and the nature of problems influences the demand for legal services. In what fields will the biggest demand for lawyers be in the next twenty years? Where will lawyers be needed in the future? Will there be too many lawyers? Too few? Anyone entering the job market should be asking these questions.

The medical profession has a much easier time predicting future demand. Medical patients, unlike lawyers' clients, are always individuals. Consequently, it is possible to take the projected population of the country, the frequency of various physical affiliations, and even projected problem areas that may arise, and come within a reasonable estimate of the demand for medical personnel.

For lawyers, a similar estimate would begin with determining what the client mix of the future might be—individuals, small businesses, corporations, government, and others—and the kinds and qualities of legal services they will require. Then you would need to predict what legislative and judicial decisions will be made in the future. Now add into the mix the entire realm of economics. The real estate market goes sour, and suddenly property lawyers face difficult times. The economy takes a downturn, and bankruptcy lawyers do extremely well. Research and development programs by corporations are cut back, and patent lawyers are in oversupply. Such economic factors touch upon all areas of practice. Fortunately, their impact is usually for a relatively short period of time. But that very uncertainty is the reason every new lawyer should remain flexible in his or her career thinking.

It is no easier to predict how future developments will lead to increased needs for legal services. Who could have predicted in 1960 the opening up of the entirely new field of computer law? Or the demand for unbundled legal services for individuals who choose to represent themselves *pro se*? Whole new areas of practice may develop within the span of your career to offer challenges no one can now foresee.

Even new applications for old practice areas may arise. Patent law, once thought of as the backwater of legal practice, has become one of the hottest areas of practice with the technology explosion in the world.

In addition to changes in the economy and profession during your career, there may be political changes, which will have an impact on you and your goals. Many lawyers have been subjected to government hiring freezes or to a change in a political party that wiped out the positions they held.

Changes on the professional level may have substantial impact on the future demand for lawyers. Among the more likely of these are the increase in law office automation, legal assistants, ancillary business ventures by law firms, multidisciplinary practice, specialization, branch offices and multijurisdictional practice, mandatory continuing legal education, and concerns about professional competency.

Even though many changes cannot be predicted, it is essential that you monitor current events and developments in the profession throughout your career so you are not caught completely off guard. In so unpredictable a world, "adaptability" and "flexibility" become career watchwords that no young lawyer can afford to overlook.

Future Practice

Within the legal profession, the growth of really large law firms with multiple branches is redefining the nature of law firms. Assembly-line procedures and other practice management improvements, including the use of paralegals, are helping to reserve the lawyer's time for more complicated legal work.

The expansion of legal departments of corporations and the employment of more lawyers in governmental agencies are affecting the traditional attorney-client relationship. An increasing number of law graduates are choosing to work in organizations outside traditional law practice. These organizational changes are touching every important activity of the individual practitioner and the environment in which he works.

Many of these changes are fueled by forces within the profession, but lawyers respond to external pressures also. Because the profession has changed and will continue to change at a rapid rate for the foreseeable future, it is important for you to critically reflect and examine the new directions the profession is taking as well as your role within it if you expect to manage change rather than simply to react when it occurs.

Where Do I Go from Here? 26

In the play *Waiting for Godot* by Samuel Becket, the two central characters, Vladimir and Estragon, stand, sit, and sleep by the road waiting for Godot, a character who never arrives, to tell them where they should go. The audience learns that the characters must decide for themselves what they are to do or they will stand by the road forever.

It's funny but the same question they asked you in kindergarten, "What do you want to be when you grow up?" perplexes the law school senior. It may be a question you have to answer several different times during the span of your professional life. It may be an answer that always somehow eludes you.

Compounding the difficulty, the choices involve a number of different factors. These have been presented in the course of this book in different ways. Essentially, however, career assessment and the job search implicate considerations involving eight distinct but overlapping concerns. These are:

- ◆ Legal skills
- ◆ Professional values

- ◆ Type of position
- ◆ Type of organization
- ◆ Substantive specialty
- ◆ Type of services rendered
- ◆ Geographic location
- ◆ Personal lifestyle

These themes have been intertwined throughout the pages of this book. The interplay of these variables offers infinite variety to the legal professional and provides constant challenges in the process of career engineering. This interconnected paradigm might be visualized as shown in Chart 19, below:

Chart 19
The Choices You Make

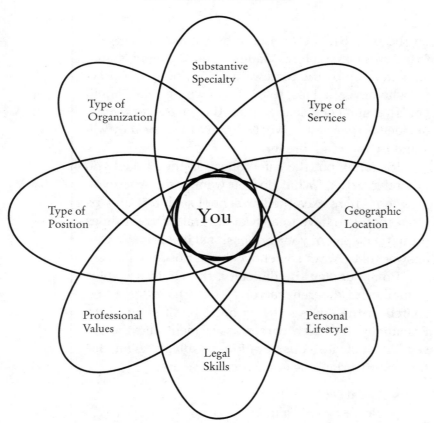

But choices present their own issues. How do we know when we are making the right choice? Will our choice make us happy? If there has been one central theme in this book, it is that most of us can do a better job of making decisions about our lives. We may not be able to eliminate the risk of making a bad choice, but we can reduce it. And while we may not be able to guarantee our future happiness, we can improve our chances of finding it.

If we accept the premise that the career choice process is inherent, complex, and ongoing, it follows that career development should become a permanent aspect of our growth as professionals.

For you, just starting your legal career, you can expect to proceed through a series of different positions as you build your skills, competitiveness, contacts, and effectiveness as a lawyer. You should be better this year then last, and better next year than this. And as long as your career evolves, you will be making choices about what to do next.

Appendix A
CAREER RESOURCES GUIDE

This resource guide is intended to give you a window into a vast array of information on legal careers, including both electronic and print media. This is not a bibliography because it does not attempt to collect in one place everything that has been written on the subject of legal careers. In fact, hardly any of the resources described is over five years old as of the publication date of this book. The more dated titles have been included because the authors believe the material retains its currency and usefulness. Many of the resources are drawn from the Internet, which is where law students today go to do their research, although print resources in the form of books, directories, and a few articles are included as well. Print resources are often available in law school libraries, career libraries, and book stores. Hopefully, this Resource Guide will help jumpstart your search. The organization eschews traditional order, alphabetized by author, title, or topic. This is because many of the resources defy placement into a particular box. The listings are more impressionistic, based on the authors' experience working with students. The authors have annotated many of the entries, however, to let you know why they were included and what you can learn from that source.

ONLINE RESOURCES

The Internet has a seemingly infinite amount of information on legal employers and career advice. These are some of the most popular Web sites for legal career information, but the list is not intended to be exhaustive. You should use it in your job search. It can also be used as a networking tool through chat groups and e-mail. The following Web sites may be useful to you in your job search:

Findlaw
This is an online database that allows you to browse legal information as well as lawyers. It is available at www.findlaw.com. In addition, you can browse job listings at www.careers@findlaw.com (includes the Greedy Associates message boards)

Rollonfriday
This Web site provides up-to-date insight on the legal profession. You can get news and information on law firms as well as current job openings. Go to www.rollonfriday.com.

Law.com
Law.com is an extensive database that provides legal news and information through a variety of online publications and information Web sites. This information is available at www.law.com.

American Bar Association
This is the official career resources Web site for the American Bar Association, which gives you access to a variety of legal resources as well as information regarding the law industry, continuing legal education, and law careers. Go to www.abanet.org/careercounsel.

New York Lawyer
New York Lawyer is a news site that gives you current information on what is happening in the law industry as well as current job openings. You can sign up for free at www.nylawyer.com.

New York State Bar Association
This is the official site of legal information for New York State. Here you can access current legal information in the law industry, obtain legal resources, browse through lists of lawyers, as well as career information and job openings. Go to www.nysba.org (click on For Attorneys, then Career Center).

Monster
An online directory of job listings is available at www.monster.com.

Hotjobs
This is another online source for job listings. Go to http://hotjobs.yahoo.com.

Vault Reports
This Web site is a career center, allowing you to research companies and industries, browse through current job listings, and also gives you job advice. Go to www.vaultreports.com. (Questionable science, but worth viewing.)

Craigslist

Go to www.craigslist.com for a list of job openings, housing listings, and other resources that would be helpful in searching for employment nationwide.

Lexis

LEXIS offers online directories and corporate annual reports for domestic and international firms. It is available at www.lexis.com.

Law Periscope

This site provides information about practice areas, clients, and diversity, and much more for the 300 largest U.S. law firms. Go to www.lawperiscope.com.

Martindale Online

This is the online version of The Martindale-Hubble Law Directory, a huge directory of lawyers and law firms, both domestic and foreign, organized into 20 volumes by region, that can be accessed free of charge at www.martindale.com. Here you may search by practice area, region, firm size, and many other criteria.

NALP Online

This online resource is useful for creating lists of legal employers based on criteria such as size and practice area. Go to www.nalp.org.

Vault Online

This is the online version of the Vault Directories in which you can obtain information on law firms in different geographic areas and practices. Go to www.vault.com.

Hoover's Online

This is the free online version of Hoover's Directories that contain comprehensive information, including contact names, for large corporations. Go to http://www.hoovers.com/free/.

Westlaw Directory

Westlaw is an online database that offers direct access to a vast range of legal information. To access the Westlaw Directory, go to www .westlaw.com and you can search a variety of legal databases. When you are unsure about which database to use, browse the Westlaw

Directory, which lists the databases and services available on Westlaw. Click Directory at the top of any westlaw.com@ page to access the Westlaw Directory. To browse the directory, click the hypertext links. Click a database name in the right frame to access a database. To access information about a database, including a description of the database, current coverage information, search tips, and available fields, click the Scope icon (1) next to the database name.

Jobs in Government
An online directory of government jobs can be found at www.jobsin government.com.

More Government Jobs
You can search for public sector jobs at www.govtjobs.com.

Courts.net
Another helpful Web site is www.courts.net. It contains links to a number of federal and state courts. Clerkship information is also available online through Lexis and Westlaw.

The National and Federal Legal Employment Report
This monthly bulletin includes current legal vacancies with the federal government and provides brief descriptions, application procedures, and deadlines. This publication is available online through Westlaw at www.attorneyjobsonline.com. Go to: http:// lawschool.Westlaw.com and click onto West Group Career Services/AttorneyJobsOnline to find job listings. Your Westlaw password is necessary to access the site.

Federal Law Clerk Information System (OSCAR)
This Web site provides a searchable database of federal clerkship opportunities, enabling visitors to create a list of judges and determine for each if a clerkship is available and, if so, the hiring schedule and application requirements. The Web site is: www.uscourts .gov. Click on the Employment button. You may also access this database via www.judicialclerkships.com, a Web site created and maintained by Professor Debra Strauss of Columbia Law School.

The Federal Judiciary Homepage
This Web site can be found at: www.uscourts.gov. It provides information of the federal judiciary, employment opportunities, and links to the Web sites of individual federal courts.

The Comprehensive Fellowship Guide, 2008–2009, The Public Service Law Network Worldwide

This resource provides lists of fellowships and information relevant to the fellowship, including application deadlines, descriptions, compensation, etc. It also contains a Fellowship Opportunity Practice Area Index, sponsoring organization indexes, and geographical indexes. Access to this information can be obtained through the Internet at www.pslawnet.org.

PSLawNet

The Public Service Law Network Worldwide helps law students and law graduates nationwide find public service opportunities with public interest organizations, government agencies, judges, and private firms with public interest or significant *pro bono* practices. The Web site is www.pslawnet.org. It is also hyperlinked to the Center's Web site, under "Internet Resources."

The Chronicle of Higher Education

For law schools and college/university teaching positions, the online version of *The Chronicle of Higher Education*, a weekly newspaper for the academic community, lists a variety of positions available. Job postings may be obtained at http://chronicle.com/jobs. Listings for these positions may also be found in The Jurist at www.jurist.law.pitt.edu.

2008 National Directory of Prosecuting Attorneys, Annual, National District Attorney's Association

This directory lists all district attorney offices nationally. You will find that many states have published their own directories. Check with the various cities and states that you have an interest in to find out if they have directories available. The information contained in this directory is also available online at www.ndaa.org (click on Publications), through the Web sites for the individual prosecutor's offices. (Click on "links" on the site map to access the Web sites of the prosecutors' offices.)

Environmental Law Guide, 2008 Yale Law School

The guide provides an overview of environmental law and the types of opportunities that exist in nonprofit and governmental organizations. It contains additional helpful information, including lists of environmental fellowships and electronic resources. This resource can be found online at the Yale Law School Web site: www.law.yale.edu/studentlife/CDOguides.asp.

International Career Employment Weekly, Carlyle Corporation
This weekly publication describes itself as the only comprehensive source of information on international career positions. This publication can also be accessed at www.internationaljobs.org.

International Public Interest Law 2007–2008 Yale Law School
Get information regarding internships, fellowships, and resource information about careers in international public interest law at www.law.yale.edu/studentlife/CDOguides.asp.

The Nontraditional Legal Careers Report
This report is now available online at www.nontradlegal.com. It contains job postings for a variety of nontraditional legal positions, including bar association positions, business positions, positions with judiciary, education positions, government positions, law library positions, legal publishing positions, policy/legislative positions, public interest positions, and international positions. It is published online by the University of Iowa College of Law.

Gay Workplace Issues Homepage
This is a comprehensive Web site filled with information on many workplace topics, such as professional groups, company policies, e-mail listserv lists and usernet groups, gay workplace chat forums, and links to other entities. Also included are links to directories of companies that provide domestic partner benefits and gay friendly companies. Go to www.gaywork.com.

LAW RELATED BLOGS (BLAWGS)

Resource list additions: As Blogs change frequently and are dependent upon the Moderator, changes in the number, scope, and focus of Blogs can change without notice.

LawSites
A listing of new legal blogs of interest to those who wish to track trends in the profession. Robert Ambrogi, Moderator. http://www .legaline.com/lawsites.html

Legal Blog Watch
Listing blogs and new commentary posted by bloggers on Law.com. Robert Ambrogi, Moderator. http://legalblogwatch.typepad.com/

Above the Law
A blog that provides advice and commentary on issues of interest to the profession. Focus is on large corporate law firms, corporate structure, compensation, and personnel changes. http://www .abovethelaw.com/

MyShingle
Advice for solos just starting or managing a firm. Carolyn Elefant, Moderator. http://www.myshingle.com/

Silicon Valley Media Law Blog
Commentary and interaction about media and technology law. Cathy Kirkman, Moderator. http://www.svmedialaw.com/content -california-enacts-violent-video-game-legislation.html

Adam Smith, Esq.
Covers the economics of law firms. Bruce MacEwen, Moderator. http://www.adamsmithesq.com/blog/

The Common Scold
Commentary on the profession with a focus on technology. Monica Bay, Moderator. http://commonscold.typepad.com/

Insurance Scrawl
Commentary focused on insurance disputes. Marc Mayerson, Moderator. http://insurancescrawl.com/

InhouseBlog
Advice and commentary directed at in-house attorneys by Geoffrey Gussis. http://www.inhouseblog.com/

Blawg Review
A review of law-related articles from around the world, guest-moderated weekly and hosted by attorneys, law students, and law professors. Anonymous Editor. http://blawgreview.blogspot.com/

LawMarketing Blog
Directed at law firm marketing and strategic planning. Larry Bodine, Moderator. http://blog.larrybodine.com/

May It Please the Court
A blog that includes commentary and observations on "law and legal news" author of "May It Please the Court" by J. Craig Williams. http://www.mayitpleasethecourt.com/journal.asp?

The BLT: Blog of the Legal Times
Washington, D.C. legal news. http://legaltimes.typepad.com/

On Point "A New Take on Legal News"
http://www.onpointnews.com/

Law Blog
Blog from the *Wall Street Journal*. http://blogs.wsj.com/law/

SCOTUSblog
Covers Supreme Court news. http://www.scotusblog.com/wp/

China Law Blog
Discusses being an American in China. http://www.chinalawblog.com/

ABA Site-tation
Covers new technology and resources. http://meetings.abanet.org/ltrc/index.cfm

Build a Solo Practice
Advice about practicing independently. http://www.susancartierliebel.typepad.com/

Jim Calloway's Law Practice Tips
Identifies new legal blogs and comments on news articles. http://jimcalloway.typepad.com/

JD Bliss Blog
Legal career trends and discussion of career satisfaction. http://www.jdblissblog.com/

Ms JD
Work-life balance discussion. http://ms-jd.org/

DIRECTORIES

GENERAL

Martindale-Hubbell Law Directory
The Martindale-Hubble Law Directory is a huge directory of lawyers and law firms, both domestic and foreign, organized into twenty volumes by region. This information is also available free of charge at www.martindale.com, where you may search by practice area, region, firm size, and many other criteria.

National Directory of Legal Employers, 2008–2009. *National Association of Law Placement.*
This directory, which is published annually, contains one-page résumés and NALP survey forms of employers who are members of the Association. The Directory includes detailed information on more than 1,200 employers of all types: private firms, government agencies, public interest employers, and corporations. Data on practice areas, hiring needs, training programs, *pro bono* policies, salaries and benefits, and more are presented for each employer. This directory may also be accessed at www.nalpdirectory.com.

Vault Directories:
These guides provide information about leading firms in different geographic and practice areas.
- *Vault Reports Guide to the Top 100 Law Firms*
- *Vault Guide to Top New York Law Firms*
- *Vault Guide to Top Boston & Northeast Law Firms*
- *Vault Guide to Top Washington DC Law Firms*
- *Vault Guide to Top London Law Firms*
- *Vault Guide to Top Texas Law Firms*
- *Vault Guide to Southern California Law Firms*
- *Vault Guide to Northern California Law Firms*
- *Vault Guide to Top Governmental and Nonprofit Legal Employers*
- *Vault Guide to Law Firm's Pro Bono Programs*
- *Vault Guide to Law Firm's Diversity Programs*

- *Vault Guide to Litigation Law Careers*
- *Q & A With Legal Women Leaders*

*See Web sites for online version of Vault

Yellow Books

Each Yellow Book contains contact information for the management of leading firms and companies in the area specified. The entire Yellow Book database is also available online.

- *Associations Yellow Book*
- *Congressional Yellow Book*
- *Corporate Yellow Book*
- *Federal Yellow Book*
- *Federal Regional Yellow Book*
- *Financial Yellow Book*
- *Foreign Representatives Yellow Book*
- *Government Affairs Yellow Book*
- *Judicial Yellow Book*
- *Law Firms Yellow Book*
- *Municipal Yellow Book*
- *News Media Yellow Book*
- *Nonprofit Sector Yellow Book*
- *State Yellow Book*

ACADEMIC

ABA-LSAC Official Guide to ABA-Approved Law Schools. *Annual, Produced by the Law School Admission Council and the American Bar Association.*
Contains a description of each ABA approved law school with a geographic guide to law schools by region.

Directory of Law Teachers. *Annual, Association of American Law Schools.*
A directory that includes biographical information on each law professor and a listing of administrative staff.

NALP Directory of Law Schools. *Annual, National Association for Law Placement.*

A description of United States and Canadian law schools that are NALP Members.

2007–2008 NALP Directory of Law Schools. *Annual, National Association for Law Placement.*
A description of U.S. Law Schools and information on Canadian law schools that are NALP members.

National Directory of Graduate Law Degree Programs. *Hermann, R.L., Linda P. Sutherland, and Jennifer L. Cox, eds. Federal Reports, Inc., 1993 (Most recent edition).*
This resource offers explanations of a broad range of graduate law programs offered by U.S. law schools.

BUSINESS

America's Leading Lawyers for Business 2006: The Client's Guide. *Chambers and Partners, 2006.*

Directory of Corporate Counsel, Vols. 1 & 2. *Aspen Publishers, 2008–2009.*
As the name states, this directory list the names of lawyers who work for corporate counsel offices, and provides biographical information on them, sort of a corporate Martindale. For those interested in corporations, this may be an easier way to approach locating contacts than sifting through more general directories, such as Martindale or state legal directories.

Hoover's Directories
These directories contain comprehensive information, including contact names, for large corporations. Basic information is searchable for free at http://www.hoovers.com/free/

- *Hoover's Handbook of Private Companies: Profiles of Major US Private Enterprises*
- *Hoover's Handbook of American Business: Profile of 750 Major US Companies*
- *Hoover's Handbook of World Business: Profiles of Major Global Enterprises*
- *Hoover's Handbook of Emerging Companies: Profile of America's Most Exciting Growth Enterprises*

The New York Law Journal 2007 Directory of Corporate Counsel for New York, *NYLJ, 2007.*
An alphabetical list of New York in-house attorneys within their corporations.

The World's Leading Lawyers for Business 2008–2009: The Client's Guide. *Chambers and Partners, 2008.*
Through interviews and "hands on" research, Chambers and Partners have compiled a guide of the world's top lawyers. This guide book includes law firms in the following areas of the world: the UK, Asia, Latin America, U.S.A., and Europe. Each listing includes a firm overview, main areas of practice and the number of partners and lawyers worldwide.

Directory of Venture Capital and Private Equity Firms. *Grey House Publishing, 2008.*
This directory contains important information on the Venture Capital industry. It offers the most extensive contact information on domestic and international venture capital and private equity firms.

The Legal Intelligencer's 2008 Law Firm Directory for Pennsylvania, Delaware, and South and Central New Jersey. *ALM, 2008.*
A directory of law firms in the central mid-Atlantic, including the corporate mecca of Delaware.

GOVERNMENT

City and County Attorney Internship Book. *Career Education Institutes, 2004 (most recent edition).*
This book gives detailed information on internships offered at the city and county levels.

Congressional Staff Directory. *CQ Staff Directories, Inc., 2008.*
Congressional Staff Directory has in-depth information on Congress members, committees, and districts. You could also subscribe to it online at www.csd.cq.com.

Directory of Legal Aid and Defender Offices in the United States and Territories, *2007–2008.*
Published annually, this comprehensive guide is useful in identifying civil legal services and legal aid offices. It also breaks down the organizations by specialty area.

Federal Staff Directory, spring 2008. *CQ Staff Directories, Inc., 2008.*
The Federal Staff Directory provides in-depth information regarding all positions within the executive branch of the United States government, such as the Executive Office of the President, Cabinet departments, and agencies. You could also subscribe online at www.cqpress.com.

International Information Directory, 2007–2008. *CQ Staff Directories, Inc., 2007 online edition.*
This reference provides you with the most current international information. Arranged by subject or individual country, this source offers information on U.S. government agency jobs as well as jobs with international organizations. Subscribe online at www.cqpress.com.

Directory of Legal Aid and Defender Offices in the United States and Territories, 2007–2008.
Published annually, this comprehensive guide is useful in identifying civil legal services and legal aid offices. It also breaks down the organizations by specialty area.

2007 National Directory of Prosecuting Attorneys, *Annual, National District Attorney's Association.*
This directory lists all district attorney offices nationally. You will find that many states have published their own directories. Check with the various cities and states that you have an interest in to find out if they have directories available. The information contained in this directory is also available online at www.ndaa-apri
.org, through the Web sites for the individual prosecutor's offices. (Click on "links" on the site map to access the Web sites of the prosecutors' offices.)

U.S. Government Manual. Federal Government, *Annual.*
This manual provides current descriptions on all agencies and departments within the three branches of the United States government as well as quasi-official agencies, international organizations, boards, commissions, and committees. It is published annually and can also be found at www.gpoaccess.gov.

Directory of National Environmental Organizations, *U.S. Environmental Directories.*
Over 775 non-governmental organizations are listed and described in alphabetical order in this directory.

Directory of Environmental Attorneys, *Aspen Law & Business.*
This directory includes information "on more than 9,265 attorneys engaged in the practice of environmental law and 4,494 law firms, companies and regulatory agencies with which the attorneys are affiliated."

Environmental Law Careers Directory, 2007–2008, *Ecology Law Quarterly.*
This directory lists more than 250 public interest organizations, private law firms, and government offices to assist law students in conducting a job search in the area of environmental law.

Environmental Law Institute Associates Directory, *Environmental Law Institute, 2001.*
The ELI Associates program is the "primary avenue for individual professionals to be involved with the Environmental Law Institute, an internationally respected center for education and research on environmental law and policy. This book is a listing of the domestic and international ELI Associates.

U.S. Environmental Protection Agency Headquarters Telephone Directory, *2008 online edition.*
A listing of EPA employees, arranged alphabetically, and regionally, by organization and by subject. It also includes organizational charts.

Conservation Directory, *National Wildlife Federation, Annual.*
This directory is a listing of organizations, agencies, and officials concerned with natural resource use and management.

JUDICIARY

(Please reference Judicial Clerkship Application section of this Resource Guide for further information on the judiciary and job opportunities in the court system, pages 321–323.)

Almanac of the Federal Judiciary, *Aspen Law & Business, 2008.*
This directory, which is published annually, contains profiles and evaluations of all Judges of the U.S. District Courts. Please note that this directory is available online at Westlaw.

The American Bench, *2008.*
This resource contains detailed biographical data on about federal judges.

BNA's Directory of State and Federal Courts, Judges and Clerks, *Bureau of National Affairs, 2008.*
"A compilation of information about the courts of record in the federal court system, the fifty states, the District of Columbia, American Samoa, Guam, the Northern Mariana Islands, Puerto Rico, and the Virgin Islands."

Federal Bar Council: Second Circuit Redbook, 2003–2004, *Federal Bar Council.*
This handbook provides detailed information (i.e., biographies of district and magistrate judges; local rules of court) on personnel and procedures in the United States Courts in the Second Judicial District.

The Judicial Staff Directory. *Congressional Quarterly, 2007.*
This directory provides a list of judges and staff within the U.S. judicial system.

The Directory of Minority Judges of the United States, *3rd Edition, American Bar Association, 2001.*
This book has been largely utilized by those seeking judicial clerkships with judges of color.

U.S. Court of Federal Claims: A Deskbook for Practitioners, *Fifth Edition, 2007.*
This book provides an overview of the Court of Federal Claims, including its history, composition, and jurisdiction.

Vermont Law School Guide to State Judicial Clerkship Procedures, *Vermont Law School, 2008.*
This guide considers itself a necessary tool for law students considering state judicial clerkships. Information on judicial clerkships in each state is provided.

Want's Federal-State Court Directory. *Want, Annual.*
These Directories provide "quick and easy access to the nation's federal and state and county courts plus federal and state enforcement officials." In addition, a guide explains how the different judicial systems operate. In addition, Want's publishes Your Nation's Courts Online (www.courts.com).

PRIVATE PRACTICE

Martindale-Hubbell Law Directory
Martindale-Hubbell is available online at www.martindale.com, which will allow you to create a customized search for employers based on many variables, including law firm size, area(s) of practice, academic backgrounds, and geographic location, among others. You may also use Lexis or Westlaw to tailor your search for your specific job search needs by entering the Martindale-Hubbell database. Martindale also comes in a print form carried by most law school libraries.

National Directory of Legal Employers, 2008–2009, *National Association of Law Placement*
This directory, which is published annually, contains one-page resumes and NALP survey forms of employers who are members of the Association. The Directory includes detailed information on more than 1200 employers of all types: private firms, government agencies, public interest employers, and corporations. Data on practice areas, hiring needs, training programs, pro bono policies, salaries and benefits, and more are presented for each employer This directory may also be accessed via the Internet at www .nalpdirectory.com.

The New York Law Journal 2007 Directory of Corporate Counsel for New York, *NYLJ, 2007.*
An alphabetical list of New York in-house attorneys within their corporations.

Asia Law Profiles 2007: The Definitive Guide to Asia's Leading Law Firms. *Euromoney Publications, 2007.*
Asialaw Profiles 2007 is a detailed reference guide of International law firms and provides editorial insight to the global legal markets.

Canadian Law List. *Canada Law Books Inc., Annual.*
Canadian Law List is a directory of Canadian judges, firms, barristers, solicitors, notaries, corporate counsels, firms, and companies.

Latin Lawyer: A Who's Who of Latin America Law Firms. *Law Business Research, 2003 (most recent edition).*

Directory of American Firms Operating in Foreign Countries, vols. 1–3. *Uniworld Business Publications, Inc., 2007.*
This is a comprehensive directory listing the contact information for more than 3,000 U.S. law firms that operate in foreign countries. It is arranged into two sections, listed by either the firm name or foreign country, alphabetically.

Directory of Foreign Firms Operating in the United States. *Uniworld Business Publications, Inc., 2008.*
This directory lists the foreign countries doing business in the United States, as well as their American affiliates.

Guide to Foreign Law Firms, 4th Edition. *Ed. Silkenat, James R. and William M. Hannay. ABA, 2005.*
This guide, published by the American Bar Association, is a comprehensive list of foreign law firms and their contact information.

Directory of Intellectual Property Attorneys, *Aspen Law & Business, 1995.*
This directory includes information on 12,000 attorneys and patent agents in nearly 4,900 firms and organizations. It includes attorneys whose practice involves copyright, patent, trade secrets, trademark, and/or unfair trade practices.

National Directory of Black Law Firms, *Marshall Williams and Gilbert Ware, 1988.*
A state-by-state listing of law firms and lawyers as well as several related chapters of advice. Also consult the *Minority Law Journal* (www.minoritylawjournal.com) National Directory of Minority Attorneys 2007.

The National Directory of Women Owned Law Firms and Women Lawyers, *National Association of Women Lawyers, 2007.*
Published by the NAWL, this directory is published annually and provides updated contact information for women lawyers and women owned law firms throughout the United States. You can find out more information about women lawyers and women-owned law firms at the National Association of Women Lawyers (NAWL) Web site www.abanet.org/NAWL.

JOB SEARCH SKILLS AND ADVICE PUBLICATIONS

America's Greatest Places to Work with a Law Degree. *Walton, Kimm Alayne. Harcourt Brace, 1999 (most recent edition).*
This book explores the best places to work with a law degree.

The American Grant and Loans Book, *Canada Books, 2007.*
This publication contains valuable information with more than 1,500 financial programs, subsidies, scholarships, grants, and loans offered by the United States federal government. It also includes over 700 financing programs put forth by various foundations and associations across the United States. Business, students, individuals, municipalities, government departments, institutions, foundations, and associations will find a wealth of information that will help them with their new ventures or existing projects.

Associate Salary Survey, 2007. *National Association for Law Placement, 2007.*
NALP's annual associate survey which includes associate salaries by years of experience for a wide range of geographic areas, salary ranges for associates through the eighth year, summer associate salaries by geographic location and year of law school, and comparisons of law firm compensation and bonus structures.

Before You Hit Send: Guidelines for Using Email Effectively for Job Search-Related Correspondence. *Katie Schendel, National Association for Law Placement, 2005.*
This brochure provides cautionary tips useful in creating positive and professional impression with potential employers.

Being an Effective Mentor: 101 Practical Strategies for Success. *National Association for Law Placement, 2006.*
The companion brochure to the publication *Working with a Mentor* described below, this brochure presents practical steps and tips on the mentoring process from the mentor's perspective.

Working with a Mentor: 50 Practical Suggestions for Success. *National Association for Law Placement, 2006.*
This brochure provides "simple, practical points that can help you work effectively with your mentors . . . and to help you take advantage of mentoring opportunities that present themselves everyday."

Being a Lawyer: Individual Choice and Responsibility in the Practice of Law. *Lesnick, Howard. West Publishing Company, 1992 (most recent edition).*
This book explores many issues and feelings, both professionally and personally, that lawyers face when practicing law.

Beyond L.A. Law: Breaking the Traditional "Lawyer" Mold. *Smith, Janet. Harcourt Brace, 1998 (most recent edition).*
This book gives you insight into the lives of people who have broken the traditional lawyer mold. Through stories from individuals about their unique path toward becoming a lawyer, you will pick up career tips that will help you succeed in your law career.

Career Opportunities in the Law and Legal Industry. *Echaore-McDavid, Susan. Facts on File Inc., 2007 (most recent edition).*
This book profiles all career opportunities within the law and legal industry with the most current and comprehensive information.

Career Change: Everything You Need to Know to Meet New Challenges and Take Control of Your Career. *Helfand, Dr. David P. Contemporary Publishing Group, 1995 (most recent edition).*
This handbook provides realistic advice for overcoming the difficulties of changing careers.

Careers in Law. *Munneke, Gary. McGraw-Hill, 2003 (most recent edition).*
This guide explores the world of law and the different careers available in the legal industry.

Changing Jobs: A Handbook for Lawyers in the New Millennium, 3rd Edition. *Staudenmaier, Heidi McNeil, ed., ABA, 1999.*
This manual is specifically geared for young lawyers who have been working for a couple of years and are in their first or second legal job. Section II of the book "covers all aspects of career planning for lawyers." Section III covers the job search process, "taking into consideration the factors that are unique to the legal profession." Section IV "provides detailed analyses of employment opportunities for experienced lawyers within various public and private sector practice settings." There are chapters that discuss specific topics, such as large law firms; small law firms; corporations; federal government; the judiciary; Legal Aid; Legal Services; and public interest organizations.

The Complete Guide to Contract Lawyering: What Every Lawyer and Law Firm Needs to Know about Temporary Legal Services. *Deborah Arron and Deborah Guyol, 2004.*

Increasingly, firms are hiring more attorneys on a temporary or contract basis. This book provides an overview of the world of contract work taken from real experiences. Contract lawyering can be useful in getting experience and as an assessment tool during a job search.

The Complete Job Search Handbook, *3rd Edition, Howard Figler, Henry Holt Books, 1999.*

In this book, the author outlines a comprehensive model of career skills. It "spells out every skill you need to conduct a successful career search."

How to Work a Room, *Susan Roane, Harper Collins Publishers, Inc., 2007.*

This book is the ultimate guide to savvy socializing in person and online.

Full Disclosure: The New Lawyer's Must-Read Career Guide. *Carey, Christen Civiletto, Esq. ALM Publishers, 2001 (most recent edition).*

This helpful guide is full of advice from legal professionals that will help you with your career search. The book also contains contact information for law firms.

It's Who You Know: Magic of Networking. *Chin-Lee, Cynthia. Book Partners, Inc. 1998 (most recent edition).*

An older title, this book still contains much useful timeless information.

Legal Ethics in a Nutshell. *Rotunda, Ronald D. West Group, 2007.*

This book describes the ABA Model Rules of Professional Conduct, while helping the reader understand the problems of legal ethics.

The Job Hunting Handbook, 2008–2009 Edition. *Dahlstrom, Harry. Dahlstrom & Co., 2006 (most recent edition).*

This book contains the skills that help any lawyer with their job search.

Jobs for Lawyers: Effective Techniques for Getting Hired in Today's Legal Marketplace. *Mantis, Hillary Jane and Kathleen Brady. Impact Publications, 1996 (most recent edition).*

Legal Interviewing and Counseling in a Nutshell. *Shaffner, Thomas. West Group, 2005.*
This book drives the point that counseling is an important resource for lawyers.

Legal Negotiation in a Nutshell. *Teply, Larry L. West Group, 2005.*
This book is everything you need to know about negotiating.

Objection Overruled: Overcoming Obstacles in the Lawyer Job Search, *Morris, Kathy. ABA, 2000.*
This practical manual discusses obstacles specific to attorneys in the job search process. It identifies ten major obstacles to effective searches and attempts to address them with specific advice and techniques for self-assessment, developing a plan and implementing a successful search.

Parting Company: How to Survive the Loss of a Job and Find Another Successfully. *Morin, William J. and James C. Cabrea. Harcourt Brace, 2000 (most recent edition).*
This book helps to deal with being fired and guides you on how to find a new job.

The Legal Career Guru's Guide to the Perfect Résumé, *J. Murray Elwood, 2000.*
Written by a lawyer who has been an editor for a legal publisher, a career "coach" and consultant, this publication offers numerous tips on how to write legal sections that address different scenarios such as résumés for partners versus associates, résumés for in-house counsel, those appropriate for different practice areas, electronic résumés, and much more.

Schmoozing: Insider Advice on Making Contacts and Building Rapport. *Vault Reports, 2002 (most recent edition).*
This "how to" book gives you basic advice on how to boost your career through making contacts, building rapport, and "schmoozing."

Should You Really Be a Lawyer: The Guide to Smart Career Choices Before, During and After Law School. *Schneider, Deborah and Gary Belsky. Decision Books, 2005.*
This book explores the question of whether a legal profession is the right path for you, and how to find a career that suits you, ultimately leading you to become a better decision maker.

Starting Off in a New Direction: Job Search Strategies for Second-Career Lawyers. *National Association for Law Placement, 2003.*
This brochure addresses the special advantages, perspectives, and challenges that second-career lawyers face.

Sweaty Palms: The Neglected Art of Being Interviewed. *H. Anthony Medley, 2005.*
"The tips and strategies in this book come from the author's experiences in counseling job hunters and employers." Topics covered include preparation for the interview, presentation, (dressing tips, small talk), and negotiation (what to do after you get a job offer). There is a checklist at the end of each chapter that recaps important points that are worth reviewing.

The 110 Biggest Mistakes Job Hunters Make (and How to Avoid Them). *Hermann, Richard and Linda Sutherland. Federal Reports, Inc., 1994 (most recent edition).*

The Vault Guide to the Case Interview. *Asher, Mark. Vault, 2008.*
This guide is compiled with information needed to prepare you for your case interview.

The Vault Guide to Finance Interviews. *Bhatawedekhar, D. Vault, 2008.*
Learn everything you need to know for your finance interview with this helpful guide.

What Law School Doesn't Teach You, But You Really Need to Know. *Walton, Kimm Alayne. Harcourt Press, 2000 (most recent edition).*
Job-hunting techniques and tactics for law students and those already practicing law, as well as some discussion of what makes a good lawyer.

You Can Pass Any Bar Exam. *Handy, Edna Wells. Practicing Law Institute, 1997 (most recent edition).*
This handbook provides you with the advice and guidance to help you pass any bar exam.

SPECIALIZED PRACTICE AREAS

The Official Guide to Legal Specialties. *Lisa Abrams, National Association for Law Placement, 2000.*
This publication offers a comprehensive look at 30 practice specialty areas. "Incorporating interviews with 130 attorneys from pri-

vate law firms of all sizes, solo practitioners, public interest organizations, and government agencies . . . (this book) is the definitive resource for pre-law students, current law students and practicing attorneys." In this book, she explores the leadership gap between men and women and introduces strategies that women are using to claim their place and rise to the top.

Careers in Admiralty and Maritime Law. *Jarvis, Robert M. ABA, 1993 (most recent edition).*
This book explores employment options and career characteristics of practicing maritime law, as well as gives advice to students and mentions future trends.

Careers in Civil Litigation. *Bay, Monica. ABA, 1990 (most recent edition).*
Although this is an old book, it provides a comprehensive look at a field of law that many law graduates enter, and although the practice has changed since 1990, it remains a good overview.

Bankruptcy Law Careers. *Stuhl, Seth. Vault, 2003 (most recent edition).*
This book explores Bankruptcy law careers and provides you with what you need to know to be successful in this area of law.

Family Law Careers. *Vlajic, Sara. ABA, 1998 (most recent edition).*
This book provides insight to the area of family law.

The Harvard Business School Career Guide: Finance. *Duncan, Ronald J. and William E. Quigley. Harvard Business School, 2002 (most recent edition).*
This book provides you with all the information you need for a career in finance.

The Harvard Business School Career Guide: Management Consulting. *Miller, Alex R., Ed. Harvard Business School, 2002 (most recent edition).*
This book provides insight into the consulting industry and gives advice to help with your job search in the consulting industry.

The Vault Career Guide to Consulting. *Shafrir, Doree, Maggie Geiger, and Hannah Im. Vault, 2008.*
This handbook is a good resource for anyone interested in a career in consulting.

Careers in Sports Law. *Shropshire, K.L. ABA, 1990 (most recent edition).*
This book explores the legal careers available in sports.

Entertainment Law Careers. *Henslee, William. ABA, 1998 (most recent edition).*

How to Build and Manage an Entertainment Law Practice. *Greenberg, Gary. ABA, 2001 (most recent edition).*
This book guides you in starting and maintaining a practice in entertainment law, as well as discusses how entertainment law is different from other practice areas.

The Sports Internship Book. *Career Education Institute, 2007.*
This book lists the internships available in the sports industry.

Patent Agent's Exam. *Patbar.com, 2008.*
This manual contains information regarding all aspects of the Patent Bar Exam including registration requirements.

PLI Patent Bar and Law School Resource Guide *Practicing Law Institute's Bar Review Course explained*

INTERNATIONAL LAW

The ABA Guide to International Business Negotiations. *Silkenat, James R. and Jeffrey M. Aresty. ABA, 2000 (most recent edition).*
This book explores the world of international business and provides you with answers to many issues you will face in this area.

Careers in International Law, Second Edition, *Edited by Mark W. Janis and Salli Swartz, American Ban Association, 2008.*
Legal practitioners discuss the profession of international law and the variety of career opportunities available in both the private and public sectors. The Appendix features Internet resources for jobseekers in international law.

ILSA Guide to Education and Career Development in International Law. *Green, Jonathan Clark, Denise M. Hodge and Robert F. Kemp, eds. International Law Students Association, 1991 (most recent edition).*

International Opportunities Resource Guide. *NALP, 1999 (most recent edition).*
This book introduces you to the world of international law practice and provides you with information that will help you have a career in this industry.

International Trade in Legal Services. *Little Brown & Company, 1996 (most recent edition).*

Internships in International Affairs. *Career Education Institute, 2006 (most recent edition).*
This book lists internships available in international affairs.

Lawyer's Register International by Specialties, Vols. 1 & 2. *Lawyer's Register Publishing Co., 2006.*

DIVERSITY ISSUES

Career and Life Planning with Gay, Lesbian, and BiSexual Persons. *Gelberg, Susan and Joseph T. Chojnacki. American Counseling Association, 1996 (Most recent edition).*

The Courts: An Excellent Place for Minority Attorneys to Launch Their Careers, *National Association for Law Placement and the American Bar Association, 2002.*
This brochure explains what clerkships are and how they benefit students of color.

To Be Out or Not to Be Out: Information for Gay, Lesbian and Bisexual Applicants in the Legal Market, *National Association for Law Placement, 2005.*
This brochure discusses various issues relevant to GLBT attorneys, including the state of the law with respect to civil rights of GLBT attorneys, disclosure issues, and choosing an employer.

LARGE FIRM/PRIVATE PRACTICE

Making Partner: A Guide for Law Firm Associates. *Sapp, John R. ABA, 2007.*
This book gives advice on how to make partner and what you should or should not be doing.

Managing Partner 101: A Guide to Successful Law Firm Leadership. *Green, Lawrence G. ABA, 2001 (most recent edition).*
This book is a good management tool, giving advice to lawyers who take on management positions. It explores four themes that are the basis for a successful law firm, which managing partners can refer to for help.

NALP Directory of Legal Employers, *Annual.*
Directory of information on large law firms who recruit at law schools and hire lateral attorneys (see listing in Directories section of this Resource Guide).

Perceptions of Partnership: The Allure and Accessibility of the Brass Ring. *NALP Foundation for Research and Education, 1999 (most recent edition).*
A discussion of how the rewards and status associated with partnership have changed in today's legal world.

Private Practice in Chicago: Strategic Choices about Firms and Career Paths. *Kimball, Frank. Kimball Legal Search, 2004.*
Insights into an urban practice.

So You Want to Be a Big Time Lawyer: The Insider's Guide to Getting Into and Surviving at a Major Law Firm. *Schwab, Solan. Lynx Media Inc., 2003.*
This a practical and balanced look at the pros and cons of going to work for a major law firm.

Vault Guide to Law Firm Pro Bono Program, *Vault Inc., 2008.*
This guide was developed to provide law students and lawyers with information necessary to evaluate the pro bono cultures and activities of large U.S. law firms nationwide. This book explores the world of women in legal professions through interviews of women who already work in the legal industry.

Developing Legal Talent: Best Practices in Professional Development for Law Firms. *Abbott, Ida O.*
NALP addresses issues such as typical pro bono assignments, recent pro bono clients, special training and supervision for pro bono cases, and average number of hours devoted to pro bono work.

Vault Guide to the Top 100 Law Firms, *Brook Moshan, Vault Inc., 2007.*
This guide "provides in-depth coverage of prestige, perks, corporate culture, and other legal lifestyle issues at close to 200 top firms." The guide includes Vault's "famous 'Top 100' prestige rankings, regional coverage and rankings, and our "Best 20" law firms to work for."

SOLO/SMALL FIRM PRACTICE

Choosing Small. Choosing Smart: Job Search Strategies for Lawyers in the Small Firm Market, *Donna Gerson, 2005.*
This book explores the ins and outs of working in a small firm environment. It provides information about understanding the small firm market, approaching firms effectively, negotiating salary and benefits, and succeeding as a small firm lawyer.

Flying Solo: A Survival Guide for the Solo Lawyer, Fourth Edition. *Edited by K. William Gibson. ABA, 2005.*
A thorough guide to practicing law on your own, many of the chapters provide insights for associate lawyers working in small firms as well, where they are, in fact, solos within the shell of an organization.

How to Start and Build a Law Practice, *2004, Platinum Fifth Edition, Jay G Foonberg*
This book is a "thorough guide to becoming a solo practitioner, covering topics ranging from office supplies to professional responsibility, client relations to time management and everything inbetween. (It) provides extensive checklists and tools for starting and managing a law office."

Full Disclosure: The New Lawyer's Must-Read Career Guide. *Carey, Christen Civiletto, Esq. ALM Publishers, 2001 (most recent edition).*
This book contains a collection of articles about today's professional development practices for attorneys.

Green Weenies and Due Diligence: Insider Business Jargon—Raw, Serious, and Sometimes Funny. *Sturgeon, Ron. Mike French Publishing, 2005.*
This hilarious book breaks down words and phrases commonly used in the business world.

Accounting and Finance for Lawyers in a Nutshell. *Meyer, Charles H. West Group, 2006.*

This book, from the Nutshell Series, is a guide to help lawyers get the most out of their finances.

Introduction to the Study and Practice of Law in a Nutshell. *Kenney Hegland. West Group, 2008.*

A great book for lawyers who are just starting their careers. This book offers advice on practicing law from case planning to closing arguments.

Guide to Small Firm Employment. *National Association for Law Placement, 2005.*

This brochure addresses the choice of a small firm career; job search strategies; characteristics valued by small firms; résumés, cover letters, interviews; and decisions.

Negotiating with Small Firms. *National Association for Law Placement, 2004.*

This brochure can be very helpful in determining whether an offer of employment with a small firm is reasonable and when negotiations are appropriate. Salary and benefits are discussed in addition to negotiating strategies and resources for further research.

GOVERNMENT

FBI Careers: the Ultimate Guide to Landing a Job as One of America's Finest. *Thomas Ackerman, 2005.*

This book contains "specific guidance through the rigorous selection process including tips on standing out from other applicants; details on positions as special agents, computer specialists, police officers, scientists, intelligence specialists, financial analysts, electronic technicians, language specialists, office and support positions; and overview of the FBI Academy and training programs; tips on getting internships (an excellent way to 'get a foot in the door') sample application forms, and tips for completing them."

2007 Federal Legal Employment Opportunities Guide. *National Association for Law Placement, 2007.*

This resource provides updated information on employment opportunities with nearly 30 federal agencies and departments. It offers job seekers a look at the government's many functions and roles as well as a glossary of terms unique to the federal application process, and tips on landing a government job.

Fedlaw: Legal Internships with Federal Agencies. *Career Education Institutes, 2004.*
This handbook contains information on various government offices (i.e., NASA, National Labor Relations Board, U.S. Attorney's Offices) located throughout the 50 states and for each such office provides the following helpful information: the name of a contact person at the organization; a description of the internship offered and the number of positions available; salary for the internship (if applicable); and a description of the application materials required and the deadline for submitting these materials.

For the Prosecution: Internships with America's Prosecutors. *Career Education Institutes, 2004.*
This handbook profiles internships with federal and state prosecutors' offices located throughout the country. It provides information on each office such as the name of a contact person, a description of the office's work, a description of the internship and the duties of the internship, the stipend amount (if any), and a description of the application materials required and the deadline for submitting these materials.

Washington, DC Internships in Law and Policy. *Career Educational Institutes, 2003.*
This book is designed to expose students to the opportunities available with 270 organizations in the nation's capital.

Legal Career Opportunities. *The New York County D.A.'s Office.*
This brochure provides an overview of the organization of the New York County District Attorney's Office.

PUBLIC INTEREST

International Public Interest Law, 2007-2008. *Yale Law School.*
This guide focuses on employment opportunities in intergovernmental organizations, U.S. government agencies and non-governmental organizations.

Pro Bono Opportunities: A Guide for Lawyers in New York City.
Association of the Bar of the City of New York and Volunteers of Legal Service, 2008.

This publication was a joint effort by the Association of the Bar and Volunteers of Legal Service. It lists specific opportunities in bar associations, legal service and public interest organizations, and court and government agencies. Probono.net/ny/nylawyer_oppsguide/

Public Service and International Law: A Guide to Professional Opportunities in the United States and Abroad. *Harvard Law School & Yale Law School, 2004.*

Recognizing that the practice of law is a global enterprise, this guide provides valuable information about legal jobs in the public sector around the world. Information regarding U.S. government, intergovernmental and non-profit organizational employment positions are described, as well as fellowship opportunities.

Serving the Public: A Job Search Guide. *Harvard Law School Office of Public Interest Law, Cambridge, MA.*

Two volumes of information and advice concerning working in the public interest.

WORK/LIFE BALANCE

The Lawyers Guide to Balancing Life and Work Second Edition. *Kaufman, George W. ABA, 2006.*

This is an updated version of the classic ABA book that first raised the consciousness of lawyers about the need to find life-work balance. For law students who find themselves wondering about this issue, this is a must read this book.

Life, Law and the Pursuit of Balance: A Lawyer's Guide to Quality of Life. *Edited by Jeffrey R. Simmons. Maricopa County Bar Association, 1996 (most recent edition).*

This book takes a look at the reasons for career dissatisfaction within the law industry and offers realistic advice on how to solve or reduce these problems.

Lawyers' Lives Out of Control: A Quality of Life Handbook. *LeVan, Gerald. WorldComm Press, 1993 (most recent edition).*

Attorney and law professor Gerald Le Van gives solid, practical advice on how to find balance between your personal and professional life in regards to the law industry.

Controlling Conflict: Alternative Dispute Resolutions for Business. *Costello, Edward J. CCH Inc., 1996 (most recent edition).*
This book explores the different methods of resolving disputes.

Should You Marry a Lawyer: A Couple's Guide to Balancing Work, Love and Ambition? *Travis, Fiona H. Decision Books, 2004.*
This book explores the concept of being married to a lawyer and is complete with tips and exercises that will help to provide balance in your marriage if one or both of you is a lawyer.

Solving the Part-Time Puzzle: The Law Firm's Guide to Balanced Hours. *Joan C. Williams and Cynthia Thomas Calvert, National Association for Law Placement, 2004.*
In this book, the authors make the case for balanced hours and provide helpful, business-savvy advice on how to create and implement a successful balanced hours program.

LEGAL EDUCATION

How to Succeed in Law School. *Gary A. Munneke. Barron's Educational Series, 2008.*
This publication offers advice on how to deal with the everyday life of law school, including "subject matter, dealing with professors, effective use of the law library, note-taking and exams." It also includes sample law essay questions, and short answer and multiple-choice questions.

Introduction to the Study and Practice of Law in a Nut Shell. *Kenney Hegland. West Group, 2008.*
A great book for lawyers who are just starting their careers. This book offers advice on practicing law from case planning to closing arguments.

Law School Competitions in a Nutshell. *Teply, Larry L. West Group, 2003 (most recent edition).*
This book is designed to prepare students for competitions such as moot court, negotiation, and client counseling.

The Academic Job Search Handbook. *Heiberger, Mary Morris and Julia Miller Vick. University of Pennsylvania Press, 2008.*
A guide to finding an academic job in today's market.

The Law of Schools, Students and Teachers in a Nutshell. *Kern, Alexander. West Group, 2003 (most recent edition).*
This book deals with some issues that face students, such as due process rights, freedom of speech, testing, and discipline.

ALTERNATIVE CAREERS

Nonlegal Careers for Lawyers. *5th Ed. Munneke, Gary, Henslee, William D., and Ellen Wayne. ABA, 2006.*
Just because you have a law degree doesn't mean you have to practice law. This book explores alternate non-legal careers and provides information on how to use your legal training to your advantage.

JD Preferred, 400+ Things You Can Do With a Law Degree, 2006, Federal Reports, Inc.
A guide describing more than 400 currently active legal employment opportunities (other than practicing law) across all employment sectors—private, public, and nonprofit. There is now a *JD Preferred, 600+ Things You Can Do With A Law Degree* that can be found at www.attorneyjobs.com, (2008). This Directory is not published in hard copy.

Judgment Reversed: Alternative Careers for Lawyers. *Strausser, Jeffrey, 1997 (most recent edition).*
This book, aimed toward law students and those already practicing law, explores and describes alternative careers.

Landing a Non-Traditional Legal Job. *Federal Reports, 1995 (most recent edition).*

Lawyer's Career Change Handbook: More Than 300 Things You Can Do with a Law Degree. *Greenberg, Hindi. HarperCollins, 2002 (most recent edition).*
This is a guide for lawyers who no longer wish to practice law. It explores alternate careers and provides information needed to pursue one.

Running from the Law: Why Good Lawyers are Getting out of the Legal Profession. *Deborah Arron. Ten Speed Press, 2003 (most recent edition).*

This book explores the rising epidemic of lawyers leaving the practice because they are unhappy and provides tips for finding alternate careers or getting over the unhappiness and learning to cope with their career.

Turning Points: New Paths and Second Careers for Lawyers. *Cain, George. ABA, 1994 (most recent edition).*
This book discusses the financial considerations and psychological matters involved in moving from private practice.

What Can You Do With a Law Degree?: A Lawyer's Guide to Career Alternatives Inside, Outside & Around the Law. *Arron, Deborah L. Decision Books, 2003 (most recent edition).*
This book sets you up with information that will be useful if you ever get fired or just decide to change careers.

Make the Right Career Move. *Canter, Rachelle J. John Wiley & Sons, Inc., 2007.*
This guide provides you with the information you need to land your dream job.

WOMEN IN THE LAW

Presumed Equal: What America's Top Women Lawyers Really Think About Their Firms? *Blohm Lindsay and Ashley Riveira. Career Press, 2006.*
This book takes a look at the role of women in today's law firms.

Closing the Leadership Gap: Why Women Can and Must Help Run the World. *Wilson, Marie C. Penguin Group, 2004.*
Marie C. Wilson argues the importance of women in leadership roles and calls to action their increased presence in filling these roles. In this book, she explores the leadership gap between men and women and introduces strategies that women are using to claim their place and rise to the top.

The Woman Advocate. *Snyder, Jean Maclean and Andrea Barmash Greene, eds. ABA, 1996 (most recent edition).* In this book, a number of women who have worked in law firms give us insight into the discrimination that women face in the legal industry.

Women-at-Law: Lessons Learned on the Pathways to Success.
Epstein, Phyllis Horn. ABA, 2004.
This book explores the world of women in legal professions through interviews of women who already work in the legal industry.

Women Lawyers: Rewriting the Rules. *Harrington, Mona. Knopf, 1994 (most recent edition).*
This book explores the obstacles women face when seeking equality in the legal profession.

A Career in the Law: A Guide for Women Law Students. *Catalyst, 2001.*
Catalyst performed a study to determine why despite the high rate of enrollment of women in law schools, there are few women in leadership positions in the legal profession. This booklet discusses the results of the study and seeks to explore how female talent can be maximized in the legal workplace.

Women in the Courts: A Work in Progress. *New York State Judicial Committee on Women in the Courts, 2002.*
This report analyzes the status of women employed in New York's court system, based on the results of two surveys designed to determine whether a woman's role in "the jurisprudential scheme in the Empire State is fair under all circumstances."

Women in Law: Making the Case. *Catalyst, 2001.*
A look at women in the legal profession, examining career paths and outcomes of women as compared to those of men in the legal profession.

Women Rainmakers: Best Marketing Tips, *2nd ed., Theda C. Snyder, American Bar Association, 2003.*
This book contains over 100 tips you can put to use right away. These are ideas that have worked for other successful rainmakers and can work for you. Learn creative marketing techniques that build your client base. Discover new action plans that fit your personal style and strengthen your rainmaking skills.

PERIODICALS

Legal newspapers and newsletters are a great place to search for additional information. Westlaw offers hundreds of publications that give you access to current information about attorneys, law firms, judges, and businesses, as well as the latest trends in hiring and employment anywhere in the country.

Below are journals with which you should become familiar and ones that contain valuable information on a variety of legal current events, as well as job postings. Job listings for *The Legal Times* can be found at www.amlawjobs.com.

American Lawyer Media (ALM.com) is the publisher of many of the nation's state or city-specific newsletters. You may search their site for job listings, local to the legal community news and other resources that may prove helpful.

The American Lawyer. ALM Properties Inc., 2008, www.american lawyer.com

ABA Journal. American Bar Association, 2008, www.abanet .org/journal/

California Bar Journal. The State Bar of California, 2008, www .calbar.org

Chicago Daily Law Bulletin. Law Bulletin Publishing Co., 2008, www.chicagolawbulletin.com

The Chronicle of Higher Education. The Chronicle of Higher Education, 2008, www.chronicle.com

The Complete Lawyer. The Complete Lawyer, LLC, 2008, www .thecompletelawyer.com

The Connecticut Law Tribune. ALM Properties Inc., 2008, www .ctlawtribune.com

Inside Counsel. WBI/CLT LLC 2008, www.insidecounsel.com

Corporate Counsel ALM. Properties, LLC, 2008 www.corpcounsel.com

CCM (American Lawyer Corporate Counsel). ALM Properties Inc., 2008, www.metrocorpcounsel.com

Crain's New York Business. Crain's Communications Inc., 2008, www.crainsny.com

Daily Report ALM Properties, Inc. 2008, www.dailyreportonline.com

Delaware Law Weekly. ALM Properties Inc., 2008, www.delaware lawweekly.com

Florida Bar News. The Florida Bar, 2008, www.floridabar.org

Focus Europe. ALM Properties Inc., 2008, www.americanlawyer .com/focuseurope/

Law Firm Partnership and Benefits Report ALM Properties, Inc. www.lawjournalnewsletters.com

Law Practice. American Bar Association, 2008, www.abanet.org/ lpm/magazine/home.shtml

Law Technology News. ALM Properties Inc., 2008, www.lawtech news.com

Legal Affairs. Legal Affairs Inc., 2008, www.legalaffairs.org

Legal Intelligencer. ALM Properties Inc., 2008, www.law.com/jsp/ pa/index.jsp

Legal Times. ALM Properties Inc., 2008, www.law.com/jsp/dc/ index.jsp

Massachusetts Lawyer Weekly. Lawyer's Weekly Inc., 2008, www .masslawyersweekly.com

Metropolitan Corporate Counsel. Metropolitan Corporate Counsel Inc., 2006, www.metrocorpcounsel.com

Miami Daily Business Review. ALM Properties Inc., 2008, www .dailybusinessreview.com

Minnesota Lawyer. Finance and Commerce Media Group 2008, www.minnlawyer.com

National Law Journal. ALM Properties Inc., 2008, www.law.com/ jsp/nlj/index.jsp

New Jersey Law Journal. ALM Properties Inc., 2008, www.law .com/njlnj.com

The New York Law Journal. ALM Properties Inc., 2008, www.lnylj.com

Newsweek. Newsweek Inc., 2008, www.newsweek.com

The Nonprofit Times. The Nonprofit Times, 2008, www.nptimes.com

Northeastern Law Magazine. Northeastern University School of Law, 2008, www.slaw.neu.edu/magazine

Pennsylvania Law Weekly. ALM Properties Inc., 2008, www.palaw weekly.com

Recorder. ALM Properties Inc., 2008, www.callaw.com (Newsletter of San Francisco Bar)

Texas Lawyer. ALM Properties Inc., 2007, www.law.com

Wall Street Journal. Dow Jones & Co., Inc., 2007, www.wsj.com

Wisconsin Law Journal. The Daily Reporter Publishing Co., 2007, www.wislawjournal.com

Kiplinger's Personal Finance. The Kiplinger Washington Editors, 2007, www.kiplinger.com

The Third Branch, Monthly Newsletter
The publication of the Federal Courts contains news on nominations, resignations, etc.

Hispanic Business
This magazine is published monthly and features Hispanic leaders in business. It is a potentially useful resource for networking and/ or conducting informational interviews.

JUDICIAL CLERKSHIP APPLICATION RESOURCES

As of this date, the Administrative Office of the Federal Courts (AO) and the Advisory Committee are working with the software vendor to combine the resources and searchable database of

OSCAR and FLCIS. Please check the AO Web site for updated information.

1. OSCAR (Online System for Clerkship Application and Review)

System allows applicants to upload application information for electronic submission to the Federal judges who have chosen to accept applications online. Judges indicate in their listing whether they participate in the OSCAR application process. http://oscar.uscourts.gov

The Federal Law Clerk Information System has been newly merged with OSCAR. This component of the OSCAR site is a searchable database for available judicial clerkship opportunities. This database allows both student and experienced attorney applicants to search the database within the following parameters: court, judge by name, year of clerkship opening, date of position posting (three days, thirty days, any date), term or career position within the federal court system. Includes: Federal Circuit, Federal District, Bankruptcy, Magistrates, Specialty Courts–Claims, International Trade. https://oscar.uscourts.gov

State court judges are not listed on OSCAR, but many accept applications either individually or through an individual law school created centralized application process.

2. The Vermont Law School Guide to State Court Clerkships

Access to this database of state court judges/systems can be obtained through an individual subscription or through the career services office of your law school. www.vermontlaw.edu/career

3. *The Almanac of the Federal Judiciary*

Includes reviews and evaluations of judges written by practitioners.

4. Federal Judicial Center

www.fjc.gov provides biographical information on federal judges. This is a resource that can be helpful when researching judges for both application and interview purposes.

5. The Judicial Yellow Book

Online and print versions provide biographical information on federal judges and lists each judge's clerks. Published yearly. http://www.leadershipdirectories.com/

6. **Handbook from your law school.**

Many schools print or post a handbook of information about their school's clerkship advice and resources. It often will include a list of faculty or alumni/ae who have clerked and might be available to provide information concerning the individual judges or the interview process.

Appendix B
PRINCIPLES AND STANDARDS FOR
LAW PLACEMENT AND RECRUITMENT ACTIVITIES

INTRODUCTION

The National Association for Law Placement (NALP) was organized in 1971 to promote the exchange of information and cooperation between law schools and employers. To advance those interests, the Association has developed these "Principles and Standards for Law Placement and Recruitment Activities."

The NALP *"Principles and Standards for Law Placement and Recruitment Activities"* were first adopted in 1978. Part V, "Standards for the Timing of Offers and Decisions," was derived from *"Interviewing Procedures for Law Students and Prospective Employers,"* a set of guidelines originally adopted in the early 1960s by a group of law schools meeting under the auspices of the Association of the Bar of the City of New York. Subsequent modifications were adopted in 1985, 1988, 1992, 1994, 2002, 2004, 2005, and 2008.

The *"Principles and Standards for Law Placement and Recruitment Activities"* are organized as follows:

    I. General Principles
    II. Principles for Law Schools
    III. Principles for Candidates
    IV. Principles for Employers
    V. General Standards for the Timing of Offers and Decisions

NALP encourages law schools and legal employers to educate all participants in the law placement and recruitment process about the spirit and the letter of these Principles and Standards. NALP urges all participants in the law student recruitment process, including members and non-members of NALP, to abide by these *Principles and Standards.*

PART I. GENERAL PRINCIPLES

Successful recruitment and placement of law students requires cooperation and good judgment from three groups—law schools, candidates, and employers. These *Principles and Standards* provide concrete guidelines for each group. Nothing in the *Principles and Standards* is intended to alter any legal relationships among the participants, but participants are urged to carry out all obligations in good faith.

Activities related to the placement and hiring of law students should be conducted on the highest ethical and professional level. Timely exchange of accurate information is essential. Recruitment activities should be scheduled so as to minimize interference with students' academic work.

Underlying these guidelines for ethical behavior is NALP's fundamental commitment to helping to make the legal profession accessible to all individuals on a non-discriminatory basis. NALP is strongly opposed to discrimination which is based upon gender, age, race, color, religious creed, national origin, physical disability, marital, parental or veteran status, sexual orientation, or the prejudice of clients related to such matters.

In addition to abiding by these guidelines, all parties concerned with placement and hiring should observe strictly all relevant laws, accreditation standards and institutional policies. A law school may deny use of its career services facilities to students and employers who fail to adhere to these Principles and Standards. If unusual circumstances or particular organizational constraints require a law school, a candidate, or an employer to modify any provision herein, every effort should be made to find an alternative acceptable to all parties concerned.

PART II. PRINCIPLES FOR LAW SCHOOLS

A. **Law schools should make career planning services available to all students.**
   1. Career planning and counseling are integral parts of legal education. Law schools should dedicate to them adequate physical space, equipment, financial support, and staff.

2. The professional services of a career planning office should be available to students without charge.

3. Law schools should strive to meet the career planning needs and interests of all students. Preferential treatment should not be extended to any student or employer.

B. Law schools should subscribe to and promote practices that protect their students' legal rights.

1. Law schools should articulate and publish meaningful policies prohibiting discriminatory hiring practices. Procedures should be developed and published whereby claims of violations can be investigated and resolved promptly and fairly.

2. Students' privacy should be protected against illegal or inappropriate dissemination of personal information. Information protected by federal, state, or municipal law must not be disclosed without proper consent. Institutional policies conforming to prevailing laws should be formulated and published to the attention of both students and employers.

C. Law schools should educate students as to proper career investigation techniques and protocol.

1. Publications and counseling provided by law schools should be designed to afford students adequate information about the variety of opportunities available to persons with legal training and proper methods for exploring such opportunities.

2. Students should be counseled to focus their career choices based on their aptitudes and career goals.

D. Students' freedom of choice in career decisions should be protected from undue influences.

1. In counseling students, career services officers and others within the law school community should avoid interposing either their own values or institutional interests.

2. Law schools should disseminate Part V: General Standards for the Timing of Offers and Decisions to students and employers and urge all participants in the law student recruitment process, including members and non-

members of NALP, to adhere to them so that students can make informed decisions.

E. Law schools should develop and maintain productive working relationships with a broad range of employers.

1. Law schools should work actively to develop and maintain employment opportunities for students and graduates. All employment opportunity notices should be publicized to all students.
2. To enhance student learning and increase career development opportunities, the office of career services should maintain good working relationships with students, faculty, alumnae/i, and other elements of the legal community.
3. In order to ensure maximum information-sharing and efficiency in the employment search process, law schools should cooperate with one another to the fullest extent possible in gathering employer information and providing interview services.
4. Law schools should not disseminate information learned in confidence from employers.

F. Law schools should establish adequate procedures to facilitate recruitment by employers.

1. Procedures to enable employers to conduct on-campus interviews, solicit direct applications or collect student resumes should be designed for maximum efficiency and fairness. Those procedures should be clearly articulated and available in writing to students and employers.
2. In dealing with employers, law schools should make maximum use of standardized forms and procedures.

G. Law schools should establish and implement practices to ensure the fair and accurate representation of students and the institution in the employment search process.

1. Law schools should adopt and enforce policies that prohibit misrepresentation and other student abuses of the employment search process, such as engaging in interviews for practice, holding more than four offers, failing

to decline offers in which there is no longer interest, or continuing to interview after acceptance of employment.

2. Law schools should provide to employers and other interested parties comprehensive information on grade standards and distribution, curriculum, degree requirements, admissions and enrollment profiles, academic awards criteria, and office of career services policies and procedures.

3. Information on employment and salaries should be collected by law schools and provided to NALP, and the survey results should be made available to employers, prospective students, and all other interested parties.

PART III. PRINCIPLES FOR CANDIDATES

A. Candidates should prepare thoroughly for the employment search process.

1. Before beginning an employment search, candidates should engage in thorough self-examination. Work skills, vocational aptitudes and interests, lifestyle and geographic preferences, academic performance, career expectations and life experiences should be carefully evaluated so that informed choices can be made. General instruction should be obtained on employment search skills, particularly those relating to the interview process.

2. Prior to making employment inquiries, candidates should learn as much as possible about target employers and the nature of their positions. Candidates should interview only with employers in whom they have a genuine interest.

3. Candidates should comply with the policies and procedures of law schools whose services they use.

B. Throughout the employment search process candidates should represent their qualifications and interests fully and accurately.

1. Candidates should be prepared to provide, at employers' request, copies of all academic transcripts. Under no circumstances should academic biographical data be

falsified, misrepresented, or distorted either in writing or orally. Candidates who engage in such conduct may be subject to elimination from consideration for employment by the employer, suspension or other academic discipline by the law school, and disqualification from admission to practice by bar admission authorities.

2. Candidates should be prepared to advise prospective employers of the nature and extent of their training in legal writing. Writing samples submitted as evidence of a candidate's legal skills should be wholly original work. Where the writing was done with others, the candidate's contribution should be clearly identified. Writing samples from law-related employment must be masked adequately to preserve client confidentiality and used only with the permission of the supervising attorney.

C. **Throughout the employment search process students should conduct themselves in a professional manner.**

1. Candidates who participate in the on-campus interview process should adhere to all scheduling commitments. Cancellations should occur only for good cause and should be promptly communicated to the office of career services or the employer.

2. Invitations for in-office interviews should be acknowledged promptly and accepted only if the candidate has a genuine interest in the employer.

3. Candidates should reach an understanding with the employer regarding its reimbursement policies prior to the trip. Expenses for trips during which interviews with more than one employer occur should be prorated in accordance with those employers' reimbursement policies.

4. Candidates invited to interview at employer offices should request reimbursement for reasonable expenses that are directly related to the interview and incurred in good faitH. Failure to observe this policy, or falsification or misrepresentation of travel expenses, may result in non-reimbursement and elimination from consideration for employment or the revocation of offers by an employer.

D. Candidates should notify employers and their office of career services of their acceptance or rejection of employment offers by the earliest possible time, and no later than the time established by rule, custom, or agreement.

1. Candidates should expect offers to be confirmed in writing. Candidates should abide by the standards for student responses set out in Part V and should in any event notify the employer as soon as their decision is made, even if that decision is made in advance of the prevailing deadline date.

2. In fairness to both employers and peers, students should act in good faith to promptly decline offers for interviews and employment which are no longer being seriously considered. In order for law schools to comply with federal and institutional reporting requirements, students should notify the office of career services upon acceptance of an employment offer, whether or not the employment was obtained through the office.

3. Candidates seeking or preparing to accept fellowships, judicial clerkships, or other limited term professional employment should apprise prospective employers of their intentions and obtain a clear understanding of their offer deferral policies.

E. Candidates should honor their employment commitments.

1. Candidates should, upon acceptance of an offer of employment, notify their office of career services and notify all employers who consider them to be active candidates that they have accepted a position.

2. If, because of extraordinary and unforeseen circumstances, it becomes necessary for a candidate to modify or be released from his or her acceptance, both the employer and the office of career services should be notified promptly.

F. Candidates should promptly report to the office of career services any misrepresentation, discrimination or other abuse by employers in the employment process.

G. Students who engage in law-related employment should adhere to the same standards of conduct as lawyers.

1. In matters arising out of law-related employment, students should be guided by the standards for professional conduct which are applicable in the employer's state. When acting on behalf of employers in a recruitment capacity, students should be guided by the employer principles in *Part IV*.

2. Students should exercise care to provide representative and fair information when advising peers about former employers.

PART IV. PRINCIPLES FOR EMPLOYERS

A. Employers should maintain productive working relationships with law schools.

1. Employers should inform the law school office of career services in advance of any recruiting activities involving their students, whether conducted on- or off-campus, and should, at the conclusion of those activities, inform the office of career services of the results obtained.

2. Employers without formal recruiting programs or whose hiring activities are sporadic in nature should notify the law school office of career services as far in advance as possible of planned recruiting activities in order that appropriate assistance might be arranged.

3. Employers who conduct on-campus interviews should refrain from making unnecessary schedule change requests.

B. Employers should respect the policies, procedures and legal obligations of individual law schools and should request only services or information that are consistent therewitH.

1. Employers should not expect or request preferential services from law schools.

2. Employers should not solicit information received by law schools in confidence from candidates or other employers.

3. Appointments with candidates for in-house interviews should be established for a mutually convenient time so as not to unduly disrupt students' studies.

4. Employers should promptly report to the office of career services any misrepresentation or other abuse by students of the employment search process.

C. **Employers should provide full and accurate information about the organization and the positions for which recruitment is being conducteD.**
   1. Employers should provide to law schools complete organizational information as contained in the NALP Employer Questionnaire well in advance of any recruitment activities. Position descriptions should include information about the qualifications sought in candidates, the hiring timetable, nature of the work, the number of available positions, and, if known at the time, the starting salary to be offered.
   2. Invitations for in-office interviews should include a clear explanation of all expense reimbursement policies and procedures.

D. **Employer organizations are responsible for the conduct of their recruiters and for any representation made by them.**
   1. Employers should designate recruiters who are both skilled and knowledgeable about the employing organization.
   2. Employers should instruct interviewers not to make any unauthorized commitments.
   3. Candidates' personal privacy should be safeguarded. Information about candidates that is protected by law should not be disclosed by an employer to any third party without specific permission.

E. **Employers should use valid, job related criteria when evaluating candidates.**
   1. Hiring decisions must be based solely on bona fide occupational qualifications.
   2. Employers should carefully avoid conduct of any kind during the interview and selection process that acts or appears to act to discriminate unlawfully or in a way contrary to the policies of a particular institution.

3. Factors in candidates' backgrounds that have no predictive value with respect to employment performance, such as scores on examinations required for admission to academic institutions, should not be relied upon by employers in the hiring process. When evaluating second and third year applicants, employers should not place undue emphasis on the nature of a first year summer job experience or on a student's decision not to work after the first year.

4. There has been a long-standing tradition that the first year summer be used to engage in public service work or to take time away from the law altogether, and, while the practice of having first year students work in private law firms provides additional employment opportunities to some students, such experiences should not be valued or emphasized inordinately.

F. Employers should refrain from any activity that may adversely affect the ability of candidates to make an independent and considered decision.

1. Employers should give candidates a reasonable period of time to consider offers of employment and should avoid conduct that subjects candidates to undue pressure to accept.

2. Response deadlines should be established when the offer of employment is made. Employers who extend offers in the fall should abide by the timetable for student response set out in *Part V* and must abide by it with respect to students enrolled in law schools that have adopted it as an employer requirement.

3. Employers should not offer special inducements to persuade candidates to accept offers of employment earlier than is customary or prescribed under the circumstances.

G. An employer should honor all commitments made on its behalf.

1. Offers of employment should be made in writing, with all terms clearly expressed.

2. If, because of extraordinary and unforeseen circumstances, it becomes necessary for an employer to rescind or modify an offer of employment, both the student and the office of career services should be notified promptly. Employers may retract any offer that is not reaffirmed by the student in accordance with Part V, Paragraphs B and C below.

PART V: GENERAL STANDARDS FOR THE TIMING OF OFFERS AND DECISIONS

Note: These Part V General Standards for the Timing of Offers and Decisions were approved by the NALP Board of Directors on February 2, 2008, and are in effect for the 2008-2009 recruiting season on a provisional basis. In April 2009, the NALP membership will vote on continuation of these provisions.

To promote fair and ethical practices for the interviewing and decision-making process, NALP offers the following standards for the timing of offers and decisions:

A. General Provisions

1. All offers to law student candidates ("candidates") should remain open for at least two weeks after the date of the offer letter unless the offers are made pursuant to Paragraphs B and C below, in which case the later response date should apply.
2. Candidates are expected to accept or release offers or request an extension by the applicable deadline. Offers that are not accepted by the offer deadline expire.
3. A student should not hold open more than five offers of employment at any one time. For each offer received that places a student over the offer limit, the student should, within one week of receipt of the excess offer, release an offer.
4. Employers offering part-time or temporary positions for the school term are exempted from the requirements of Paragraphs B and C below.
5. Practices inconsistent with these guidelines should be reported to the student's career services office.

B. Full-Time Employment Provisions

1. Employers offering full-time positions to commence following graduation to candidates not previously employed by them should leave those offers open for at least 45 days following the date of the offer letter or until December 30, whichever comes first. Offers made after December 15 for full-time positions to commence following graduation should remain open for at least two weeks after the date of the offer letter.

2. Students may request that an employer extend the deadline to accept the employer's offer until as late as April 1 if the student is actively pursuing positions with public interest or government organizations. Students may hold open only one offer in such circumstances. Employers are encouraged to grant such requests.

3. Employers offering full-time positions to commence following graduation to candidates previously employed by them should leave those offers open until at least November 15 of the candidate's final year of law school.

4. Employers offering candidates full-time positions to commence following graduation and having a total of 40 attorneys or fewer in all offices are exempted from the provisions of this section. Offers made on or before December 15 should remain open for a minimum of three weeks. Offers made after December 15 should remain open for at least two weeks.

C. Summer Employment Provisions for Second- and Third-Year Students

1. Employers offering positions for the following summer to candidates not previously employed by them should leave those offers open for at least 45 days following the date of the offer letter or until December 30, whichever comes first. Offers made after December 15 for the following summer should remain open for at least two weeks after the date of the offer letter.

2. Students may request that an employer extend the deadline to accept the employer's offer until as late as April 1

if the student is actively pursuing positions with public interest or government organizations. Students may hold open only one offer in such circumstances. Employers are encouraged to grant such requests.

3. Employers offering positions for the following summer to candidates previously employed by them should leave those offers open until at least November 15.

4. Employers offering candidates positions for the following summer and having a total of 40 attorneys or fewer in all offices are exempted from the provisions of this section. Offers made on or before December 15 should remain open for a minimum of three weeks. Offers made after December 15 should remain open for at least two weeks.

D. Summer Employment Provisions for First-Year Students

1. Law schools should not offer career services to first-semester first year law students prior to November 1, except in the case of part-time students who may be given assistance in seeking positions during the school term.

2. Prospective employers and first-year law students should not initiate contact with one another and employers should not interview or make offers to first year students before December 1.

3. All offers to first-year students for summer employment should remain open for at least two weeks after the date made.

Appendix C
TRENDS IN GRADUATE EMPLOYMENT (1985–2007)
NALP Bulletin, July 2008

The first table shows employment trends for new law graduates from 1985 to 2007. Because of changes in how jobs are classified, exact comparisons will not be available for all trends effective with the Class of 2001. It is evident, however, that the market for new law graduates has been quite strong in recent years with overall employment close to or above 89 percent since 1997, and increases over the prior year in 2005, 2006, and 2007. The employment rate for the Class of 2007 was almost 97 percent, the highest in twenty years. More than half of employed graduates obtain their first job at a law firm—a fact that has not changed in the thirty-four years that NALP has compiled employment information.

A further analysis of law firm employment shown in the second table reveals that, in many of these years, small firms of two to ten lawyers have supplied relatively more jobs than any other size firm. After declining through much of the 1980s and reaching a low of about 25 percent in 1989, the percentage of jobs in this category climbed back to about 41 percent in 1993. Another decline started in 1996 and continued through 2001. After a few years of growth, the figure declined again starting in 2006. These changes were mirrored by opposing changes for firms of more than one hundred lawyers. The percentage of law firm jobs accounted for by these firms doubled during the 1980s, dropped noticeably between 1990 and 1993, and started to rise again in 1994. For the last ten years, the number of jobs taken in firms of more than one hundred lawyers has outnumbered those taken in firms of two to ten, although the differential has fluctuated. Also of note is the growing proportion of jobs in either very small or large firms, which since 2000 have accounted for more than 70 percent of law firm jobs taken by new graduates.

Employment Trends: 1985–2000

OF THOSE FOR WHOM EMPLOYMENT STATUS WAS KNOWN

Year	% Employed	% Employed Legal Full-Time	% Employed Legal Part-Time	% Employed Other Full-Time	% Employed Other Part-Time	% Not Working	% Pursuing Advanced Degree	% of Jobs in Law Firms
1985	91.5	81.6	2.6	6.7	0.8	7.0	1.5	60.6
1986	91.3	81.8	2.5	6.2	0.8	7.2	1.5	62.3
1987	92.2	84.1	2.0	5.6	0.5	6.6	1.2	63.5
1988	92.0	84.5	2.0	4.9	0.5	6.9	1.1	64.3
1989	90.8	82.7	2.2	5.2	0.5	7.9	1.3	62.4
1990	90.3	82.1	2.4	5.2	0.7	8.2	1.4	62.9
1991	85.9	76.1	3.3	5.6	0.9	12.6	1.5	60.8
1992	83.5	72.5	4.0	5.9	1.1	14.5	1.9	59.0
1993	83.4	70.3	4.6	7.0	1.5	14.6	2.0	57.1
1994	84.7	69.6	5.2	8.1	1.8	13.1	2.2	55.0
1995	86.7	70.7	5.4	9.0	1.6	11.2	2.1	56.1
1996	87.4	71.4	4.7	9.7	1.6	10.5	2.1	55.7
1997	89.2	73.6	4.4	9.9	1.5	8.6	2.2	55.6
1998	89.9	74.9	3.7	10.0	1.4	7.9	2.2	55.0
1999	90.3	75.5	2.9	9.8	1.1	7.8	1.9	55.1
2000	91.5	77.3	2.5	9.6	1.0	6.4	2.1	54.8

Employment Trends: 2001–2007

OF THOSE FOR WHOM EMPLOYMENT STATUS WAS KNOWN

Year	% Employed	% Employed in Positions Requiring Bar Passage	% Employed in Positions Where JD Is Preferred	% Employed in Other Professional Positions	% Employed in Non-Professional Positions	% Not Working	% Pursuing Advanced Degree	% of Jobs in Law Firms
2001	90.0	75.9	6.0	5.5	1.5	7.6	2.4	57.8
2002	89.0	75.3	5.2	5.8	1.6	8.5	2.5	58.1
2003	88.9	73.7	6.5	5.7	1.6	8.4	2.7	57.8
2004	88.9	73.2	7.5	5.3	1.4	8.6	2.5	56.2
2005	89.6	74.4	7.5	5.1	1.4	8.2	2.2	55.8
2006	90.7	75.3	7.9	5.1	1.3	7.0	2.2	55.8
2007	91.9	76.9	7.7	5.1	1.3	5.8	2.3	55.5

Note: Overall employment rates for 1990-1998 are based on all graduates for whom employment status was known, excluding a small number known to be employed but for whom basic job type was not known. Overall rates for all other years include such graduates, and thus may not necessarily be obtained by adding up figures for individual job types. Also, in 1985 and 1986, multiple jobs held by one person were reported separately; hence legal and other employment percentages for these years reflect positions taken rather than individuals and cannot be added to obtain the overall employment rate. The percentage not working includes graduates seeking employment as well as those neither working in any capacity nor actively seeking a job. New job classifications effective with the Class of 2001 preclude direct comparisons of job types with prior years.

Law Firm Jobs by Firm Size—Classes of 1982–2007
(percent of law firm jobs taken in each size firm)

	SIZE OF FIRM (NUMBER OF LAWYERS)					
Year	Solo	2-10	11-25	26-50	51-100	101+
1982	7.6%	40.3%	14.8%	11.1%	10.7%	15.6%
1983	7.1	41.1	15.1	11.2	10.1	15.4
1984	6.6	39.7	15.0	11.1	10.4	17.2
1985	5.0	35.7	15.1	11.7	12.0	20.6
1986	4.3	32.4	15.6	12.0	12.5	23.2
1987	3.3	31.6	15.3	12.9	12.8	24.1
1988	2.7	28.6	14.5	12.2	13.4	28.6
1989	2.8	24.6	15.0	12.6	14.8	30.2
1990	3.6	28.7	13.1	11.6	12.2	30.8
1991	5.2	33.1	12.5	10.3	10.0	28.9
1992	6.8	38.0	13.5	9.1	9.1	23.6
1993	7.5	41.5	13.1	7.8	7.9	22.2
1994	6.2	41.0	12.2	7.6	8.1	24.9
1995	6.0	40.9	12.3	7.5	7.5	25.8
1996	6.1	39.3	11.8	7.4	7.5	27.9
1997	5.7	36.4	12.0	7.7	7.6	30.6
1998	3.8	33.5	11.5	7.7	8.0	35.5
1999	3.2	31.4	11.1	7.4	7.7	39.1
2000	2.7	30.2	10.8	7.7	7.6	41.0
2001	2.8	29.9	10.3	6.9	7.4	42.6
2002	2.4	31.4	10.7	7.0	7.3	41.2
2003	3.3	34.5	11.6	7.2	6.8	36.6
2004	3.6	34.9	11.5	7.2	6.4	36.4
2005	3.2	36.0	10.7	6.8	6.0	37.3
2006	2.9	34.3	10.4	6.9	5.9	39.5
2007	3.0	33.2	9.6	6.1	5.8	42.3

Note: Figures for 1989 and 1990 reflect only full-time law firm jobs; for all other years, figures reflect all law firm jobs acquired by graduates. Figures in this table differ slightly from those published in national reports (*Employment Report & Salary Survey/Jobs & JDs*) because law firm jobs for which firm size was not reported are excluded from the base.

Appendix D
LAW FIRM PRACTICE STUDY

The information in Appendix D was developed by Major, Lindsey & Africa, a leading legal search firm. The study describes a broad range of substantive practice areas with key elements of each. The authors appreciate this contribution to *The Legal Career Guide* by MLA.

ADMINISTRATIVE LAW

Practice Area	Description
Administrative	• These attorneys represent companies before government agencies such as the FCC, FTC, FDA, Consumer Product Safety Commission, etc. They aid clients who are the subject of enforcement actions, ensure corporate compliance with regulation and challenge regulation. Challenges are typically brought on constitutional grounds. • Federal practice is heavily concentrated in Washington, D.C. There are smaller state practices in state capitals. • Attorneys in this practice typically focus on one agency, so there are FDA attorneys, FTC attorneys, etc. The SEC is the most glamorous. • The day-to-day work involves drafting, negotiation and client counseling. The drafting includes a wide variety of documents, including everything from constitutional briefs to license applications to disclosure documents. • People who like this profession like working at the intersection between government and business, and appreciate that this is a recession-proof industry. Many partners in these practices come from agency commissions. • People who leave this practice typically do so because they are frustrated by governmental bureaucracy.

BANKRUPTCY LAW

Practice Area	Description
Bankruptcy	• This practice combines the representing and counseling of clients who are considering or going through bankruptcy, or the represen- tation of creditors of such companies. The basic premise is that there is a limited pool of assets and all the creditors are fighting to get the greatest amount possible. This prac- tice is a hybrid litigation/counseling/contract practice. • The day-to-day work includes standard litiga- tion tasks plus drafting agreements such as loans documents, licenses, etc. The trials, though, are not jury trials, and there is only a limited right to appeal. There is a lot of nego- tiation involved in this practice. • Bankruptcy is governed by a special set of rules and can take a while for new attorneys to master. • This practice is great for people who like deals and who enjoy negotiation. Also, the lawyers tend to drive the terms and take much more of a business role than most liti- gation attorneys. • People who don't like this practice can be frustrated by the litigation process (the judge has a lot of discretion so parties tend to raise arguments without much merit), by the complexity of the practice, or by the lack of a predictable schedule. The cases move quite quickly and demand a great deal of time. • This practice is counter-cyclical.

CORPORATE LAW	
Practice Area	**Description**
Asset Finance	• Help companies finance the purchase of equipment (e.g., aircraft, trucks, etc.). • Parties are banks on the one hand and large companies on the other. Relatively balanced negotiating power between sophisticated parties. • Like many finance practices, this practice is focused in New York but appears in some other major markets to a lesser degree. • Demands logistical organization skills as there are often multiple people involved (sometimes in many countries), each responsible for a portion of the transaction. • Requires excellent drafting skills as contracts tend to be fairly complicated. • Reward is helping businesses obtain a significant tangible asset. Attracts people who like to be able to touch the results of their efforts. • Very detail-oriented practice, contracts must all align with each other so not the most creative drafting in some cases. • It is primarily a project-based practice; deals take a couple months to close. There are ongoing compliance and maintenance responsibilities because the assets may need to be repossessed at the end of the lease or upon default.

CORPORATE LAW

Practice Area	Description
Banking/Finance	• Representing banks or companies with respect to lender agreements (lines of credit, loans, restructurings). • Wide range in size of transactions, traditionally focuses on large series of loans. • Transaction, contract driven, restricted by banking/contract law. • Small firms may not have as a separate group. • New York is the geographical heart of this practice. New York attorneys represent the major banks. • When operating in support of another practice, the deadlines can be tight. Schedule can fluctuate dramatically between busy and quiet periods. • This practice tends to be a support or ancillary practice in many markets.
Broker-Dealer	• This is a subset of securities law in which the focus is on SEC broker-dealer rules. • Typically these attorneys represent investment banks. Most client contact is with the in-house lawyers at the bank. • A lot of broker-dealer work is compliance work. Successful broker-dealer attorneys must be comfortable with rules and regulations. • Investment banks also have in-house litigators to handle arbitration regarding typical-broker dealer claims including fraud, churning, NASD violations, etc.

CORPORATE LAW

Practice Area	Description
Capital Markets	• Facilitates movement of money from one place to another within the market. This practice overlaps with securities practice. • There is a New York City focus to this practice, although it can be found in some other major markets. • The practice divides into both public and private deals. The typical scenario is that an individual or a fund is purchasing an interest in a company. • There is a compliance piece to this work involving applicable state, federal and foreign securities laws, SEC rules, etc. • Clients are often investment banks.
Cross-Border	• The deals in this practice area can vary widely, but always involve transactions with foreign entities. • Although U.S. attorneys must be familiar with the applicable foreign law, they often work with local counsel who advise them. • Currently, hot countries include Israel, Canada, China, and India. Much of the work in Europe is done in or through New York City and a lot of the work in Asia funnels through the West Coast. • The deals can be more challenging than domestic deals. You have to understand the needs and challenges of dealing with a company in a foreign country, not just laws but also cultural and communication differences. Also, there can be gray areas when the foreign laws are not as well developed. • This practice can create a crazy schedule (e.g., conference calls at 3:00 a.m.).

CORPORATE LAW

Practice Area	Description
General Corporate	• What constitutes a general corporate practice varies by geography. New York/East Coast practice tends to focus more on finance; Silicon Valley/West Coast practice tends to focus more on venture, securities, IPOs, start-up and high tech counseling. New York attorneys tend to specialize more. There is more private company work on the West Coast. • A corporate generalist deals with a number of different practice areas and can often serve as an "outside general counsel" to a firm. • Client relationships tend to be positive. Companies are glad to have your help and view you as part of the team seeking to get the deal done. • Corporate law is a substantive field and you can become expert in it (most people say it takes ten years). • The practice is collaborative in general, although direct negotiation can sometimes be adversarial. • People who like corporate practice tend to get satisfaction from helping companies grow and protect themselves. In the grand scheme, corporate practice is a practice that deals with money. • People who don't like corporate practice complain that they always have to think negatively (e.g., what could go wrong here?) and do not to get satisfaction from the nebulous nature of the work or from helping corporations.

CORPORATE LAW

Practice Area	Description
Investment ('40 Act)	• An investment practice combines the corporate, tax, and ERISA practices. • The practice divides between registered and unregistered funds. For mutual funds (registered), both the Investment Advisors Act and the Investment Companies Act apply. For hedge funds and private equity funds (unregistered), only the Investment Advisors Act applies. • This practice is more prevalent in major markets. Secondary markets may have only a few firms that offer this practice. • Day-to-day work focuses on drafting and reviewing documents, negotiations, and answering clients' questions. There is not a lot of research after you become familiar with the Act. • Registered work involves SEC filings and can be somewhat repetitive. Unregistered work is slightly more complex, involves tax issues, ERISA and allows more flexibility in structuring relationships (partnerships, LLCs, etc.). • Intense client contact and the deadlines can be short. It can be a high-stress practice and is best for people who enjoy the service aspect of law.

CORPORATE LAW

Practice Area	Description
M&A	• Help companies acquire, be acquired by or merge with other companies.
	• This practice can allow an attorney to work on big deals that make headlines and are significant events for the client.
	• Day-to-day work involves a lot of drafting and revision of documents, negotiation, due diligence and overseeing compliance with applicable law. At senior levels, there is significant client contact. Also, these attorneys often supervise or organize the service contributing attorneys (tax attorneys, etc.) on the deal.
	• The general feeling of the transaction and the client relationship is win/win. All parties and attorneys are working to get the deal done. This is not to say there won't be acrimony, just that the overall practice is constructive as opposed to destructive.
	• Intellectual challenges from rules changing/different geographic rules. There is more of an emphasis of business issues as opposed to strictly legal ones.
	• Project-based work can be slow at times and hectic at other times. Attorneys have very little control over their schedule.
	• Deals often take place over holidays to lower risk of press.

CORPORATE LAW

Practice Area	Description
Municipal	• In this practice, attorneys represent a governmental entity or agency or a party acting on behalf of or dealing with such an entity or agency. For example, in addition to cities and counties, these attorneys could be dealing with utilities.
	• This is fundamentally a general transactional practice. There is a lot of contract work involved, though the subjects can range from real estate to bonds to corporate work to other types of matters.
	• In many markets, there are certain firms that are known as municipal practice boutiques; not many big firms have a municipal practice group.
	• People who like this practice enjoy that they are acting in best interest of people or local/regional governments and like the variety of work. They also can feel that they are working on matters that will really affect people's lives.
	• People who are frustrated by this practice may not like the fact that there is not much work with companies and may be frustrated by dealing with bureaucracy and politics.

CORPORATE LAW

Practice Area	Description
Outsourcing	• The outsourcing attorney helps a company move a portion of its operations (typically manufacturing or a call center, etc.) overseas. This is a recently created and still developing practice area. • This function is sometimes fulfilled by technology transaction attorneys rather than devoted, full-time outsourcing attorneys, although the latter do exist. Tech trans attorneys do this because outsourcing deals create an ongoing relationship between the parties just as a license does. • This practice area is relatively narrow. Although the outsourcing itself contemplates a variety of areas such as real estate, employment, etc. The agreements themselves are unlike most other agreements. Think of them as complicated, cross-border service agreements. • Because it is a relatively new area of importance to many major companies, attorneys tend to work very closely with their clients. Clients tend to be major companies. • This is a contract driven practice. It requires great attention to detail. The deals tend to take a fairly long time to negotiate and implement and the expense to the company can be great.

CORPORATE LAW

Practice Area	Description
Private Equity/LBO	• This is a subset of an M&A practice. These attorneys work with banks, companies, and funds who want to invest in companies or perform leveraged buyouts or management buyouts to obtain control of a company. • This practice is centered geographically in New York, though it can appear in other major markets. It is not as common in Silicon Valley. • These deals break into two parts: the M&A part of the transaction and the finance part of the transaction. The M&A part is similar to a public M&A, except there are continuing covenants and warranties between the parties. The debt finance piece involves getting a loan against the assets of the acquired entity and is typically done by finance attorneys. • This is a deal-based practice so the schedule can fluctuate some, but not as much as the debt finance attorneys' schedule. • People who don't like this practice are often frustrated by its narrowness.

CORPORATE LAW

Practice Area	Description
Project Finance	• The goal is to finance the construction of large construction projects such as power plants, dams, etc. • The practice is geographically focused in large markets. • This practice can involve a significant international component: Africa, Middle East, Latin America. Can involve a lot of travel. • Day-to-day work involves document drafting and negotiation. Typical closing for a big New York deal can have a 50-page closing checklist of documents. It's a very document intensive practice. • In-house opportunities can include development banks like World Bank, so can be good for people interested in such public interest positions. • Attractive to people because it incorporates political components and international components that allow the attorney to interact with governments and large international institutions. • Challenges include the fact that the deals can take years to close, are very complex and require extraordinary organizational skills.

CORPORATE LAW	
Practice Area	**Description**
Securities	• The primary division is between '33 Act (issuance of securities) and '34 Act (reporting and compliance, mostly public companies) and practices differ geographically. Securities work is still centered on the East Coast, particularly in New York. On the East Coast, most junior associates start by working almost exclusively on due diligence. On the West Coast, attorneys represent more private companies and junior associates get more responsibility earlier. West Coast attorneys often act as "outside general counsel" to companies.
• Day-to-day work involves due diligence, drafting documents, interfacing with SEC, negotiating the offerings and/or financing documents, writing memos, etc. On the West Coast, attorneys can also handle stock plans, option plans, employment matters, and the entire gamut of corporate issues.
• Good for people who like to be experts, and enjoy rule-driven practices. Attorneys handle strategy questions when dealing with the SEC. You are helping corporations to run smoothly and obtain capital.
• People who leave this practice don't like that the practice can be repetitive, especially with public company reporting, and that it is very deadline-driven, particularly under Sarbanes-Oxley.
• Private company work is great for someone who wants to be a general advisor but can be frustrating to others because there's a lot of hand-holding involved.

CORPORATE LAW

Practice Area	Description
Structured Finance	• Basic concept is the securitization and sale of loans to manage the risk of default. The attorney documents the parceling up of the loans and ensures compliance with SEC rules and state laws. • Day to day work involves drafting of offering memoranda, interacting with rating organizations, representing buyers or sellers, maybe even with negotiations of loans that are securitized. • The principles in these transactions, banks and experienced investors, are sophisticated entities. • This is a project-based practice. It usually two to three months to close a sophisticated deal. • There can be ongoing compliance obligations, but unlike some other practice areas, the problems can usually be solved with money. • Structured finance can be frustrating for people who want to see a tangible benefit or who don't like complicated transactions.

EMPLOYMENT LAW

Practice Area	Description
Employment	• Employment law offers a mix of litigation and counseling. In large firms, the litigation work tends to dominate and it is unusual for a large firm to maintain a purely counseling position. The proportion of each type of work varies from firm to firm. Employment attorneys also can support corporate deal teams on due diligence and drafting of executive employment agreements and handbooks. • Counseling can be rewarding because the attorney can encourage their client to resolve employee issues in an equitable and efficient manner. • Complex regulatory schemes, evolving laws and differing state provisions provide some intellectual challenge. • These attorneys can become experts in a discrete area of law. • Many employment lawyers provide training to clients and their employees. • It's usually a low-profit margin, service practice where it can be tough to make partner and there is an increased pressure to be efficient. • This can be an emotional practice area.

ERISA LAW

Practice Area	Description
ERISA Litigation	• ERISA litigation involves administrative agencies and courts. • Cases are almost always in federal court. • The ERISA Bar is relatively small. The attorneys tend to know each other and behave in a civilized and friendly manner. • Day-to-day work consists mostly of research and writing. • ERISA trials often do not involve any dispute of fact, so trials are often held on a written record and not conducted live in court. • ERISA litigators don't acquire traditional litigation skills. There is no examination of witnesses and discovery is very restricted. There are very few, if any, depositions. • People who don't like this practice say it can be isolating or too narrow.
ERISA Counseling	• This practice involves employee benefit plan drafting and requires an understanding of code provisions. Similar to tax practice in that much is governed by codes. • There has been increased scrutiny of pension plans and 401(K) plans since Sarbanes-Oxley. • These attorneys often support M&A departments. This support involves review of seller's plans for funding/diligence/compliance issues and review of buyer's plans for integration/comparison purposes. • There is not much in-house demand for ERISA lawyers. • It's not an adversarial practice. • These attorneys face economic challenges similar to employment lawyers.

ERISA LAW

Practice Area	Description
Executive Compensation	• Very rule-driven practice (securities, tax, corporate and accounting rules). • These attorneys are usually part of the employee benefits or tax practice. • This practice is rather lawyerly, less business-like. • Since Sarbanes-Oxley, shareholders have sued over allegedly excessive compensation. • Also, there is a right answer to most of the legal issues raised and the hours are more predictable than in many areas. • This practice can have an international aspect if the client has executives abroad.
Immigration	• Immigration attorneys help individuals in most cases, even when the work is company-sponsored. • Day-to-day work involves research and drafting, client counseling, court appearances. • People enjoy this work because it can often help to reunite families, etc. Also, cases are leanly staffed and young attorneys get a lot of client contact and take on a great deal of responsibility, including appearances at hearings. • People who don't like this practice get frustrated by the statutory framework and tire of wading through bureaucracy. • This practice is done mainly by small firms and solo practitioners, though some big firms have a small department.

ERISA LAW

Practice Area	Description
Labor	• This is a subset of employment law that deals mainly with labor unions and unionized employees. The work here is governed by the National Labor Relations Act, though the decisions are often affected by politics. • The day-to-day practice involves a heavy counseling component as well as quasi-litigation. Cases are usually arbitrated or handled by an administrative law judge, which allows for fewer formalities and rules than ordinary litigation. Provides a chance for young attorneys to appear at hearings. • Elections, picketing, and grievances can be intense. Personal campaigns against client representatives are not unusual. Election and campaign work allows attorneys to be creative and to work with other professionals (such as public relations people, etc.)

ENVIRONMENTAL LAW

Practice Area	Description
Environmental	• This practice differs greatly depending upon the type of client. Attorneys can defend/counsel big companies or work for a public interest group trying to preserve the environment. • Typically this practice involves both counseling and litigation. • Environmental assessments and remediation efforts are commonly part of a real estate development plan, especially in urban areas. • It's a regulatory practice with a host of federal and state laws governing air, water, waste disposal, etc. The practice can also be extremely political. • These attorneys should be comfortable with science and numbers. • There is some cross-over with the "takings" cases, especially when development or use is halted by protection efforts, so there can be some interesting appellate work. • This tends to be a practice that generates strong feelings. Small businesses can be wiped out by preservation efforts or species can be eradicated by development. • Working for big industry can be frustrating for those who wish to work more actively to preserve the environment.

ENERGY LAW

Practice Area	Description
Energy	• This practice divides between old energy (oil, gas, electricity) and new energy (deregulated gas and power as a commodity).
	• Old energy practice deals with exploration, production, property and mineral rights, maritime (offshore drilling), environmental, eminent domain, even probate. Day-to-day involves coordinating logistics, drafting documents, conducting diligence and dealing with geologists. Many of these lawyers are in-house at oil companies. Also includes pipeline work, which is a highly regulated area.
	• New energy practice breaks down into project development, buying and selling energy commodities and monetization of the energy commodity (derivatives, swaps, hedging, etc.). The new practice began twenty years ago when natural gas was deregulated. Parts of the practice are heavily regulated (FERC) and contain a finance aspect.
	• These practices are geographically concentrated in Texas, Oklahoma, etc., except that New York investment banks are getting into the new energy practice. FERC litigation is very specialized and located primarily in Washington, D.C.
	• Unique overlay in this practice are the complications of power transmission and how you buy/sell it. Electricity, for example, is not a tangible asset like pork bellies. CFTC regulates the trading of energy commodities.
	• This is a good practice for someone who wants a balanced practice, dealing with both tangible assets and sophisticated finance. Compensation for new energy practice is very high on the in-house side.
	• Challenges are that the industry is cyclical and that there has been a lot of consolidation recently so there are fewer clients to go around.

ENTERTAINMENT LAW

Practice Area	Description
Entertainment	<ul><li>Geographically centered in Los Angeles and, to a lesser extent, New York City.</li><li>Very hierarchical and sometimes crass industry with lawyers at the bottom of the heap. Every lawyer wants to be a business-person, every business-person wants to be creative (a producer or studio executive).</li><li>The day-to-day work can involve drafting agreements, negotiation, counseling clients, researching IP questions, and drafting memoranda.</li><li>Agent-style star representation can feel like babysitting, but does occasionally provide contact with the stars.</li><li>Work for studios is like normal contract and corporate work, except the people have bigger egos.</li><li>This practice is very competitive and it can be difficult to get into.</li><li>Challenges are the lack of respect, the large egos and the simplicity of the practice.</li></ul>

FAMILY LAW

Practice Area	Description
Family	• These attorneys assist clients with child custody, divorce, child support, paternity, guardianship, and other matters. They can also assist in dealing with the tax and financial aspects of these events.
	• This is a highly emotional practice. The attorney is at the center of life's most personal disputes. There is a lot of client counseling that is not limited to legal discussions.
	• Clients are mostly individuals, there is a lot of client contact and good people skills are required.
	• Most of the work can be highly confrontational, although recently collaborative approaches have been growing in popularity. Practitioners can specialize in either the more combative or more collaborative approach.
	• This practice is found almost exclusively at small firms and boutiques. A few large firms have small family law groups, and these groups tend to focus on the financial aspects of family events.

HEALTHCARE LAW

Practice Area	Description
Healthcare	• This practice divides into three pieces: transactional (provider operations counseling, standard corporate work), regulatory and litigation. • This is a highly regulated environment. • The standard hospital practice can include a significant amount of work for non-profit institutions. The day-to-day work centers on disputes regarding medical reimbursement, allegations of fraud, compliance with regulatory issues, etc. • In Washington, D.C., some healthcare practices focus on compliance issues for the National Institute of Health and can include such cutting-edge issues as stem cell research. • Successful attorneys are typically interested in the subject matter and the primary exit paths are to healthcare providers and hospitals. • Provider operations is a low-profit margin practice, corporate practice is higher margin. • Geographically centered in state capitals and Washington, D.C., although some big firms in other markets have small departments. • This practice tends to be a service practice and it can be difficult to make partner.

INSURANCE LAW

Practice Area	Description
Coverage	• Most attorneys do both insurance coverage and insurance litigation. • This practice is very contract driven. The meat of the work is interpretation of the scope of coverage of insurance contracts (auto, home owners, renters, general, employers, directors and officers, etc). Directors and officers liability insurance, or "D&O," is the hot area since Sarbanes-Oxley. • Attorneys in this practice review the facts of insurance claims in conjunction with insurance contracts and advise insurers or insureds with respect to coverage questions. • This is a good practice for people who like contracts and who don't want to do only litigation. • The practice can be intellectually challenging because the coverage disputes arise in a variety of areas. Also, resolving issues can involve untangling layers of verbiage. • People who don't like this practice find analyzing and debating over insurance contacts to be tedious.
Defense	• Most attorneys do both insurance coverage and insurance litigation. • These attorneys litigate whether the insurer's decision regarding coverage was appropriate under the language of the policy. • It is a good litigation practice for someone who wants to limit themselves to a discrete subject matter. It's better for someone who wants to lean towards becoming an expert. • One challenge with this practice is that insurance claims may be gory, heart-wrenching and the insurer's position may be distasteful. Also, these cases tend to be very large and move very slowly; they rarely go to trial, so practice focuses on prep work and motion practice.

INTELLECTUAL PROPERTY LAW

Practice Area	Description
Licensing and Technology Transactions	• This practice can include licensing, supporting M&A and even outsourcing. • Straight licensing is a very discrete body of law. Not many terms vary between agreements. It's mostly negotiation with light drafting. Patent and biotech work may require a technical degree. • Geographically centered in technology areas (Silicon Valley, Boston, etc.). • Great for someone who wants to focus on negotiation and deal-making and for someone who enjoys learning about technology. • These attorneys are sometimes responsible for cease and desist letters, although litigators can also do that work. The language of the letter must be carefully crafted to avoid giving the other side a chance to seek a declaratory judgment. • This is project-based work that typically demands a very quick turnaround time. • When operating in support of another practice, the deadlines can be especially tight. Attorneys' schedules tend to fluctuate, with busy and not-so busy periods.

INTELLECTUAL PROPERTY LAW

Practice Area	Description
Litigation	• This practice divides into patent, copyright, trademark, and trade secrets. Patent and copyright disputes are governed primarily by federal law. Trademarks and trade secrets arise mostly under state law. Most litigation is done in federal courts.
	• This is a very adversarial practice. The stakes are high and for technology companies this can be "bet the company" litigation.
	• Special hearings, such as claim construction hearings are required in this litigation.
	• Research involves not only legal issues, but also factual issues such as the scope of the market, competitors, and competing technologies and products.
	• These actions are generally not very document intensive.
	• This practice is good for people who are interested in learning about new technologies, products, businesses and markets. These attorneys work with experts often.
	• People who dislike IP litigation generally don't like the adversarial nature of the practice or are not interested in technology.

INTELLECTUAL PROPERTY LAW

Practice Area	Description
Prosecution	• This practice is divided by type of product: biotechnology, electrical, mechanical, medical devices, software, etc.
	• Most attorneys who prosecute patents have advanced degrees, often Ph.D.s.
	• These attorneys must be qualified with the Patent and Trademark Office. A science degree is required to sit for the Patent Bar Examination. It is possible (and advisable) to sit for the Patent Bar before passing a state bar examination.
	• This is administrative work. Attorneys assist clients in obtaining patents (and occasionally trademarks, although that is relatively simple work). They evaluate whether the client's request impinges on other intellectual property, defend against opposition to client's applications in administrative trials, and oppose applications that impinge on the client's property.
	• This is a very detail oriented practice that requires knowledge of new technologies, businesses and markets There is not much interaction with other people.
	• The deadlines in this practice are long and rather flexible.

INTERRNATIONAL TRADE LAW

Practice Area	Description
International Trade	• These lawyers help facilitate the movement of goods and technology across borders. Deals with import-export laws, trade laws, tax laws, many of which are derived from treaties or national statutes of different sovereigns. • This is a mix of counseling and litigation. Counseling clients on how to import or export and defending them against allegations of breaching regulations. Hot area now is compliance with security laws. • Unfair trade laws play a large part in the litigation aspect of this practice. These cases tend to look like antitrust cases. These complicated actions involve economic analysis and depend upon expert testimony. The litigation itself takes place before administrative agencies, including International Trade Commission. • Geographic gravity of this practice is in Washington, D.C. Very few practices elsewhere. • The day-to-day work includes counseling clients and engaging in most litigation activities, similar to administrative law attorneys. The litigation cases tend to be very intense: the relevant statute provides for very tight timelines. All proceedings have to be concluded in less than eighteen months. • There is an overlap with intellectual property because U.S. laws are designed to prevent importation of infringing goods. • People who like this practice enjoy the international aspects of the practice, there's some travel involved but it's not constant usually, and the demands of the practice change with the international ebb and flow of global economics and politics, so it is always changing and interesting. • People who don't like this practice often would prefer to work with smaller businesses or individuals.

LITIGATION LAW

Practice Area	Description
Antitrust	<ul><li>These attorneys help companies navigate restraint of trade issues, including those created by organic growth or acquisition.</li><li>The practice focuses primarily on litigation, although there can be some counseling involved as well. The litigation tends to be very high stakes for the companies and can be civil or criminal in nature.</li><li>Many antitrust attorneys come from the Department of Justice or spend at least part of their careers working for state or federal government. These cases are often litigated against the federal government.</li><li>This is a complicated area of law that is good for people who like sophisticated issues, who want to learn about industry segments and who like economics, market analysis and intellectual property.</li><li>Antitrust suffers from the same challenges as any general litigation practice, with the addition that since you are litigating against the government, success rates can tend to be rather low.</li></ul>

LITIGATION LAW

Practice Area	Description
Appellate	• This practice is very prestigious and hard to break into. • The day-to-day work involves only legal research and writing. There is no fact development work such as discovery, depositions, etc. • It is not as adversarial or time-sensitive as trial litigation; it's great for introverts who want a predictable schedule. • Pure appellate practice is focused in Washington, D.C. There is some pure appellate in New York and Los Angeles, but not that much. Appellate work in other cities tends to mix with trial practice. • These cases can be morally difficult. The defendants appeal because they were hit with large damages because they did something very bad. Damage reduction cases can involve difficult arguments regarding how valuable a person's life was. • Aside from damage reduction cases, questions can be arcane: such as, how the 7th Amendment would have been interpreted in 1791 on a subject it doesn't directly address. • Discrete projects tend to be shorter than general litigation. • Students interested in this should try to write for a law review and obtain a federal appellate clerkship, if possible.

LITIGATION LAW

Practice Area	Description
General Litigation	• These attorneys are the consummate generalists. They're always learning something new and never expected to be an expert at anything. • This is the quintessential adversarial practice. The interactions between the parties can be rancorous. This means you can spend a lot of time drafting arguments that you may never need to use. • The reward is victory. You must get satisfaction from winning. • People who like this practice like the intellectual diversity and the fact that the attorneys have more direct influence over the case than the client. It's also easier to bill hours as a litigator than it is in many practice areas (depositions, hearings, strategy meetings can involve hours of sitting around, all of which is billed). • People who are dissatisfied with litigation typically don't like the fact that matters can last for years, the overall practice can feel destructive rather than constructive, it can be difficult to predict your schedule (fires tend to flare up and need attention), and you can spend hours, days, or weeks working on items that may never be used. • Clients can look at you as an unwanted but necessary expense.

LITIGATION LAW

Practice Area	Description
Product Liability/ Toxic Tort	• Product liability practice is litigation involving the production, manufacturing, marketing and use of a business product or service. It may involve anything from traditional product liability theories such as design defect or strict liability to antitrust and consumer class action claims. • Toxic tort practice typically involves harmful agents such as asbestos, etc. • People who like this practice enjoy the fact that there are lots of depositions and that that they are allowed to assume every role from scientist to corporate counsel. Also, these attorneys feel that they are essential to a company's business. The lifeblood of many businesses is the revenue from goods sold, and product liability lawyers are seeking to protect that revenue flow. • People who don't like this practice are frustrated because these cases rarely go to trial and they typically involve graphic personal injury and death. Also, the cases are very document intensive, sometimes involving literally millions of documents and take a long time to resolve.

LITIGATION LAW

Practice Area	Description
Securities	• These attorneys represent individuals and corporations in securities class actions, stock-drop cases, and derivative actions. They perform internal investigations on behalf of corporate audit committees (whistleblower investigations), represent audit committees, individuals and companies in SEC investigations, advise corporations regarding director and officer liability insurance, and advise law-firm corporate departments regarding disclosure questions.
	• The day-to-day work involves most usual litigation tasks with a focus on pre-trial activity. Associates spend a lot of time drafting, counseling and interviewing clients and on factual development (these cases can have intense discovery demands). Partners spend a lot of time on the telephone advising clients in addition to drafting. The hours can be fairly long and the cases can be rather complicated.
	• Attorneys who like this practice enjoy helping accused individuals: this is closest you can get to doing criminal defense work without worrying that your client will go to jail. Client relationships with the individuals and company management tend to be very close. These attorneys also enjoy working in a variety of industries and learning about various companies' businesses.
	• People who don't like this practice are frustrated because these cases rarely go to trial. Also, it is a lawyer-driven industry.

LITIGATION LAW	
Practice Area	**Description**
White Collar Crime	• This is narrow practice area and is very different from other litigation practices, which tend to be civil in nature if not in tone. Criminal rules differ from civil rules.
	• The community of white collar practitioners is usually relatively small. They all know each other and, for the most part, behave with a higher degree of civility than general litigators.
	• Day-to-day is similar to civil litigation with research, drafting, factual development and argument, but with more significant client contact.
	• This can be a tough practice area for associates because there is not much leverage: clients whose lives are on the line want to work with partners. The usual path is to come from government practice, so the practice contains many senior attorneys.
	• Client relationships tend to be very close.
	• These attorneys have to like battling the government. They see themselves as "The Fixer," called in at the last minute to clean up a bad situation. Crisis management.
	• Clients require 24-hour access to you because of the stakes. High stress practice.

REAL ESTATE LAW

Practice Area	Description
Finance	<ul><li>The goal of this practice is to help clients finance construction of hotels, office buildings, business campuses, even residential development and baseball parks. It is similar to project finance, though the types of projects tend to be slightly different.</li><li>This work divides between attorneys who represent borrowers and those who represent lenders. When the attorney is representing the borrower, this work can be done by the same attorneys who do transactional practice. Lender work is a separate practice (that conflicts with representation of borrowers).</li><li>On the borrower side, clients tend to be developers.</li><li>On the lender side, the work can be very routine. Large banks will have standard agreements and standard concessions. It is easy for a junior associate to learn.</li><li>Real estate finance attorneys are attracted by the size of the projects, which can be significant, news-making buildings. There is a great sense of accomplishment when the building is built and these attorneys like the tangible results.</li><li>Attorneys who don't like this practice can be frustrated by the repetition.</li></ul>

REAL ESTATE LAW

Practice Area	Description
Land Use	• This practice focuses primarily on helping real estate development companies use or develop their property. It's common for this practice to have a transactional aspect as a follow-up to the permitting process. • This is a pseudo-governmental practice as these attorneys help clients manage the local and state approval processes. • The day-to-day work involves project management, organizing logistics with regard to a wide range of professionals on a schedule to get the development through approvals, counseling clients with regard to these processes, presentation to and negotiation with governmental agencies, and advising regarding local and state regulations regarding development and use of property. This practice is less drafting intensive than the transactional practice but these attorneys do review documents drafted by experts such as architects and planners. • People who are drawn to this practice are interested in public policy. The results are very tangible. There is a lot of opportunity for coming up with creative solutions and a fair amount of negotiation. • Partner intensive practice. It demands experience and connections. Can be tough to break into. • People can get frustrated in this practice because they are dealing with bureaucratic agencies.

REAL ESTATE LAW

Practice Area	Description
Transactional	• In this practice, there are three fundamental tasks: help entities acquire property, help them lease it, and help them dispose of it. The attorneys also work on property rights and easements, but that's usually a smaller portion of the practice. This practice can include finance work if the attorney represents borrowers. • The day-to-day work focuses on negotiation and documentation of transactions. • People who like this practice like the fact that you can see the results of your work, buildings are tangible. It's a practice area where you can become an expert. • This practice provides a great deal of client contact, for better and worse. • This work is project-based with a pretty quick turnaround, which gives you a feeling of accomplishment. • People who are frustrated by this practice are bored by the repetition. The deadlines can be tight, particularly in leasing.

TAX LAW

Practice Area	Description
Tax	• In big firms, this work divides up into federal and state/local tax. State/local tax attorneys tend to work more on litigation issues (mostly people seeking refunds or appealing an assessment). Federal tax attorneys divide up into tax controversy (audit and litigation support) and transactional.
	• The federal transactional practice varies by firm and can include cross-border transactions, M&A support, REITs, mutual fund work, etc.
	• These attorneys do not handle tax returns for companies and individuals. Those are usually done by accounting firms.
	• This is a very complex, regulation and rule-driven practice. There are many state-by-state differences and the federal law changes all the time. There is a heavy burden to keep with current developments (daily).
	• Day-to-day work for tax controversy or state tax practice is similar to litigation. For federal transactional, there is a lot of research (more than in most practices), drafting of memoranda, and reviewing documents from other departments.
	• There is not much client contact as a tax associate at a big firm.
	• It's a service practice and it can be difficult to make partner because the departments tend to be smaller.
	• This practice can be extremely deadline intensive. Business lawyers tend to consult tax lawyers at the last moment.
	• People who like this practice like the intellectual challenge and like being the expert in an arcane area. It is perfect for those who enjoy intellectual challenge and like problem-solving.
	• People who leave the practice do so because it can be exhausting mentally, because they don't like the statutory work, or because they feel like they're not really building anything (deals tend to be business-driven, not tax-driven).

TRUST & ESTATE LAW

Practice Area	Description
Trusts & Estates	• The goal is to efficiently transfer wealth between generations and within families. • Similar to tax practice, this is a complex, statutory practice. The law evolves very quickly and there is a wide variety of authority, including case law, revenue rulings, statutes, etc. • This is mostly a non-adversarial practice. • The day-to-day work involves drafting of estate plans and sub-documents, counseling clients, and administering estates both in and out of court. • This practice does not have many deadlines. • This practice is most commonly found in boutiques, although most big firms have a small group. It's a service practice and it can be difficult to make partner. • The goal is to preserve client wealth. • People who fail in this practice sometimes have problems discussing the complex law in plain English, don't like the complexity, or get pigeon-holed into one small section of the practice, which can be boring. • This can be a tough practice to break into. It can sometimes be class-oriented. Interested students should spend a summer doing T&E and take appropriate classes or have a financial background.

Please contact your local Major, Lindsey & Africa office for further details (www.mlaglobal.com).

Appendix E
REPRESENTATIVE SKILLS USED BY LAWYERS
(ACTION VERBS)

This list includes a collection of action verbs that may also be defined in terms of skills employed by lawyers in a variety of work settings. The list will be useful in skills identification, career assessment, résumé and cover letter drafting, interviewing, and analyzing employment openings. It is intended to be representative rather than exhaustive.

accelerated	balanced	defined
accepted	briefed	defended
accomplished	brought	demonstrated
accounted	budgeted	derived
achieved	built	designed
acquired	catalogued	determined
acquitted	categorized	developed
addressed	chaired	devised
adjusted	challenged	devoted
administered	charted	directed
advised	clarified	disseminated
advocated	collected	documented
allocated	compiled	donated
amassed	completed	drafted
amended	computed	edited
analyzed	conceived	effected
annotated	conducted	enforced
anticipated	consolidated	engaged
applied	constructed	enhanced
arbitrated	continued	enlarged
argued	contracted	entered
arranged	contributed	established
assembled	controlled	executed
assessed	convicted	exercised
assigned	coordinated	expanded
assisted	corrected	expedited
attended	counseled	experienced
attracted	created	experimented
authored	critiqued	explained
backed	cross-examined	explored

exposed
facilitated
figured
filed
financed
focused
forecasted
formulated
fought
functioned
generated
governed
grouped
handled
headed
identified
illustrated
implemented
improved
increased
initiated
innovated
inquired
instituted
instructed
interpreted
intervened
interviewed
introduced
investigated
judged
lead
litigated
maintained
managed
marketed
maximized
mediated
mobilized
modeled
modified
monitored
motivated
named

negotiated
noted
observed
obtained
operated
ordered
organized
originated
outlined
performed
persuaded
planned
pledged
predicted
prepared
presented
presided
printed
propossed
produced
prosecuted
protected
provided
publicized
pursued
questioned
raised
recommended
recorded
recreated
recruited
reduced
refined
rendered
renewed
repaired
reorganized
reported
represented
reproduced
researched
resolved
responded
restored

restructured
retained
retrieved
revealed
reviewed
revised
revitalized
rewrote
scheduled
searched
selected
served
settled
simplified
solicited
solved
specified
spoke
sponsored
started
stimulated
strengthened
structured
studied
suggested
summarized
supervised
supported
synthesized
systemized
targeted
taught
took charge
took over
trained
transacted
tried
updated
upgraded
upset
utilized
won
wrote

Index

Nonlegal Careers for Lawyers, Fifth Edition

By William D. Henslee, Gary A. Munneke, Ellen Wayne

In this guide, the authors lead you step by step through the process of assessing the special skills that legal training provides, choosing a nonlegal career, and conducting a nonlegal job search. In addition, they provide you with essential information about a variety of careers in business and industry, government and public service, associations and institutions, and entrepreneurial ventures. To help you with the task of locating additional useful information on nonlegal careers, the book also contains a valuable resource section featuring surveys, descriptions of nonlegal careers, and a listing of publishers and publications, as well as suggested readings on nonlegal careers.

Women-at-Law: Lessons Learned Along the Pathways to Success

By Phyllis Horn Epstein

Discover how women lawyers in a wide variety of practice settings are meeting the challenges of competing in an often all-consuming profession without sacrificing their desire for a multidimensional life. Women-at-Law provides a wealth of practical guidance and direction from experienced women lawyers who share their life stories and advice to inspire and encourage others by offering solutions to the challenges—personal and professional. You'll learn that, with some effort, a motivated woman can redirect her career, her home life, and her interests, in the long journey that is a successful life. If you are a law student, a practicing lawyer, or simply a woman considering a career

The Lawyer's Guide to Balancing Life and Work, Second Edition

By George W. Kaufman

This newly updated and revised Second Edition is written specifically to help lawyers achieve professional and personal satisfaction in their career. Writing with warmth and seasoned wisdom, George Kaufman examines how the profession has changed over the last five year, then offers philosophical approaches, practical examples, and valuable exercises to help lawyers reconcile their goals and expectations with the realities and demands of the legal profession. Interactive exercises are provided throughout the text and on the accompanying CD, to help you discover how to reclaim your life. New lawyers, seasoned veterans, and those who have personal relationships to lawyers will all benefit from this insightful book.

How to Build and Manage a Personal Injury Practice, Second Edition

By K. William Gibson

Written exclusively for personal injury practitioners, this indispensable resource explores everything from choosing the right office space to measuring results of your marketing campaign. Author Bill Gibson has carefully constructed this "how-to" manual—highlighting all the tactics, technology, and practical tools necessary for a profitable practice, including how to write a sound business plan, develop an accurate financial forecast, maximize your staff while minimizing costs, and more.

How to Build and Manage an Entertainment Law Practice

By Gary Greenberg

This book addresses a variety of issues critical to establishing a successful entertainment law practice including getting started, preparing a business plan, getting your foot in the door, creating the right image, and marketing your entertainment law practice. The book discusses the basic differences between entertainment law and other types of law practice and provides guidance for avoiding common pitfalls. In addition, an extensive appendix contains sample agreements, forms, letters, and checklists common to entertainment law practitioners. Includes a diskette containing the essential appendix templates, forms and checklists for easy implementation!

How to Build and Manage an Estates Practice, Second Edition

By Daniel B. Evans

Whether you aim to define your "niche" in estates law, or market your estates practice on the Internet, this valuable guide can help you make a practice a success. Chapters are logically organized to lead you through the essential stages of developing your specialty practice and include practical, proven advice for everything from organizing estate planning and trust administration files . . . to conducting estate planning interviews . . . to implementing alternative billing strategies . . . to managing your workload (and staff!). Appendices include such sample documents as: an estate planning fee agreement, an estate administration fee agreement, an estate administration schedule, will execution instructions, and more.

LawPracticeManagementSection

MARKETING · MANAGEMENT · TECHNOLOGY · FINANCE

The Successful Lawyer: Powerful Strategies for Transforming Your Practice
By Gerald A. Riskin
Available as a Book, Audio-CD Set, or Combination Package!
Global management consultant and trusted advisor to many of the world's largest law firms, Gerry Riskin goes beyond simple concept or theory and delivers a book packed with practical advice that you can implement right away. By using the principles found in this book, you can live out your dreams, embrace success, and awaken your firm to its full potential. Large law firm or small, managing partners and associates in every area of practice—all can benefit from the information contained in this book. With this book, you can attract what you need and desire into your life, get more satisfaction from your practice and your clients, and do so in a systematic, achievable way.

How to Start and Build a Law Practice, Platinum Fifth Edition
By Jay G Foonberg
This classic ABA bestseller has been used by tens of thousands of lawyers as the comprehensive guide to planning, launching, and growing a successful practice. It's packed with over 600 pages of guidance on identifying the right location, finding clients, setting fees, managing your office, maintaining an ethical and responsible practice, maximizing available resources, upholding your standards, and much more. You'll find the information you need to successfully launch your practice, run it at maximum efficiency, and avoid potential pitfalls along the way. If you're committed to starting—and growing—your own practice, this one book will give you the expert advice you need to make it succeed for years to come.

The Lawyer's Guide to Marketing on the Internet, Third Edition
By Gregory Siskind, Deborah McMurray, and Richard P. Klau
The Internet is a critical component of every law firm marketing strategy—no matter where you are, how large your firm is, or the areas in which you practice. Used effectively, a younger, smaller firm can present an image just as sophisticated and impressive as a larger and more established firm. You can reach potential new clients, in remote areas, at any time, for minimal cost. To help you maximize your Internet marketing capabilities, this book provides you with countless Internet marketing possibilities and shows you how to effectively and efficiently market your law practice on the Internet.

The Lawyer's Guide to Fact Finding on the Internet, Third Edition
By Carole A. Levitt and Mark E. Rosch
Written especially for legal professionals, this revised and expanded edition is a complete, hands-on guide to the best sites, secrets, and shortcuts for conducting efficient research on the Web. Containing over 600 pages of information, with over 100 screen shots of specific Web sites, this resource is filled with practical tips and advice on using specific sites, alerting readers to quirks or hard-to-find information. What's more, user-friendly icons immediately identify free sites, free-with-registration sites, and pay sites. An accompanying CD-ROM includes the links contained in the book, indexed, so you can easily navigate to these cream-of-the-crop Web sites without typing URLs into your browser.

The Lawyer's Guide to Marketing Your Practice, Second Edition
Edited by James A. Durham and Deborah McMurray
This book is packed with practical ideas, innovative strategies, useful checklists, and sample marketing and action plans to help you implement a successful, multi-faceted, and profit-enhancing marketing plan for your firm. Organized into four sections, this illuminating resource covers: Developing Your Approach; Enhancing Your Image; Implementing Marketing Strategies and Maintaining Your Program. Appendix materials include an instructive primer on market research to inform you on research methodologies that support the marketing of legal services. The accompanying CD-ROM contains a wealth of checklists, plans, and other sample reports, questionnaires, and templates—all designed to make implementing your marketing strategy as easy as possible!

The Lawyer's Guide to Creating Persuasive Computer Presentations, Second Edition
By Ann E. Brenden and John D. Goodhue
This book explains the advantages of computer presentation resources, how to use them, what they can do, and the legal issues involved in their use. This revised second edition has been updated to include new chapters on hardware and software that is currently being used for digital displays, and it contains all-new sections that walk the reader through beginning and advanced Microsoft® PowerPoint® skills. Also included is a CD-ROM containing on-screen tutorials illustrating techniques such as animating text, creating zoomed call-out images, insertion and configuration of text and images, and a sample PowerPoint final argument complete with audio, checklists, and help files for using trial presentation software.

30-Day Risk-Free Order Form
Call Today! 1-800-285-2221
Monday–Friday, 7:30 AM – 5:30 PM, Central Time

Qty	Title	LPM Price	Regular Price	Total
_____	Nonlegal Careers for Lawyers, Fifth Edition (5110567)	$ 34.95	$ 29.95	$_____
_____	Women-at-Law: Lessons Learned Along the Pathways to Success (5110509)	39.95	49.95	$_____
_____	The Lawyer's Guide to Balancing Life and Work, Second Edition (5110566)	29.95	39.95	$_____
_____	How to Build and Manage a Personal Injury Practice, Second Edition (5110575)	64.95	54.95	$_____
_____	How to Build and Manage an Estates Practice, Second Edition (5110591)	64.95	44.95	$_____
_____	How to Build and Manage an Entertainment Law Practice (5110453)	54.95	64.95	$_____
_____	How to Start and Build a Law Practice, Platinum Fifth Edition (5110508)	57.95	69.95	$_____
_____	The Lawyer's Guide to Creating Persuasive Computer Presentations, Second Edition (5110530)	79.95	99.95	$_____
_____	The Lawyer's Guide to Fact Finding on the Internet, Third Edition (5110568)	84.95	99.95	$_____
_____	The Lawyer's Guide to Marketing on the Internet, Third Edition (5110585)	84.95	74.95	$_____
_____	The Lawyer's Guide to Marketing Your Practice, Second Edition (5110500)	79.95	89.95	$_____
_____	The Successful Lawyer—Book Only (5110531)	64.95	84.95	$_____
_____	The Successful Lawyer—Audio CDs Only (5110532)	129.95	149.95	$_____
_____	The Successful Lawyer—Audio CDs/Book Combination (5110533)	174.95	209.95	$_____

*Postage and Handling		**Tax	*Postage and Handling	$_____
$10.00 to $24.99	$5.95	DC residents add 5.75%	**Tax	$_____
$25.00 to $49.99	$9.95	IL residents add 9.00%	TOTAL	$_____
$50.00 to $99.99	$12.95			
$100.00 to $349.99	$17.95			
$350 to $499.99	$24.95			

PAYMENT

❑ Check enclosed (to the ABA)

❑ Visa   ❑ MasterCard   ❑ American Express

_____
Account Number   Exp. Date   Signature

Name _____ Firm _____

Address _____

City _____ State _____ Zip _____

Phone Number _____ E-Mail Address _____

Guarantee

If—for any reason—you are not satisfied with your purchase, you may return it within 30 days of receipt for a complete refund of the price of the book(s). No questions asked!

Mail: ABA Publication Orders, P.O. Box 10892, Chicago, Illinois 60610-0892
♦ Phone: 1-800-285-2221 ♦ FAX: 312-988-5568

E-Mail: abasvcctr@abanet.org ♦ Internet: http://www.lawpractice.org/catalog

About the CD

The accompanying CD contains sample résumés, charts, checklists, and Appendix A from *The Legal Career Guide: From Law Student to Lawyer*, Fifth Edition. The files are in Microsoft Word® format.

For additional information about the files on the CD, please open and read the "**readme.doc**" file on the CD.

NOTE: The set of files on the CD may only be used on a single computer or moved to and used on another computer. Under no circumstances may the set of files be used on more than one computer at one time. If you are interested in obtaining a license to use the set of files on a local network, please contact: Director, Copyrights and Contracts, American Bar Association, 321 N. Clark Street, Chicago, IL 60654, (312) 988-6101. **Please read the license and warranty statements on the following page before using this CD.**

CD-ROM to accompany
The Legal Career Guide: From Law Student to Lawyer, Fifth Edition

Defending Liberty
Pursuing Justice

WARNING: Opening this package indicates your understanding and acceptance of the following Terms and Conditions.

READ THE FOLLOWING TERMS AND CONDITIONS BEFORE OPENING THIS SEALED PACKAGE. IF YOU DO NOT AGREE WITH THEM, PROMPTLY RETURN THE UNOPENED PACKAGE TO EITHER THE PARTY FROM WHOM IT WAS ACQUIRED OR TO THE AMERICAN BAR ASSOCIATION AND YOUR MONEY WILL BE RETURNED.

The document files in this package are a proprietary product of the American Bar Association and are protected by Copyright Law. The American Bar Association retains title to and ownership of these files.

License

You may use this set of files on a single computer or move it to and use it on another computer, but under no circumstances may you use the set of files on more than one computer at the same time. You may copy the files either in support of your use of the files on a single computer or for backup purposes. If you are interested in obtaining a license to use the set of files on a local network, please contact: Manager, Publication Policies & Contracting, American Bar Association, 321 N. Clark Street, Chicago, IL 60654, (312) 988-6101.

You may permanently transfer the set of files to another party if the other party agrees to accept the terms and conditions of this License Agreement. If you transfer the set of files, you must at the same time transfer all copies of the files to the same party or destroy those not transferred. Such transfer terminates your license. You may not rent, lease, assign or otherwise transfer the files except as stated in this paragraph.

You may modify these files for your own use within the provisions of this License Agreement. You may not redistribute any modified files.

Warranty

If a CD-ROM in this package is defective, the American Bar Association will replace it at no charge if the defective diskette is returned to the American Bar Association within 60 days from the date of acquisition.

American Bar Association warrants that these files will perform in substantial compliance with the documentation supplied in this package. However, the American Bar Association does not warrant these forms as to the correctness of the legal material contained therein. If you report a significant defect in performance in writing to the American Bar Association, and the American Bar Association is not able to correct it within 60 days, you may return the CD, including all copies and documentation, to the American Bar Association and the American Bar Association will refund your money.

Any files that you modify will no longer be covered under this warranty even if they were modified in accordance with the License Agreement and product documentation.

IN NO EVENT WILL THE AMERICAN BAR ASSOCIATION, ITS OFFICERS, MEMBERS, OR EMPLOYEES BE LIABLE TO YOU FOR ANY DAMAGES, INCLUDING LOST PROFITS, LOST SAVINGS OR OTHER IN-CIDENTAL OR CONSEQUENTIAL DAMAGES ARISING OUT OF YOUR USE OR INABILITY TO USE THESE FILES EVEN IF THE AMERICAN BAR ASSOCIATION OR AN AUTHORIZED AMERICAN BAR AS-SOCIATION REPRESENTATIVE HAS BEEN ADVISED OF THE POSSIBILITY OF SUCH DAMAGES, OR FOR ANY CLAIM BY ANY OTHER PARTY. SOME STATES DO NOT ALLOW THE LIMITATION OR EX-CLUSION OF LIABILITY FOR INCIDENTAL OR CONSEQUENTIAL DAMAGES, IN WHICH CASE THIS LIMITATION MAY NOT APPLY TO YOU.